Praise for *A New Kind*

"Rarely do people become Christians after being ~~...~~
book, by leading thinkers, calls for a Christian apologetics rooted in humility and love. Read this book and be armed to defend the faith and to love the lost. This is the kind of apologetics book that calls us not just to defend Jesus with our arguments but to follow Jesus in our argumentation."

Russell Moore, president,
Southern Baptist Ethics & Religious Liberty Commission

"Apologetics saved my life! As a young struggling believer in an academic environment, I floundered in my faith until I found good answers to the good questions that unbelievers were asking me. But I began to love apologetics for all the wrong reasons. I wanted to prove my point, win the argument, and leave people reeling from the encounter. What Sean McDowell and his team have done in *A New Kind of Apologist* is give us a fresh look at what a defender of the faith ought to be and how to speak the truth in love."

Skip Heitzig, senior pastor, Calvary Albuquerque

"If you know someone with no background in apologetics, this is a great resource to get them started. It breaks out of the box by embracing what, in my classes, I call 'worldview apologetics'—showing how biblical truth makes better sense in diverse realms such as economics, politics, literature, science, gender, and race relations. Instead of crafting arguments in abstraction, it includes interviews with atheists to help Christians learn how to talk to real people. Under Sean McDowell's skillful editing, the style is clear, accessible, and most of all, inviting."

Nancy Pearcey, author, *Total Truth* and *Finding Truth*

"Sean and friends welcomes a fresh approach to defending the faith that is long overdue. Thankful for this book!"

Josh Griffin, high school pastor, Saddleback Church,
and cofounder of Download Youth Ministry

"New eras bring new challenges to Christianity, and new challenges require new apologetic approaches. With its collection of diverse voices approaching apologetics from a myriad of angles, *A New Kind of Apologist* is exactly the sort of resource Christians need to respond winsomely to the unique topics, and the unique tone, of our time. This comprehensive, accessible, practical book is a worthy addition to any Christian's library."

Brett McCracken, author of *Gray Matters: Navigating the Space Between Legalism and Liberty* and *Hipster Christianity: When Church and Cool Collide*

"In this book, you'll find excellent contributions from young, winsome voices speaking about the best ways to make a case for Christianity in a 21st-century secular age. Compassionate and convictional—the words on these pages exude joy and confidence in the gospel."

Trevin Wax, managing editor of The Gospel Project,
blogger for The Gospel Coalition, and author of
Clear Winter Nights: A Journey into Faith, Doubt, and What Comes After

"Every generation of Christians faces its own set of challenges and opportunities. The church sometimes seems like it's playing 'catch-up' as it tries to provide answers to old objections from new atheists. It's time for a new approach, with a new methodology, to address the new issues facing believers today. *A New Kind of Apologist* has been written for this very purpose. Sean McDowell has assembled an all-star group of apologetic thinkers and practitioners. Get ready to rethink the way you've been defending the faith."

J. Warner Wallace, cold-case detective
and author of *God's Crime Scene* and *Cold-Case Christianity*

"*A New Kind of Apologist* is a treasure of a resource! No matter what sphere of ministry God has called you to, these chapters will surely equip you to be a more prepared and gracious ambassador of Jesus."

Maya Moore, WNBA champion, finals MVP, WNBA All-Star MVP,
gold-medal Olympian, UCONN's all-time leading scorer,
and first female basketball player to sign with Jordan Brand

"In a world that is constantly fighting for our heart's affections, it is pertinent that we know why we believe what we believe, and are able to communicate it in a way that is filled with grace and respect. Sean, alongside some of the leading apologists of the day, did a masterful job with this book! It will give you a passion for apologetics and encourage you to defend your faith, but to do so sounding more like a melodious instrument rather than a clanging gong."

Adam Donyes, founder/president of the Kanakuk Link Year

A NEW KIND

—— *of* ——

APOLOGIST

SEAN McDOWELL

GENERAL EDITOR

HARVEST HOUSE PUBLISHERS
EUGENE, OREGON

Cover by Dual Identity, Inc,

Cover photo © Brayden Heath / Lightstock

A NEW KIND OF APOLOGIST
Copyright © 2016 Sean McDowell
Published by Harvest House Publishers
Eugene, Oregon 97402
www.harvesthousepublishers.com

Library of Congress Cataloging-in-Publication Data
A new kind of apologist / Sean McDowell, PhD, general editor.
    pages cm
ISBN 978-0-7369-6605-4 (pbk.)
ISBN 978-0-7369-6606-1 (eBook)
1. Apologetics. 2. Christianity and culture. I. McDowell, Sean, editor.
BT1103.N484 2016
239—dc23

2015021781

Printed in the United States of America

16 17 18 19 20 21 22 23 24 / LB-JC / 10 9 8 7 6 5 4 3 2 1

To my son, Shane.

I pray that you will be the kind of apologist
that your generation needs.

I love you and am so proud of you.

Contents

PART 2   New Methods in Apologetics

PART 3 New Issues in Apologetics

— Introduction —

A New Kind of Apologist

SEAN MCDOWELL

During a trip to Breckenridge, a beautiful ski town in the mountains of Colorado, a friend and I decided to get our hair cut at one of the little shops downtown. As we waited our turn, I read another chapter of the book I had brought along with me, a book whose title clearly indicated my interest in spiritual things.

When my turn came and I settled into the chair, the young hairstylist noted that I was reading a Christian book and wondered if it would be okay for her to ask me a question about God that had been on her mind. Of course I said yes, relishing the opportunity to talk about theology. After all, I had been studying apologetics and was ready with all the right answers. *Bring it on*, I thought, smiling to myself.

"Well," she started, with just a hint of hesitation, "why does God allow so much evil and suffering in the world?"

Really, that's all you got? raced through my mind. *Why is this such a big problem?* It's one of the most oft-asked questions in apologetics, and I was ready with the classical free-will defense—emphasizing that God desires a relationship with us, which is possible only if we have free will. I made the point that evil can exist only if there is first a standard of objective good and there can be good only if there is a God. In other words, her very question, I pointed out, presupposes the existence of God.

This led to more questions, and I found I could answer each one pretty easily. She'd ask a question, and I had an answer ready at hand.

Things were going extraordinarily well, I thought, until she paused for a long moment, lifted the scissors away from my head, and then began to cry. She stepped back from cutting my hair and said in a quavering voice, "This is a bunch of bs! You've got an answer for everything. It *can't* be that easy. You just don't understand."

I was speechless (and a bit nervous, since she was clearly upset and had very sharp scissors poised not far from my head).

What had just happened? It seemed like we were having a great conversation...and now this. Well, I quickly changed the topic and made sure to give her a big tip on the way out. Outside the shop, I turned to my friend and asked him why he thought she had been so defensive. He took a deep breath and looked me in the eyes, probably trying to determine if I was ready to hear the truth.

"Well," he said, as gently as he could manage, "do you have any idea how arrogant you were toward her?"

I was taken aback. But as we walked along the streets of Breckenridge, I thought about the encounter and realized he was absolutely right. Rather than really listening to her, asking questions, and trying to learn from her, I was more interested in scoring points and winning the argument. My replies had come across as prepackaged sound bites rather than compassionate and respectful responses. What I saw, maybe for the first time, is that truth must be wedded to grace, and that what we say is important...but *how* we say it is equally critical.

If we have the best arguments but not love, our arguments will often fall on deaf ears (1 Corinthians 13:1-3). A new kind of apologist must have both truth and love. This is why the apostle Paul said,

> And the Lord's servant must not be quarrelsome but kind to everyone, able to teach, patiently enduring evil, correcting his opponents with gentleness. God may perhaps grant them repentance leading

to a knowledge of the truth, and they may come to their senses and escape from the snare of the devil, after being captured by him to do his will (2 Timothy 2:24-26).

Whenever the problem of suffering and evil come up, I try to avoid simple answers. I typically respond with a question: "Of all the things you can ask about God, why that one?" Occasionally people have a genuine intellectual issue they want to wrestle with, and I am more than happy to help. But more often than not, the intellectual question masks a deep personal wound. When I ask this question, I often hear painful stories of sickness, broken relationships, and abuse. The Christian response is not to simply give a reason, although there may come a time for that, but to "weep with those who weep" (Romans 12:15) and to show comfort and care to the afflicted (Psalm 82:3).

Caught Off Guard

Not long ago I attended a conference put on by the Reformation Project, which is part of a larger movement committed to reforming the church's traditional views on homosexuality.[1] My goal was simply to meet people and learn about the movement from the inside. Along with worship, testimonies, and lectures, there were multiple ninety-minute sessions focused on helping people rebut biblical arguments against homosexuality and to make the most compelling case for the compatibility of Christianity and same-sex relationships. These sessions were led by Matthew Vines (*God and the Gay Christian*) and James Brownson (*Bible, Gender, Sexuality*).

Afterward the leaders broke us up into small groups and sent us to classrooms to practice role-playing what we had learned. As the group session started, the teacher went to the front of the class and said, "Before we begin the role-play, it would be great if each of you could share your story of why you are here and why you care so much about this movement." Inside I was thinking, *You've got to be kidding me. How did I get myself into this situation? What should I say?* Fortunately I was fifteenth out of twenty people, so I had some time to think and pray for wisdom.

Even though I had serious theological reservations with the views of others in the group, I was heartbroken at many of their stories. One young man shared how his church kicked him out when they found out he was gay. Another young woman shared how her parents rejected her when she came out as a lesbian. An older man shared how he had experienced same sex attraction his entire life, and because of his shame, he had never told anyone until last week. He first told his mother when he was about sixty years old. My heart broke for many of these people.

It was finally my turn. I started with: "My name is Sean McDowell and I teach at Biola University." Many of them must have known about Biola and its conservative biblical stance, since half of them looked at me with an expression of surprise and bewilderment, as if they were wondering, *Who let this guy in here?* I continued, "If you are familiar with Biola, then you probably realize I am not theologically where you want me to be. In fact, I have serious theological reservations about what I am hearing here. But I want to read you something."

I pulled out the worship packet we were given at registration and read the opening words, "There is love for one like you. There is grace enough to see you through. And wherever you have walked, whatever path you choose, may you know there is love for one like you." I then asked, "We may disagree theologically, but there's a place for me here, right?" At that point they had to say yes, or they would have betrayed their message of inclusion and tolerance. And many of them graciously welcomed me.

I went on, "Like you, I am here because the church desperately needs to get this answer right. I have seen the pain firsthand that many of my students and friends with same-sex attraction have experienced. I am here to meet many of you, learn about your views firsthand, and to understand where you are coming from so maybe I can gain some insight about how to best address this issue."

I paused and then made my final point: "The narrative that is often told is that those who don't affirm homosexuality are hateful, bigoted, homophobic, and intolerant. I want you to know that this is not always true. There are Christians who have serious reservations about your theology but still love you as people. I am not homophobic or I wouldn't be here. There are many Christians who deeply care about each one of you. And I am sorry many of you have experienced such hurt at the hands of believers, but please don't be tempted to think we hate you just because we disagree with your views."

Unfortunately, I had to leave soon afterward to catch a flight. But I have been in touch with a handful of people in that classroom since, and from what I can tell, they were touched by my comments.

A New Kind of Apologist

In our increasingly post-Christian culture, each one of us may find ourselves in a variety of difficult situations. Will we be ready? Will we respond with both grace and truth?

Apologetics has been a staple of the church since the time of Jesus and Paul. More than ever before, we need Christians who will both live and proclaim the Christian worldview. Apologetics is critical for that task. Apologetics is not a spiritual gift for some; it's something we are *all* called to do. As C.S. Lewis said, the question is not if we are apologists, but what kind of apologist will we be.

And yet *how* we do apologetics must change. And that is exactly the goal of this book.

My hope is that you will be challenged and equipped to defend classical Christianity in a manner that is relevant for today. My prayer is that your heart will be broken for the lost, and that your eyes will be opened to seeing how effective and important apologetics is for ministry today. While the gospel message is eternal (Galatians 1:6-9), our methods must adapt. The following characteristics define *a new kind of apologist*:

Humble. Jesus was the first Christian apologist. In John 5–8, Jesus reasoned with the religious leaders of his day, providing multiple lines of evidence that he is the Son of God. And yet, even though he was divine, Jesus willingly humbled himself for the sake of loving others (Philippians 2:5-7). We can do no less.

Relational. While labels can sometimes be helpful, it is easy to depersonalize people by putting them into various boxes. If our labels cause us to ignore the unique personhood of *every* individual, then we need to reexamine how we use them. I work hard to have genuine relationships with people who are atheists, Mormons, agnostics, and a variety of other worldviews. My goal is not simply to convert them, but I value them as human beings. Apologetics is not an abstract discipline for me, but relates to people I deeply care about. If you want to be a new kind of apologist, it is vital to build relationships with people of varying faiths so you can speak from a heart of genuine care.

Studious. Apologists today must do their homework. We must critically examine our arguments and read both sides of every issue. We must know what we are talking about and do proper research to back up our claims. This younger generation has been raised with endless information in the palm of their hands, and they frequently check the veracity of what they hear. If we make a claim that is not true, our credibility will go out the window. Apologists today must do the hard work of learning a discipline and presenting the truth fairly and accurately.

Practitioner. Authenticity is highly prized among young people. They want to know not only if we can make a good argument, but also if our lives reflect the truth we proclaim. If our lives don't reflect our truth claims, what we say we believe will fall on deaf ears. Thus, prolife apologists must not merely make the case for the value of the unborn, but they must actively care for the vulnerable. Apologists for creation must not only present their arguments, but also help protect creation. We must actively live the truth we proclaim.

There are many more important aspects of being a new kind of apologist. In this book, you will see the intersection between apologetics and important topics such as economics, politics, and race. You will learn how to tackle thorny matters of our day such as the transgender issue and religious liberty. You will gain a model for answering tough questions such as the exclusivity of Christ and new challenges to the Bible. And you will learn practical skills such as having apologetics conversations, asking good questions, using social media, and mentoring the next generation. All of these skills, and more, are important for apologists today.

Are you ready to make a difference in the lives of people? Are you ready to become a new kind of apologist?

As you glean from the wealth of wisdom in the pages that follow, I'm convinced it will help you avoid a repeat of my Breckenridge blunder. And most importantly, it will equip you to lovingly speak truth to our broken and hurt-ing world.

SEAN MCDOWELL is an assistant professor in the Christian apologetics program at Biola University and a popular speaker at schools, churches, and conferences nationwide. He holds master's degrees in theology and philosophy from Talbot Theological Seminary and a PhD in apologetics and worldview studies from South-ern Baptist Theological Seminary. Sean's website, www.seanmcdowell.org, offers his blog, articles, videos, and additional curriculum.

PART 1

A New Approach to Apologetics

SEAN MCDOWELL

Jesus was an apologist. He used logical reasoning to respond to criticism (e.g., Matthew 22:23-32) and he put forth various lines of evidence to demonstrate that he was the Messiah (John 5–8).[1] Along with loving people, healing people, and proclaiming the kingdom of God, Jesus thought it was important to defend the truth of the Scriptures and to provide positive evidence in support of his worldview.

His goal was not simply to win arguments for their own sake. Rather, his greater goal was to see people follow him and to experience eternal life (John 17:1-5). And yet to accomplish this end, Jesus utilized apologetics as one important tool.

Jesus had a unique approach to apologetics, notes the late philosopher Dallas Willard: "Jesus' aim in utilizing logic is not to win battles, but to achieve understanding or insight in his hearers...He presents matters in such a way that those who wish to know can find their way to, can come to, the appropriate conclusion as something they have discovered—whether or not it is something they particularly care for."[2]

Jesus was much more than an apologist, but he was no less than one. Peter, Paul, and the rest of the apostles utilized apologetics in their early ministry (Acts 2:14-41). And so did many of the early church fathers. My point is simple: *apologetics has been one important staple of the church since its inception.*

And yet today we find ourselves at a unique cultural crossroads. The world is more connected and diverse than ever. While Christianity is growing worldwide, in Western culture, those who embrace the Christian worldview are increasingly labeled hateful, bigoted, and intolerant. How will we respond?

As you will learn in this section, it is more important than ever that the church embrace apologetics. And yet our approach to apologetics must change. We simply cannot keep doing business as we have in the past. Rather than seeing outsiders as enemies, which often creates an "us versus them" mentality, we need to reach out with a posture of humility, generosity, and openness. As Biola University president Barry Corey says, *we need to have a firm center and yet soft edges.*

My prayer is that this section will encourage you to rethink your approach to apologetics. Ultimately, the most important question is: "How would Jesus do apologetics today?" I think you will find some hints in the following chapters.

— 1 —

Christians in the Argument Culture:
Apologetics as Conversation

TIM MUEHLHOFF

What's stopping you?"

During a training session for those interested in apologetics, I asked if anyone knew of family members, classmates, or coworkers who did not have a relationship with Jesus. Hands went up throughout the audience.

"What's stopping you from sharing the Christian perspective with them?" I asked. When I present this question to audiences, several responses surface. Some answer, "I tried to bring up God with a family member, but he quickly became defensive, so I changed the subject. I have yet to bring up the issue again." Others, "I imagine having a conversation with a coworker, but always envision it going poorly. I continually psych myself out." Last, and most common, "I have no idea how to organize such a potentially explosive conversation."

Can you relate?

Is there someone you want to share the Christian perspective with but have yet to do it? If so, what's stopping you? Have you psyched yourself out or just lack a clear strategy for how to engage?

Most of us—through participating in social media or watching cable news shows—are aware of the *argument culture,* which Georgetown University linguist Deborah Tannen defines as a pervasive war-like atmosphere that makes us approach anything as if it were a verbal fight. "The argument culture urges us to regard the world—and the people in it—in an adversarial frame of mind."[1] Regularly witnessing such incivility makes us want no part of contentious conversations, so we get into the habit of ignoring certain topics.

For the past couple of years, as I have watched our culture simultaneously lose the ability to have respectful conversations *and* become more hostile to Christian beliefs,[2] I have found myself wrestling with perplexing questions:

How can I remain faithful to my convictions but communicate in a way that produces dialogue, not uncivil debate?

How can I balance truth and love when discussing my worldview with people who disagree with me?

What if the person I'm struggling with is a spouse, family member, coworker, or neighbor? Can I protect our relationship while sharing a worldview people increasingly find offensive?

Most importantly, where can I look for guidance?

I found the communication principles I needed in the book of Proverbs. This unique book is the collective counsel of teachers to their students. Israel's teachers were watching their best and brightest leave to take leadership positions in Jerusalem. This move put young Israelite men in touch with non-Israelites who did not share the sacred beliefs of the Jewish community. The writers of Proverbs faced the same challenge we do: How do we prepare individuals to meet and engage people whose beliefs are radically different from our own? These wise teachers knew they could not write a script for every interpersonal situation their pupils would encounter. People then were too diverse, just as they are now. Instead, they carefully crafted broad principles and sayings, which we can use today.

These proverbial principles are expressed in four essential questions that we must ask during a conversation with someone whose beliefs are different from our own.

Question 1: What does this person believe?

Proverbs 18:13 (NASB) states that "He who gives an answer before he hears, it is folly and shame to him." In almost every personal interaction mentioned in Proverbs, the first step is listening. Why is listening so crucial? Because to neglect it is to respond to a person in both folly (speaking without knowing all the facts) or shame (treating the person as an inferior). Rather than talking prematurely, the wise conversationalist will "store up knowledge" (10:14 NASB). The importance of listening cannot be overstated. Before you respond to a person find out *exactly* what he or she believes.

Many Christians, however, view listening as an unnecessary and unwelcome step in sharing the Christian worldview. Humorist Dave Barry made this stinging observation about people who are eager to start religious conversations: "People who want to share their religious views with you almost never want you to share yours with them."[3]

Why is that? In apologetic conversations, why do we Christians usually find ourselves doing most of the talking?

I think most of us suffer from what one communication scholar described as "agenda anxiety," which he defines as the overwhelming anxiety to "get across all points" of a subject regardless of the spiritual state of the person we are speaking with.[4] Let's face it, most of us struggle with guilt at having not said more concerning spiritual issues with friends and family, and we desire to relieve that guilt by sharing *everything* we've always wanted to say about God in one conversation. The problem is "one can be satisfied with his coverage of content and still fail to communicate."[5]

In the end, listening is sacrificed when so much needs to be explained and opportunities are few and far between. To listen to a person will require that we temporarily set aside our objections to what a person is saying and allow him or her to speak openly without fear of being challenged. After listening to a person's perspective, we need to dig even deeper.

Question 2: Why does this person believe?

Scholars at the Harvard Negotiation Project have served as mediators in thousands of difficult cases. They argue that when we discuss differences, most of us make the mistake of only trading conclusions, not how we *arrived* at those conclusions. In the heat of the moment, we merely give another person the bottom line of our convictions, not the backstory of how those convictions developed.

Proverbs 16:25 (NIV) tells us, "There is a way that appears to be right, but in the end it leads to death." During this crucial step in the conversation, we need to resist the urge to explain to a person why we think his position will lead to intellectual or spiritual death. Rather, we need to first understand *why* this way seems right to him. What a person believes is deeply entwined with his or her personal and social history. The goal is to understand why a person has embraced convictions or behaviors we find unreasonable or offensive.

Psychologist and gender scholar Carol Gilligan states, "you cannot take a life out of history."[6] All of our convictions and passions have a history to them that can be traced back to the influences of our family, personal experiences, and influential people.

All three of these influences were on display with the death of Steve Jobs. While Jobs is considered one of our finest American inventors, his perfectionism and bouts of anger made it nearly impossible to work with him resulting in his once being fired by the very company he created. Understanding what fueled his anger and impossible standards would have been crucial in attempting to engage him. Biographer, Jeff Goodall, after being given unprecedented access to Jobs in the last years of his life, offers this insight:

> The central trauma of his life, after all, was being given up for adoption by his parents, and now he was being kicked out of his second family, the company he founded. A close friend once speculated to me that Steve's drive came from a deep desire to prove that his parents were wrong to give him up. A desire, in short, to be loved—or, more precisely, a desire to prove that he was somebody worth loving.[7]

What impact does it have on you to know that what in part undergirded Jobs's perfectionism and anger was not narcissism but the desire of an adopted kid to prove to himself and others he was worthy of love? How much would this insight change how you interacted with him?

If we want to effectively engage people from differing perspectives, we must first create thick, not thin, impressions by asking: "When did you first start to think this way?" "Who has influenced your thinking the most concerning this issue?" "What books or movies have shaped your perspective?" "Does your perspective deviate from your parents' perspective?"

The next question is perhaps the most neglected by Christian apologists.

Question 3: Where do we agree?

The book of Proverbs extols wisdom and encourages its readers to pursue it at all costs. Wisdom is personified as a woman calling above the roar of a busy street inviting all to come to her. The writers of Proverbs firmly believed that her voice could be found not only in Israel but far beyond her borders as well. That is why the words of two non-Israelite leaders, Augur (chapter 30) and Lemuel (chapter 31), appear in the inspired book of Proverbs. "All truth belonged to and ultimately derived from their Lord no matter who experienced and expressed it," suggests Old Testament scholar David Hubbard.[8]

The greatest skill needed by Christians in today's argument culture will not be the ability to debate but the ability to recognize and affirm God's truth buried in the perspectives of our neighbors and friends. In today's vitriolic communication climate, differences will be apparent; it will take skill to cultivate common ground. Like the writers of Proverbs, we need to seek out and affirm God's truth in each perspective we encounter. My ability to discover where a person's worldview overlaps with the Christian worldview often depends on where I focus the conversation. Do I focus on a person's questions or on his or her answer?

Students taking my introduction to communication theory class are surprised to see one particular textbook: the Qur'an. They are even more surprised when they learn that the first assignment isn't to attack it but to find common ground. Even though most have never read the Qur'an, they are convinced there can't possibly be agreement between it and the Bible. To start their assignment I share a quote from C.S. Lewis: "The man who agrees with us that some question, little regarded by others, is of great importance can be our friend. He need not agree with us about some answer."[9]

As they begin reading, students soon learn that while the two faith traditions often have differing answers,[10] they ask and value similar questions. "What is God like?" "Who is Jesus?" "What is our responsibility to the poor?" "What is the role of prayer?" "Is there an afterlife?" "Is there a final judgment?" "If so, how can one be saved?"

Focusing on common questions allows us to recognize our similarities while probing our real differences.

Question 4: Based on this knowledge, how should I proceed?

What should the Christian communicator do once he or she has listened and cultivated common ground? In other words, what should you do when it's your turn? The answer in part comes in the book of Proverbs' careful description of how a discerning person sets out to build a house of wisdom. "By wisdom a house is built, and by understanding it is established; and by knowledge the rooms are filled with all precious and pleasant riches" (Proverbs 24:3-4 NASB). This proverb mirrors the communication strategy we have been considering. In step one, by asking, "What do they believe?" we are gathering *knowledge*—facts, information, beliefs, and convictions. In steps two and three, the answers to "Why do they believe?" and "Where do we agree?" help us prioritize facts and cultivate common ground, which is the foundation of true *understanding*. Step four requires that we allow our personal communication to be molded by *wisdom*—in this case, the artful application of knowledge and understanding to people.

Step four requires that we ask the oft-neglected question: "With this person, at this time, under these circumstances, what is the one thing I should say?" Notice the question asks what is the *next thing*, not three or four things, you want to say. When teaching this method to others, I force them to identify a single communication goal—to rebut, clarify, cultivate more common ground, gather more information, affirm the relationship, or set up the next conversation.

When I was in grad school first developing this strategy, I had a memorable opportunity to apply this question. During a public speaking course, a young woman began her speech by lifting up a Bible and saying, "The holy Word of God." She then threw it on the floor and proceeded to kick it across the room. With each kick pages were sent flying. In her speech, with powerful emotions surfacing, she argued that the Bible was an intolerant book that had emotionally damaged thousands of individuals. When she finished, all eyes turned toward me. How would their self-professed Christian professor respond? How would you respond in such a situation?

I was angry and insulted. I sat there, eyes looking down on some incoherent notes scribbled on a legal pad. Then, God powerfully brought to mind Proverb 12:16: "Fools show their annoyance at once, but the prudent overlook an insult." Still not looking up, I thought to myself, *At this time (class is almost over), under these circumstances (roomful of watchful students), with this woman (I didn't know her well), what should be the one thing I say?* I chose to dig deeper rather than challenge her harsh claim about the Bible.

I applauded her for the passion she put into her presentation. I asked her where the passion came from. What had happened in her life to foster such anger? She told the class that last year her younger sister had courageously confessed to being gay. Her small church responded by excommunicating her on Christmas Eve. You could see the hurt and anger etched on her face. Along with the class, I sat and listened as the period ended. By temporarily overlooking her offensive actions, I had preserved the relationship for future interaction.

I wish I could say that I always respond in such a way toward those who belittle or attack things dear to me. I don't. Sometimes I surprise myself how easily I respond to anger with anger or I choose debate over listening. And yet, I find that the four questions explored in this chapter give me tracks to run on when engaging situations such as this one.

The Power of Communication

As followers of Christ, we are desperate to share our story with a world that seems to be rapidly moving away from God. However, in our zeal we forget that communication is a give-and-take proposition, a right to be earned. The communication strategy we have been considering is grounded on the central presupposition of the book of Proverbs—our personal actions operate according to a cause-and-effect pattern. Theologian Cornelius Plantinga describes this universal pattern:

> Like yields like. You get back what you put in. What goes around comes around...No matter what we sow, the law of return applies. Good or evil, love or hate, justice or tyranny, grapes or thorns, a gracious compliment or a peevish complaint—whatever we invest, we tend to get it back with interest. Lovers are loved; haters, hated.[11]

If we want our friends and neighbors to listen to *our* story, then we must listen to theirs. If we want others to attend to *our* convictions, then we must first attend to theirs. If we desire for others to cultivate common ground with us, we must do so *first*. In doing so, we will create a communication climate in which we can fulfill our deepest longing—engaging others in a respectful, civil way that allows us to share a perspective that has changed our lives.

TIM MUEHLHOFF (PhD, University of North Carolina at Chapel Hill) is a professor of communication at Biola University in La Mirada, California. He is the author of *I Beg to Differ: Navigating Difficult Conversations in Truth and Love; Authentic Communication: Christian Speech Engaging Culture;* and *The God Conversation: Using Illustrations to Explain your Faith* (coauthored with J.P. Moreland).

— 2 —

Apologetics and New Technologies

BRIAN AUTEN

n the early fifteenth century, a German blacksmith named Johannes Gutenberg invented the printing press, a new technology that allowed for the production and distribution of the printed word like never before.

Every so often technologies arise that seem to change everything. The telephone, radio, television, the Internet...each new technology brings with it the possibility of a new means of interaction, a new platform for communication. Today, social media has changed how people stay in touch, as well as how we receive news about the world. Some have called this the golden age of communications.[1] Access to information is greater than it has ever been, and in many ways this has created a cacophony of voices and opinions, which thrust many toward the path of skepticism.

But how can the Christian apologist effectively utilize new technologies to defend the faith? In this chapter we will explore this question, as well as look at some practical ideas for making the most of the new media available to us today. For the apologist, new technologies can change everything.

Find Your Role

For the Christian apologist looking at today's technological landscape, the opportunities are endless. This global platform has made it possible for a single individual to reach the same audience as only Hollywood could have just decades earlier. The only question is where to start.

That's a tough question, because we could explore any number of possible outlets for reaching people. If we started listing the possibilities, we might quickly get overwhelmed: websites, blogs, audio, video, podcasts, social media, Twitter...the list goes on. Here we'll take a different approach by first looking at the *role* you can play.

As I see it, there are four main roles available to the apologist when it comes to using technologies, whatever those outlets might be:

- Content Authors
- Content Artists
- Content Communicators
- Content Propagators

Content authors create the information or the message. Content artists shape that information into various media. Content communicators reach people through direct interaction. Content propagators take the message and make it more widely available through sharing or multiplying it.

The apologist can take on any or all of these roles when using technology. The purpose of this differentiation is to make it easier to get started. Instead of starting with the question, "How can I use technology to reach people?" we ask, "How am I gifted when it comes to apologetics?"

Some are more inclined to study and write and do research. They would tend toward the *content author* role. Some are gifted or skilled in using tools to build websites, edit audio, or shoot video. They would land in the *content artist* role. Others seem gifted and drawn to speaking on a one-to-one level with people, asking questions and answering challenges. They would fall into the *content communicator* role. Finally, there are those who don't have to be great experts, but they have a passion for apologetics and have found answers to other people's questions while doing their own investigation. They would land in the *content propagator* role.

There are no hard borders between roles; they overlap. This is just a useful tool for finding a starting place when it comes to how apologists might use technology. The main thing to think about at this point is which role you think you are most drawn to based on your unique gifts and skills.

Now we'll unpack each of these ideas a bit more.

Content Authors

When we talk about *content*, we are talking about the message or the information that's being communicated. Everything on the web is content, whether audio, video, or text. But someone had to create that content. When it comes to doing apologetics, content authors are those who write articles for blogposts, write book reviews, create scripts for interviews or videos, or do any other authoring of content not already available.

If this area seems to match your skills, gifts, and interests, then being a content author is perhaps the first way to delve into harnessing new technologies for apologetics. I know some prolific writers who can, with very little effort, generate reams of content for blogposts and articles. They can team up with content artists to shape that content into the various media outlets, such as online resource pages, podcasts, teaching curriculum, PowerPoint presentations, videos, and the like.

Content Artists

Content artists use their skills and gifts to make the message or information available. They may use a blogging platform, podcasting software, a video editing suite, graphic design tools, or other means to present the message. The content artist knows how to shape the message and make it available across various outlets.

Think about it. A content *author* may be skilled in research and writing, but may have few skills or know-how beyond that. But the content *artist* can take an article, make it into a blogpost, an infographic, an animation, a YouTube video, a podcast, a PowerPoint presentation, or an iPhone app. Often in the apologetics world, we have already authored plenty of good content; we just need content artists with a creative vision who can create an accessible way for people to interact with that content through the various media.

Content Communicators

The content communicator is more gifted or drawn to personal interaction, and so they can find their outlet for doing apologetics through social media, Twitter, blog comments, Internet forums, and message boards. This role requires patience, wisdom, and tact. It requires patience because interactions on the Internet can sometimes feel fruitless when discussing issues with obstinate individuals. However, sometimes these online conversations have more benefit for those reading the interactions than for those engaged in the actual discussion.

The content communicator needs to be wise in choosing topics to interact with, people to interact with, and what platforms to interact on. Trying to have a debate on Twitter with an angry atheist is not usually the most productive use of time, nor does the platform lend itself to discussion.

Wise communicators can discern the best places to interact and just how much time to spend. Tact is required because online interaction lacks the visual cues of body language and the verbal cues of tone of voice. Words must be chosen carefully, not quickly. And what is on the Internet is there to stay. The Internet doesn't forget. Content communicators (or online apologists) take their time and are careful with words.

Content Propagators

The content propagator multiplies the reach of the resources already available. On the Apologetics 315 website (www.apologetics315.com), for example, much of what you find there—a great lecture, a powerful debate, a helpful podcast—are simply resources that have been propagated. Great content is of no use unless others find it, so the job of the content propagator is essential to share content.

Think of how many times you have come across a video that went viral. It wasn't because you went to YouTube and searched for it. It's because someone shared it with you via Facebook, Twitter, or it was linked to on a blog or a website. Then you went on to share it with others. Now millions of people have viewed the video because of the viral effect of multiplied sharing.

The content propagator can use platforms such as blogs, webpages, Facebook, and other social media to point people to resources, links, articles, and videos of great content that is already out there.

Tying It Together

For the next generation of Christian apologists to make a maximum impact using technology, it will become essential to build a strategic synergy between teams of people working together as content authors, content artists, content propagators, and content communicators. By bringing all of these roles together, networks of apologists can fully utilize the content by bringing it to bear on every available media outlet.

Know Your Tools

Not long ago my wife and I bought an iPad as a gift for a family member. Although they were excited about all the possibilities of this wonderful new device, certain walls immediately went up: "How on earth do I use this? I'm not a computer person. I'll never be able to understand this thing." The same walls can go up when we look at unfamiliar technology. Someone who has never used Twitter or Facebook is overwhelmed at the thought of it, simply because they have never used it. This problem needs to be overcome to reach the world through new technologies.

For the apologist, the best starting point is to use the tools that are already familiar to them. For example, someone may be comfortable using a word processor. They can easily write an article defending the resurrection of Jesus. It's not a difficult jump from word processing to a blogging platform. That authored content can then be published and shared online. Not too much of a problem.

Let's say that blog continues and the blogger wants to expand their reach by using that same content for a YouTube channel. They are familiar enough with PowerPoint that they can make that defense of the resurrection into a slide presentation...but there's more. They will need to record themselves narrating the presentation. They will need to edit the slides together into a video. They will need to upload it onto YouTube. As soon as they want to expand the impact, they either need to upgrade their skill set or work together with a content artist.

Some people have the ability to easily take on new skills. For others, this is more of a challenge. I encourage people first off not to be intimidated or afraid of learning new skills. After all, apologists tend to be learners and self-taught in many areas. Why not let that ability to learn challenging subjects carry over to learning a challenging technology?

If learning how to record, edit, or design seems absolutely out of the question, then I encourage a general familiarity with various tools that are required for creating audio, video, and web-based content. However, it's extremely useful for apologists to be able to interact with social media tools like Facebook for the purpose of sharing content and networking.

Know How to Interact

For the apologist, clear communication and winsome interaction are key. Greg Pritchard offers a definition of apologetics as "the art and science of Christian persuasion." I like the threefold appeal to heart, head, and emotion in that definition. Like Aristotle's rhetoric, it entails *ethos, logos,* and *pathos.* For the Christian ambassador, it's critical to know both the art (the heart and emotional aspects) and the science (the logical, technical aspects) of persuasion.[2]

When it comes to technology or interactions on the Internet, these principles carry over and play out in a unique way because of the nature of the medium. So how do we interact when it comes to using the Internet? Here are a few tips to consider.

The Internet Never Forgets

Remember, what you say on the Internet is forever. Once you publish your blogpost, it is there to be scrutinized by everyone. Even if you delete it, it may be archived or already copied elsewhere. With this in mind, *take your time.* One of the benefits of interacting on the Internet is that there is time to think carefully about your replies, your answers, and your questions. This is not the time to rush, get carried away by emotion, or try to make quick replies. Once you say it, it's out there. So just take your time and respond well.

Know the Strengths and Weaknesses of the Medium

It's important to consider the strengths and weaknesses of the medium you are using. As mentioned before, Twitter is not the most effective tool for debating others. The strength of Twitter might be more suited to propagating links to resources. The comments section on YouTube also isn't the best place for trying to carry on a deep discussion. Using those places for linking back to more appropriate discussion forums (where anonymity isn't possible) can make interaction more productive. The point here is that we want to use the right tool for the job.

Watch Out for Pitfalls

Perhaps you've seen the Internet cartoon that goes something like this:
Wife: "Honey, can you come to bed now?"
Husband: "Not yet dear, this is more important."
Wife: "What is it?"
Husband: "Someone is wrong on the Internet."
For those doing apologetics on the Internet, perhaps you can relate to this. It's very easy to spend inordinate amounts of time on emotionally charged issues, to try to win arguments instead of winning people, and to forget about the larger picture and try to be a lone-ranger apologist. But often what is needed is for us to step back and consider what it is we are trying to do and how we are trying to do it.

The pitfall of new technologies is that they can easily breed isolation, anonymity, and imbalance. However, the new kind of apologist realizes the importance of community, accountability, and balance.

Conclusion

We live in a day when the opportunities to reach the world for Christ are greater than they have ever been. The tools at our disposal are manifold, and are only going to continue to grow. Apologists today can find their role in using new technologies based on their particular gifts and skills, and find a wide variety of outlets for apologetic interaction. We can be strategic in our outreach by utilizing teams of apologists in coordinated efforts to make a maximum impact.

BRIAN AUTEN is the founder of Apologetics 315, an apologetics resource hub featuring interviews with over 175 Christian apologists. Brian holds a master's degree in Christian apologetics and is director of Reasonable Faith Belfast.

Interview with Bart Campolo
SEAN MCDOWELL

You grew up in the Christian subculture and were even an evangelist, and yet now you no longer believe in God. What happened?

It's a long story, but the bottom line is that I gradually lost the ability to believe the supernatural parts of the Christian narrative, despite having every incentive to stay in the faith. Eventually, all the doctrines I used to rely on seemed so clearly fabricated by human beings that I wondered how I ever managed to believe them. I ended up feeling about Christianity the way most Christians feel about Islam and Hinduism.

What label do you prefer for yourself?

I call myself a secular humanist these days, not because I'm angry or fed up with the church, but because I want to attract folks who no longer or never could believe in supernatural forces but still want to actively pursue goodness as a way of life. Such people have very few spiritual leaders, so I'm just trying to let them know where they can find one. That said, I'm still grateful for Christianity, since that's where I learned almost everything I know about love. Just as I no longer live in Philadelphia, but still speak with that accent and root for the Eagles, I'm proud of where I came from spiritually and I still support the best kinds of Jesus followers.

Why *humanist* instead of an *atheist*, *skeptic*, *agnostic*, or *freethinker*? Well, every label has its drawbacks, but I avoid *atheist* and *skeptic* because they sound negative and because they're too easily confused with antitheism, which doesn't work for someone like me. Technically I'm *agnostic*, but that word suggests way more uncertainty than I actually feel. Even if it didn't sound hopelessly old-fashioned, I'm too aware of my cognitive biases to call myself a freethinker. I'm not fully sold on *humanist* either, but at least it immediately communicates (a) that I don't believe in God and (b) that I'm actively committed to a positive value system.

What advice would you give Christian apologists?

Honestly, I think you folks should stop trying to reason with thoughtful nonbelievers. After all, hardly anyone decides to follow Jesus because Christianity simply makes so much more sense to him or her than every other worldview. On the contrary, people become Christians because they are born into or enfolded into a loving community that provides meaning and purpose to their lives, and they are able to believe the Christian narrative because it makes sense in the context of that community. The primary value of your work as apologists lies in enabling your fellow Christians to stand confidently, secure that their faith is not unreasonable even though—or perhaps because—it is founded on the divine revelation of a supernatural God. You're wasting your time with the rest of us.

BART CAMPOLO was a popular writer and speaker in Christian circles before becoming the first humanist chaplain at the University of Southern California and the University of California, Los Angeles (UCLA).

— 3 —

Servant Apologetics

TOM GILSON

Apologetics has a reputation problem. We're the ones who "like to argue." We're the ones with a need to win. We're the people who don't understand people, though we claim to understand everything else.

That may be distorted, but it's not entirely off the mark. Those of us who care about the ministry of apologetics need to take it seriously. We do have a problem. Part of the difficulty, I believe, is that we haven't understood where the problem comes from. Much of it can be attributed to some very normal and very human motivations—motivations so human, in fact, I doubt there's any human way to escape them.

The human motivation I'm speaking of here is our tendency to turn inward, to do what meets our own needs, even in our ministry of apologetics. It stands in contrast to a more biblical approach, which I call *servant apologetics*.

I'm going to explain that contrast in more detail in a moment, but first I want to give you an actual picture of what I mean by servant apologetics, in the person of Matt Burford of Montgomery, Alabama.

A Servant Apologist

Matt Burford is a young guy, or at least he looks that way to me, being in my late fifties as I am. Trained as a computer network administrator, Matt has made some career transitions lately, and now he's a preacher doing pulpit supply work on weekends. He's also a seminary student, and he's the president of a grassroots apologetics organization called Tactical Faith.

I first encountered Matt in connection with a conference he was helping to run in Alabama. When I got to know him better, I found out he was uniting people to do apologetics events all over the state and occasionally beyond. As of early 2015, there were about twenty-five people directly involved with Tactical Faith, and together they've led or facilitated almost fifty apologetics events, large and small, since 2011.

No one draws any salary from Tactical Faith, including Matt. In that sense, he's not much different from most of the rest of us. He calls it a "ministry hobby." I'd say it must be quite a hobby to reach that many people with that much impact.

I spent some time on the phone with Matt recently, talking about how he does it. That was when I found out what an excellent model he was of a servant apologist. There were three main themes in what he shared that day: listening, giving, and growing.

Listening

I asked Matt to describe the kind of work he does with Tactical Faith, and he started out by telling me story after story of sitting down with other Christians and listening to them.

"I'm intentional in what I do," he told me. "Every aspect is about networking, having an attentive ear, listening, hearing their stories, and being open to them and saying, 'If you like apologetics, how can I help you?' Because it's not about me, it's about saying, 'You have these options, how can I help position you to be useful for the kingdom? What can I do to help you succeed?'"

I'd like to echo Matt on the importance of listening. One of my favorite things to do is to take pastors out to lunch. Maybe you've heard it said that pastors have the hardest job in the world. I agree, and I speak from a knowledge base, having been trained in organizational psychology and consulted with some of the largest mission organizations in the world. There really is no other job as complicated as a pastor's.

So I go to lunch with pastors, armed with two kinds of answers. On the one hand I have training and experience in organizational leadership, and on the other hand, I've got a bagful of apologetics answers.

Sometimes pastors are interested in those things. More often by far, though, what they need is someone who will listen. Every pastor I've ever met with is dealing with a lot; every one of them needs someone who will show they care.

Now I've also found that once I've listened long enough so they know I care, sometimes they'll ask me about a challenge they're facing, one that happens to be related to a field I've studied. They welcome my answers, if I have any, to questions they're *actually* dealing with.

Here's another way to look at it. We're in the research and communication business: we discover and we communicate reasons for confidence in Christianity. Communication can be speaker-centered or audience-centered (or a mix of the two, but I'm simplifying to make the point). Speaker-centered communication starts with the communicator and what he thinks is important. Audience-centered communication starts with what the audience is dealing with, what they're concerned with at the moment, and what they really need deep inside.

Of course we know that everyone, without exception, needs the gospel in all its fullness. We can't just deliver the same message to everyone, though. Jesus certainly didn't. We need to connect our message with their current questions and concerns. That requires an attitude of servanthood expressed in the act of listening.

Giving

Back to my conversation with Matt, I noticed him returning repeatedly to another theme: *giving*. I don't mean financial giving (although Tactical Faith does that). I mean something more like what he was getting at when he said,

"Collaboration is about being in mutual submission [an allusion to Ephesians 5:21], being able to let the light shine on others brighter than on you." He gives others opportunities. He gives them credit. He gives them honor. Take a look again at my first quotation from our conversation and you'll see he loves to help others succeed.

Woven throughout the Bible is a principle of blessing. It starts in Genesis 12:3 and continues without pause or interruption to the book of Revelation. We're blessed for a reason: so that we can pass a blessing along to others. This applies to apologetics as much as it does to anything else. If God has gifted us to enjoy and excel at apologetics, he's done it so that we can equip, encourage, teach, and otherwise be a blessing to others.

I appreciate Frank Turek in this regard too. He's written some great books, he's a popular speaker, and he has a radio show. Still, he and several prominent apologist friends of his take time out every year to equip other young apologists, through the Cross-Examined Instructors Academy.

I could name many others with similar giving attitudes, but I'm simply trying to illustrate a point. This kind of giving lines up well with a servant approach to apologetics.

Growing

Toward the end of our conversation, Matt Burford added this word. He emphasized it, actually, as he's been realizing lately it's important above everything else. It's about "using apologetics in a right manner. My advice," he said, "is to be really looking at virtue, character development, and what it means that the fear of the Lord is the beginning of wisdom."

That's one way of looking at what it takes to be truly caring and giving. It comes out of a heart molded by the Word of God and the work of the Holy Spirit.

Another Look at Servant Apologetics

Not everyone is a Matt Burford, though. Not everyone is running multistate conference support efforts. What about the rest of us? How can we be servant-like in our approach to apologetics at church, on campus, or in our communities?

I'm sure there are more ways to answer that than I could begin to think of, much less include in this chapter. Instead of trying to name them, I'm going to offer a general framework to help you think it through for yourself in your own situation.

One way to think about our apologetics audiences is their level of interest. What follows here is an informal description of different attitudes Christians (and some non-Christians) might have toward apologetics. This isn't a comprehensive list by any means: even some of my closest working associates, Ratio Christi chapter directors, fall somewhere between level 1 and 2. My purpose here isn't to develop new labels for people, but to help us think about who we're ministering to and what their key apologetics-related needs might be.

These, then, are five levels of apologetics interest to think about, and a few thoughts about what people at each level might need.

1. Core leaders. These are the scholars, teachers, speakers, and writers who produce most of the apologetics material the rest of us use. What core leaders need most in their ministry is mutual encouragement, opportunities to study, a well-developed strategic platform from which to present their material, and a heart to serve the rest of the body of Christ.

2. Enthusiasts and local leaders. Enthusiasts are the ones who go to conferences, buy books by the armload, write or comment on blogs, and so on. Local leaders are enthusiasts who have also taken up a significant leadership role teaching in Sunday schools, leading community apologetics groups, and so on. Enthusiasts often need encouragement and training to step up to a leadership role. Local leaders and enthusiasts both need a network of encouragers, and they need their steady supply of books to read and conferences to attend. They need a way to minister to others as well.

3. Questioners. Everyone has questions, but some people are more open to exploring them than others. Questioners care about answers—but they might not know there are any. They might include teenagers (or even preteens) who have reached the point of wondering whether their parents' faith can be their own. They might include parents who wonder what to tell their drifting teens to keep them in the faith. Questioners might find apologetics to be mentally challenging, but still they might well be interested in apologetics-style answers if they knew such a thing existed. They need someone to patiently show them those answers do exist, and help them understand.

4. *The inoculated.* These are people who know about apologetics and have a bad opinion of it. They may know some apologetics themselves, but for whatever reason, they don't see much value in pursuing or promoting it; it's as if they've been inoculated against it. The best way I know of to help the inoculated, and what they might need most, is a kind of double exposure. The first exposure is to tough, real-world questions, issues, and problems that demand seriously thoughtful answers. Painful though it may be, the inoculated need to become uncomfortable in their apathy toward answers. The second exposure involves a deeply relational connection with someone who can represent apologetics wisely, lovingly, and thoughtfully toward them.

5. *The closed.* These fellow Christians aren't at all interested in apologetics and wouldn't respond to anything we have to offer. Maybe they'll get along just the way they are until God calls them home, or maybe God will bring them face-to-face with a hard question someday. Unless and until that happens, there's not much we have to offer them as apologists. We may still have a lot to offer them as friends in the Lord, but not so much as apologists.

That list is obviously incomplete, but there's enough there to give us some conceptual material to play with. Suppose you're an enthusiast: apologetics may not be your greatest love in life, but it's close. You read a book a week (though you really wish you had time to read two or three). You've got Gary Habermas's minimal facts down pat, and you know William Lane Craig's kalam cosmological argument well enough to throw in names like Hilbert and Vilenkin. You enjoy apologetics so much you made sure you got a copy of this book.

If something like that describes you, I have two questions for you:

1. *Who needs your apologetics skills and insights the most?* Hint: it isn't other enthusiasts. They're getting their apologetics fix the same way you are: books, the Internet, and conferences.

2. Who do you find most motivating to be with? The answer to that question will reveal whether you're a servant apologist or not.

If your answer is "other enthusiasts," or even "core leaders," you might want to take a careful look at yourself. There's nothing the least bit wrong with enjoying fellowship; it's a matter of purpose and balance. If you're there for mutual refreshment, great! If you're there to get equipped to serve others elsewhere, that's great too.

If you're there to get a pat on the back for coming up with a new twist on an old argument, that might be okay if you keep it in perspective. If, however, you're there to escape the realms of the unenlightened and bask in the warmth of some real intellect, take a close look at yourself: that's old-fashioned pride taking over. And if you're there without giving a second thought to those who aren't, then I suggest you think very hard about what Jesus meant when he said, "For even the Son of Man came not to be served but to serve, and to give his life as a ransom for many" (Mark 10:45).

Servant apologists look for ways to use their gifts to help those who actually need what they have to offer: questioners, the inoculated, and even the closed. They find ways to serve even if they don't get pats on the back for their clever new arguments. They do it even if the people they're ministering to think they're a little bit weird.

They do it because they know service means meeting others' needs ahead of their own.

Breaking the Cycle

I don't know of any other ministry quite like apologetics. The people who need our gifts and skills the least are the ones who appreciate them the most, and the ones who need our gifts and knowledge the most are the ones likely to appreciate them the least.

I wonder whether there's a self-reinforcing cycle operating to keep it that way. We apologetics enthusiasts have trouble finding real encouragement from anyone except other apologetics enthusiasts. So we find ways to connect with each other online or in person. When we do, we speak in our esoteric language about arguments and inferences and evidences, and in our weaker moments we criticize the church's lack of interest in what concerns us most.

The church sees us doing that from a distance and finds it foreign and more than a little bit distasteful. So when we come back down to earth (to our churches, that is) we feel even more estranged. It makes us want to just go right back to our connections with apologists, which is where the cycle began. The whole thing repeats itself. No wonder we have a reputation problem.

It doesn't have to be that way. We can break the cycle by living in our churches as servants: listening, caring, loving, and always remaining available to teach and to give answers when the need arises.

That's why I like Matt Burford's approach. First, he tries to understand what makes people tick, and then he tries to help them succeed. It isn't about the answers he can give; it's about the people he can build. It's about growing in Christ, to rise above the human tendency to meet our own needs, meeting others' needs instead.

> *"For even the Son of Man came not to be served but to serve,*
> *and to give his life as a ransom for many."*

TOM GILSON is the vice president for strategic services for the Ratio Christi student apologetics alliance, a columnist at BreakPoint online, and coeditor of *True Reason: Confronting the Irrationality of the New Atheism.* He blogs at www.Think ingChristian.net. He and his wife, Sara, and their two grown children live in southwestern Ohio.

— 4 —

Motivating Others to "Give an Answer"

MARK MITTELBERG

You've gotten this far in a book on Christian apologetics, so I can now safely state a fact: *You're not normal.*

Congratulations! We don't need more "normal" Christians. We need more *extraordinary* ones. Specifically, the kind who:

- take seriously biblical commands like the one Peter issued to every believer: "Always be prepared to give an answer to everyone who asks you to give the reason for the hope that you have" (1 Peter 3:15 NIV)

- follow the example of Paul in learning how to "demolish arguments and every pretension that sets itself up against the knowledge of God, and...take captive every thought to make it obedient to Christ" (2 Corinthians 10:5 NIV)

- build their life around Jesus's command to "go and make disciples of all nations, baptizing them in the name of the Father and of the Son and of the Holy Spirit, and teaching them to obey everything I have commanded you" (Matthew 28:19-20 NIV).

See what I mean? Doing all of that isn't normal in the church today—though it should be. I hope, though, that it describes you in increasing measure.

More than that, I hope you're becoming a *new kind of apologist*—one who lives out the full challenge of 1 Peter 3:15, including the last part that tells us to answer people "with gentleness and respect." And I hope you're following the example of Paul, who opened his bold passage about demolishing arguments with these words: "By the humility and gentleness of Christ, I appeal to you..." I also hope you're emulating Jesus, who "made himself nothing" and "humbled himself" (Philippians 2:7,8 NIV).

That combination of godly motivation and godly attitude is truly powerful in God's hands. I trust you've already begun to see the fruit of it in your own life.

But this brings us to our central question: How can we help more and more Christians catch the infectious spirit that we've already caught? What can we do to motivate our brothers and sisters in Christ to "be prepared to give an answer to everyone who asks...with gentleness and respect"?

Let's look at some ways we can motivate several different groups of people: church leaders, church members, parents and grandparents, and students. Then we'll end by discussing what should motivate us to do all of this.

Motivating Church Leaders to "Give an Answer"

Whether or not you're a leader in your church, a key to helping any congregation reach its evangelistic and apologetic potential is helping its top leaders, especially the senior pastor, to increasingly adopt and live out these values in their own lives.

There's no getting around the axiom: *Speed of the leader, speed of the team.* People don't do what the leaders *say* as much as they do what the leaders *do.* That's why evangelist and apologist Lee Strobel says that senior leaders invariably "set the evangelistic high-water mark" for their church or ministry.

As Jesus explained in Luke 6:40 (NIV): "The student is not above the teacher, but everyone who is fully trained will be like their teacher."

So how can we "lead up," helping those who shepherd our churches to set the bar high in these areas? Here are some ideas.

Give Old-Fashioned Encouragement

While many leaders will be guarded about being challenged in an area outside their expertise, almost all are receptive to genuine encouragement. So, as Ken Blanchard advises in his classic book *The One-Minute Manager*, try to catch them doing something right! Whenever they teach, tell a story, or recommend a resource in the area of apologetics or evangelism, affirm them. Tell them how encouraging you thought it was, or how you saw it helping someone else. Reinforce what you'd like to see more of. Your enthusiasm alone will help energize them.

Provide Key Information

Leaders will be spurred to action if we expose them to studies and statistics that show how our society is becoming increasingly secular, and how so many church members—especially students—are walking away from their faith. For example, research by the Barna Group revealed that intellectual concerns underlie half of the top six reasons that young Christians gave for why they are leaving the church.[1] Information like this, gently delivered, can heighten the leaders' awareness of this problem and stir their desire to do something about it.

Expose Them to Great Information and Tools

Many teachers and leaders avoid apologetics, not necessarily because they don't find it important, but because they don't feel equipped in this area. Often that's because they're not aware of the many articles, books, seminars, and online resources that could quickly help them come up to speed. You can become a solution to this problem. If you provide timely, relevant, and measured information to help them with upcoming messages or classes, you'll help them succeed in this area and feel a growing sense of excitement to teach about it further. But don't miss a key word in that list: *measured*. That means you need to be careful not to overload them with too much information. They might need a chapter, or an article, or even a well-crafted paragraph or two—but rest assured they don't want you to haul your five-volume encyclopedia of philosophy into their study!

Provide Living Examples

They might not come right out and say it, but some church leaders suspect that apologetics is mostly an intellectual exercise for eggheads and not highly relevant for the average believer. We need to prove them wrong—first, by showing how the evidence often helps clear the path for people to come to Christ, and second, by introducing them to the stories of people who have come to faith, in part, by having their intellectual questions answered. These could include classic testimonies of people such as Lee Strobel (*The Case for Christ*), Josh McDowell (*More than a Carpenter*), J. Warner Wallace (*Cold-Case Christianity*), Holly Ordway (*Not God's Type*), or Nabeel Qureshi (*Seeking Allah, Finding Jesus*). Ideally, you should also feature people from your own church or community whose journey toward Christ has been helped by apologetics. Hearing such accounts, and seeing the examples right before their eyes, makes it hard to argue about whether or not apologetics is still relevant today.

Offer Godly Exhortation

This must be used sparingly, and only after prayer and preparation, but there is a place for challenging a leader to do more in these areas. This must be done in private and in a spirit of humility—and always with the offer to help become part of the solution to the problem you're raising. Don't go to complain and lay a burden on them; instead, go to raise an important need and to help them seize opportunities to make a difference.

Practice Focused Prayer

It's interesting to note that the passage we quoted earlier, where Paul talked about demolishing arguments and taking thoughts captive, begins with a discussion about spiritual warfare. One verse earlier, Paul said, "For though we live in the world, we do not wage war as the world does. The weapons we fight with are not the weapons of the world. On the contrary, they have divine power to demolish strongholds" (2 Corinthians 10:3-4 NIV). Paul explained elsewhere, "Our struggle is not against flesh and blood, but against the rulers, against the authorities, against the powers of this dark world and against the spiritual forces of evil in the heavenly realms" (Ephesians 6:12 NIV). So while the intellectual angle is important, we must engage in the spiritual battle as well by praying for God's wisdom and intervention—including in our efforts to sound the alarm about the importance of apologetics and evangelism.

Motivating Church Members to "Give an Answer"

After helping leaders heighten their commitment to apologetics and evangelism, here are some ideas for how we can partner with them to motivate the entire congregation in these areas.

Underscore the Church's Vision

Without regular reminders, congregations tend to lose their focus on what the church—and we as individuals—are called to accomplish. Unfortunately, the part that fades away first is the most important: *Reaching our world for Christ.* How quickly we forget our mission and fall back into mundane church activities.

Churches need to be reminded of why they are here. Evangelism and apologetics, which is the handmaiden to evangelism, are not optional activities. They are at the very core of our mission, which is to reach our world with the gospel. That's why Jesus spelled it out so clearly: to go into all the world (including next door or down the hallway) to reach everyone we can for him (Matthew 20:18-20). This Great Commission wasn't one choice among many options. *It's what we're here to do.*

Church members quickly forget this, and so we must patiently but persistently remind them. As we do, the Holy Spirit will echo our challenge in their hearts as God's Word underscores it in their minds.

After all, this is God's will—let's be bold about it.

Provide Living Examples

Again, people need role models. We, and the leaders of the church, need to become examples of what evangelism and apologetics can look like in the real world. Even if it doesn't come naturally to us or it's not our gift, we need to strive to teach and defend truth as we point people to the salvation offered through Christ. When we try, they'll try.

Teach Strategically

The church's evangelistic lifeblood will most naturally flow through regular, passionate teaching about our predicament of sin, the solution of the cross, God's offer of unmerited grace, and the adoption into his family that God so freely offers. These are themes that must be hit consistently from the pulpit as well as in classes, small groups, youth groups, children's ministries, and special outreach events. As we do so, we can count on God's promise in Isaiah 55:11 (NIV):

> "So is my word that goes out from my mouth:
> It will not return to me empty,
> but will accomplish what I desire
> and achieve the purpose for which I sent it."

Tell Stories of Life Change

Apologists thrive on truth, logic, information, and evidence. But as I already mentioned, *we're not normal*. Other people in the church tolerate these things, but they gravitate instead toward stories of God's love and transforming power. Let's give them both, including a steady stream of testimonies about how God is reaching people who were filled with spiritual doubt, disbelief, and disobedience. This will touch the hearts of Christians and motivate them to consider our classes and seminars that are designed to equip them to "give an answer to everyone who asks." Having both, they'll begin to bear fruit through their own efforts to talk to others about their faith. Soon they'll have their own first-hand stories to tell.

Offer Ongoing Training

A common mistake is to confuse *teaching* with *training*. Here's the difference: *training always involves trying*. If we want to help church members become confident in talking to others about their faith, then we need to let them try it first—in a safe, affirming environment. That's what training seminars are for, like the *Becoming a Contagious Christian* training course I developed with Lee Strobel and Bill Hybels. It's designed to help ordinary Christians develop the skills to effectively and naturally share their faith with others.[2] Another example is Sean McDowell's *GodQuest* curriculum, which equips entire churches to defend biblical truth.[3] These and similar tools can train and embolden the people in your church—but only if you present them over and over in order to reach increasing numbers of your congregation.

Motivating Parents and Grandparents to "Give an Answer"

Parents and grandparents are part of the churches we're committed to revitalizing, but I want to add some extra advice for motivating them: *Tell them you want to help them reach and retain their own offspring.* Yes, the world matters, but nothing motivates people like concern for their own flesh and blood. So emphasize that benefit of apologetics. Help them understand the risks of losing their children or grandchildren to secular influences. Then covenant with them to pray, prepare, and partner together to intellectually immunize their kids and grandkids so that their faith can withstand the challenges it will surely face.

Motivating Students to "Give an Answer"

Too often our students are unprepared for the onslaught of secular ideas that will buffet them in the future. This is yielding disastrous results. Instead, let's train them to answer the arguments they will inevitably encounter. We can start by showing them video clips of skeptics and proponents of other world religions, or presenting their arguments in a role-play situation, as I've often done with high school groups. Let them feel the challenge.

Better yet, instead of being so quick to spoon-feed them answers, have them wrestle with how they would respond to these arguments. Don't let them languish too long, but after they've grappled with the objections for a while, discuss what the Bible says and where the evidence really points. By then they will truly be listening—and they'll be ready to learn what you want them to know. Later, when they hear these same objections in the real world, they will be much more prepared. They "will no longer be infants, tossed back and forth by the waves, and blown here and there by every wind of teaching and by the cunning and craftiness of people in their deceitful scheming" (Ephesians 4:14 NIV).

Finding the Right Motivation to "Give an Answer"

I hope some of these ideas will help you motivate the people in your church to become much more prepared to give an answer to everyone who asks them for a reason for their faith.[4]

I'll end with a word about the best motivation for us and our fellow Christians we're seeking to encourage. Far too often we've been compelled in these areas by a desire for knowledge alone. Or, more candidly, by a quest to win arguments and to display our impressive intellectual acumen for others to see.

This is *pride*, and it's a dead end. "Knowledge puffs up while love builds up," Paul warns in 1 Corinthians 8:1 (NIV). If we stay on that path, we'll end up winning debates but alienating people.

I've seen it. Frankly, I've done it. The other person ends up begrudgingly admitting, "You may be right," though they don't usually voice the rest of their thoughts out loud: "but I don't want to be like you."

We win the battle but lose the war.

Yes, prevailing in an argument can be important, but much more important is winning the *person*. How can we do this? By changing our motivation—what it is that fuels us. We must stop being motivated primarily by knowledge, or by clinching a debate, or by power or pride. Instead, we must be motivated by one little word: *love*.

"God is love," 1 John 4:8 assures us.

"God so loved the world," says the best-known verse in the Bible, John 3:16.

"Therefore be imitators of God, as beloved children," admonishes Paul in Ephesians 5:1.

We must speak God's truth, and give an answer for the reason for the hope we have in Christ—but we must do so gently, with respect, and always motivated by *the love of God*.

MARK MITTELBERG is a bestselling author, international speaker, and a leading strategist in the area of apologetics-oriented outreach. His books include *Confident Faith*, *The Questions Christians Hope No One Will Ask*, *The Unexpected Adventure* (with Lee Strobel), and *Becoming a Contagious Christian* (with Bill Hybels). He serves as the executive director of the Center for American Evangelism, in partnership with Houston Baptist University.

— 5 —

Social Justice and a New Kind of Apologist

KEN WYTSMA AND RICK GERHARDT

*"You are the light of the world...let your light shine
before others, so that they may see your good works and
give glory to your Father who is in heaven."*[1]

JESUS OF NAZARETH

*Oh, I don't reject Christ. I love Christ. It's just that so many
of you Christians are so unlike Christ. If Christians would
really live according to the teachings of Christ, as found
in the Bible, all of India would be Christian today.*[2]

MOHANDAS GANDHI

We get apologetics.

We understand the need for Christians to be able to give a reasoned formulation and winsome presentation of a rational defense of the Christian world-and-life-view. Whatever ministries we have helped to birth or nurture have been grounded in our conviction that Christianity provides a uniquely accurate understanding of the real world we all live in.

We have graduate degrees in philosophy and apologetics. We have devoured the arguments of C.S. Lewis and of older apologists like Augustine and Blaise

Pascal, who describe the realities of human existence with stunning accuracy. We have conducted "skeptics' balls," opportunities for anyone—seekers, believers with doubts or questions, true skeptics—to interact with the claims of the Bible in raw, open honesty.

Eventually, Christ called us to plant a church in Bend, Oregon, in one of the most unchurched regions of the country. From its inception, Antioch has had an apologetics component. At any given time, we are offering a skeptics' Sunday school series, a learning group centered on apologetics, or a full-semester apologetics course at Kilns College,[3] the school we founded during Antioch's first year of existence. The skeptics' balls have since morphed into *Redux*, a question-and-answer service that we hold most Sundays after the regular worship service.[4]

Enter "The Justice Conference"

But a funny thing happened on our way to an apologetically grounded local church and college.

We had hosted two successful citywide apologetic conferences through Kilns College. We brought in leading apologists from around the country, and together we offered a powerful defense of the reliability of the Gospel accounts of Jesus's life, the historicity of the resurrection, the reconciliation of science and the Bible, and Christianity's uniqueness in explaining reality and human experience.

But before we could begin planning a third such conference, another conviction took root. We were defending important aspects and truth claims central to historical Christianity, but the Lord urged us that contemporary evangelical Christianity was missing one central aspect for a true and authentic Christian witness.

One of the tasks of the Christian apologist is to accurately articulate what it is Christians believe, what the Bible teaches, and what God has revealed to us of himself. And the Lord was convicting us that our tribe had been failing to articulate—for at least most of the last hundred years—one of his essential, inseparable attributes: his concern for justice. In lieu of yet another conference offering a general apologetic for Christianity, the Lord called us to gather a wide variety of Christian scholars, teachers, pastors and leaders, NGOs, field workers, and lay people from every walk of life for a conversation about the theology and practice of social justice.

We partnered with World Relief to host the Justice Conference in Bend, Oregon, in February 2011, and we were awed and humbled by the response. In 2012, the Lord greatly multiplied the number of attendees and the overall impact as we moved the conference to Portland. Since then, there have been Justice Conferences in Philadelphia, Los Angeles, and Hong Kong. As we write this chapter, the run-ups to Chicago 2015, Melbourne, Australia, and a second Hong Kong Justice Conference are under way.

Along the way, we have met thousands of passionate followers of Christ, and many unbelievers who, while extending the practical compassion of Christ, had not yet acknowledged him as their redeemer. Many Christians we met were already involved in efforts to relieve poverty and suffering—the results of injustices—across the world. Others knew they were called to a life of selfless service to others, but found no encouragement from their Christian communities to follow that call to the brothels of Cambodia, the villages of northern Uganda, or the complex web of social injustices in the city centers of the United States.

Indeed, many experienced a disconnect between the discipleship the Lord was calling them to and an articulation of Christianity that had everything to do with saving souls and nothing to do with redeeming the whole person, much less the rest of creation. For the Christians involved, the overwhelming success of the Justice Conference is quite simply because the form of Christianity that acknowledges that God in Christ is establishing his justice "on earth as it is in heaven" is a more holistic, truer form of Christianity than the version that, in much of evangelicalism, had come to ignore this deeply biblical truth.

Lest You Missed It...

Justice in the social realm is a thread running through all of Scripture. Justice is at the very heart of God's character and at the core of what he desires from his people.[5] According to the psalmist, "The LORD is known by his acts of justice"[6] and "a scepter of justice will be the scepter of [his] kingdom."[7] The Creator executes justice for the oppressed, gives food to the hungry, sets the prisoner free, and watches over the immigrant, the widow, and the orphan.[8]

The Lord says, "Justice, and only justice, you shall pursue, that you may live and possess the land,"[9] and he ties the future of his people to their treatment of the oppressed, the immigrant, the orphan, the widow.[10] What he wants from mankind is that we do justice, love mercy, and walk humbly with him.[11] When God's people fail to act justly, they are disciplined or separated from him.[12] In commending King Josiah, God equates knowledge of himself with defending the cause of the poor.[13]

Jesus's own mission statement[14] incorporates healing and social justice, and his followers will be recognized by their feeding the hungry, clothing the poor, welcoming the immigrant, and visiting the sick and the prisoner.[15] Whereas we evangelicals have sometimes made the good news all about an otherworldly heaven,[16] Jesus's own gospel was of the in-breaking of God's kingdom on earth.[17] Paul's understanding was that Christ's redeeming work applied to all of *this* creation,[18] and that his followers—those saved by grace—would be ambassadors of reconciliation,[19] doing the works of justice to which he calls them.[20]

Social Justice and Apologetics

Most of us would agree that the best apologetic is a life well lived. Our character and relationships with others have a greater capacity for attracting those around us to the Christian message than do our arguments or rhetoric.

We also know that many intellectual or academic objections to Christianity usually mask deeper reasons for rejecting Christ. You may have experienced this in your conversations with friends. One such common reason to reject Christianity is the hypocrisy of his followers—failure to live according to the teachings of Jesus and to the worldview we espouse. This is reflected in many of our personal interactions, and it's also the conclusion of a 2007 poll designed to identify the most common perceptions of Christianity among young adults—in which 85 percent viewed Christians as being hypocritical.[21]

Our experiences throughout the United States and around the world have led us to some clear conclusions about the generation now growing up and the reasons they are suspicious of Christianity and the church. Let's look at three of these, because they have important implications for doing effective apologetics today.

First, young people are globally aware to a degree unimaginable just a few years ago. The Internet and social media have provided the tools for keeping on top of current events around the world. These include not just the high profile and political events and issues that would always have made headlines. They include the more hidden goings-on unearthed by the isolated fieldworker, the personal friend on vacation, or the unknown blogger.

Second, what provides purpose and meaning for many is a variety of ongoing critical problems in the way people are being treated by others. Slavery and human trafficking are occurring at a greater rate than at any time in human history, and young Westerners know this. Poverty, malnutrition, lack of clean drinking water, abuse and exploitation of women and children, denial of property rights, government corruption that leads to squalor and destitution—all of these are occurring in our messy fallen world and being made increasingly visible in the flat world of modern technology. Racism is alive and well, not just in twentieth-century Germany or South Africa, but today in our own cities and towns. Issues that rightly fall into the category of social justice—justice in the realm of social relationships—are at the center of the individual and corporate consciousness of young people today.

The Justice Conference has always been organized and hosted by passionately and overtly Christian people and organizations. Nonetheless, many who are not (or were not) followers of Christ have been drawn to that conversation and have attended those conferences. The reason is simple: all humans are made in the image of the one true God, who cares about justice. All people share with their Creator (at least to some degree) a sense of right and wrong, fairness and unfairness, justice and injustice. Therefore, given the knowledge of and ability to expose social injustices with global media, it is not at all surprising that many people today find their purpose in combatting what the God of creation detests.

Third, for most people, the truth of any worldview is logically linked to its practical applications. If Christianity is—as its apologists claim—the accurate understanding of reality, then it ought to result in practices that offer hope and solutions to the obvious brokenness of our world. If we want to remove the obstacles preventing people from following the One who cared about "the least of these" and commanded his disciples to do the same, we ought to be aligning our lives with that command.

Social Justice and a New Kind of Apologist

From an apologetics perspective, there are at least two reasons for a renewed commitment to social justice. On the positive side, justice is a fundamental attribute of God and an inseparable part of the gospel of Christ. If it is Christianity we defend, our arguments and lives must include the teaching and practice of the social justice that Christianity necessarily entails. As John Perkins has it, "Preaching a gospel absent of justice is preaching no gospel at all."[22]

On the negative side, inattention to social injustices and apathy toward God's creation represent the sort of hypocrisy that prevents our defense of Christian truth from being heard.

Everything we are arguing on behalf of social justice could be urged on behalf of caring for the creation as well. As those who claim an intimate personal relationship with the Creator, we Christians—of all people—ought to respect, enjoy, and care for creation, to be concerned about and leading the conversation regarding environmental problems and potential solutions. Christ created all things, sustains all things, and died to reconcile and redeem all things,[23] and works through his followers to actualize this ministry of reconciliation.[24]

A new generation of Christian apologists will be able to relate to the newer generations in the language they speak and about the issues that motivate them. That means recognizing and living according to the truth that God cares deeply—and commands his people to care deeply—about justice in the social realm, about the flourishing (*shalom*) of whole people, communities, and nations, and all of his creation.

We have witnessed this in the lives of Christians pursuing justice all over the world, but let us share a single example, that of the Association for a More Just Society (AJS) in Honduras.[25] In some of the most dangerous neighborhoods on earth, AJS workers minister to and fight for justice on behalf of victims of violence and corruption. As they do so, they frequently watch those victims discover (or rediscover) a vibrant Christian faith.

As they work tirelessly to reform the systems that perpetrate injustice, AJS team members present to the UN representatives, government officials, and foreign ambassadors with whom they interact a truer, more Christlike Christianity than these folks have ever seen. And many of the young people who come to participate in such justice work—whose prior church experience has offered little to attract them—find a faith worthy of the dedication of their lives.

Though the founders and workers of AJS are merely living out the call of Christ on their lives, the result is that they are frequently asked for "the reason for the hope" that is in them.

For the younger generations (and increasingly for people of all ages), our best articulation of the cosmological argument for the existence of the Creator will not receive a hearing if our actions demonstrate a disregard for the creation itself.

Our most robust defense of the reliability of the Gospel accounts of Jesus's life and teaching will fall on deaf ears if we ignore his commands to plead the cause of the poor, the orphan, the widow, the immigrant, and the prisoner.

Our clearest argument for the historicity of Jesus's resurrection will sound hollow if we are not going forth in the promised power of that resurrection to establish his kingdom "on earth as it is in heaven."

And our best theodicy—our most satisfactory defense of God's goodness and power despite the pain and suffering in the world—will be seen as empty words if it doesn't cause us to join with him in alleviating some of that pain and redressing the injustices from which that suffering results.

We believe and pray that the Lord is raising up a new generation of apologists whose rhetorical defense of Christian truth will be accompanied by just and compassionate living, and that as a result, a broken world might see our good works and glorify our Father who is in heaven.

KEN WYTSMA is the founder of the Justice Conference, the president of Kilns College, and the lead pastor at Antioch Church in Bend, Oregon. Ken is also the author of *Pursuing Justice: The Call to Live and Die for Bigger Things* and *The Grand Paradox: The Messiness of Life, the Mystery of God, and the Necessity of Faith.*

RICK GERHARDT is a research and conservation biologist, and has an MSc in raptor biology from Boise State University. He has published nearly two dozen journal articles and chapters on natural history and conservation. He also has an MA in Christian apologetics from Biola, is a cofounder of Kilns College, where he serves as a professor, and is a teaching elder and director of apologetics at Antioch Church in Bend, Oregon.

Interview with J.P. Moreland
SEAN MCDOWELL

How has apologetics changed since you began?

When I started, most people believed in God and historical apologetics, and questions about people who never hear the gospel were front and center. Now, the question of God needs to be defended, issues of science and Christianity, and topics about pluralism and relativism regarding worldviews and religions are important. Also, people don't believe in truth, so that needs to be defended and clarified.

What big issues do you think apologists should be focusing on?

I think we need to focus on the idea that Christianity is a source of knowledge of reality and not just a set of mere true beliefs. Also, we need to defeat scientism and show that there are other ways of knowing besides the hard sciences. Several ethical issues have come up, especially homosexuality and gay marriage.

What advice would you give apologists?

Two things. First, continue to cultivate a gentle approach to people. Read Dallas Willard's new book *The Allure of Gentleness*. Part of this requires the development of emotional intimacy with God. Second, apologetics is cross-country not a hundred-meter dash. Stay at it. Slowly, keep reading and growing. Never settle for where you are currently.

J.P. MORELAND, PhD, is the distinguished professor of philosophy at Talbot School of Theology and the author or coauthor of thirty books, including *The Kingdom Triangle*.

— 6 —

"Don't Blame Us, It's in the Bible" Understanding New Strategies for Shaking Up the Faith of New Generations

DAN KIMBALL

I have been serving in youth and college ministry for over twenty years and have seen trends come and go. Some pass quickly, but they are actually needed and helpful to notice. Generally they impact ministry more in regards to stylistic changes in methodology for greater effectiveness. The reason for new methodology is to see new generations reached for Jesus and made into his disciples. So I do want to always be scanning the land to see what is happening for us to most effectively serve on mission.

But something of great importance is happening now that is unlike anything I have observed before. If you know me, you know I am not a sensationalist or an alarmist. But I have never sensed such a crisis as the need for apologetics of a different kind for this generation.

Junior Highers and the Levitical Holiness Code

I received an email from someone I didn't know named Brad who said he's part of our church and wanted to ask me some questions. He emailed me some very detailed questions from Leviticus 19:28 asking why Christians get tattoos when the Bible says we shouldn't. He also asked why Christians eat shrimp when Leviticus 11:12 says not to eat shellfish.

I took time to respond as thoughtfully as I could. After I sent the email, it seemed only a matter of seconds before I got an email back from him thanking me, then asking more questions about passages in the Old Testament that seemed to support slavery and genocide.

I emailed him back and asked if we could meet in person so we could talk, and he agreed. After the service the following Sunday, I heard someone say, "Hi, Dan. I'm Brad." Much to my surprise, this was not a college-age or older adult standing there, it was a young teenager. "You're Brad?" I asked. It turned out he was in eighth grade and was coming with his parents. I asked him how was he coming up with all these questions, and he smiled and told me they were all from a website called evilbible.com. He said he was cutting and pasting things from that website and sending them to me as questions.

Now I know that the average eighth grader is not sending their pastor questions about dietary laws from the book of Leviticus, but I realized anyone can find websites dedicated to highlighting strange passages that seem to discredit the Bible and thus discredit the Christian faith. This eighth grader was mostly just having fun with this, it turned out, but not all stories are like his.

Beyond Good Worship Bands and Even Loving Churches

I recently spent over three hours talking to a college student who sees himself as an atheist. Two years earlier, he was a leader in his college ministry group on campus. He grew up in a Christian home and was highly involved as a leader in his youth group. I was meeting with him because his campus leader put him in contact with me because she wasn't sure how to respond to what was happening.

In his case, he was studying the Bible in his campus group when he noticed the Exodus story of the firstborn in Egypt being killed—a story he had read and heard multiple times about God rescuing Israel and putting more and more pressure on Pharaoh. But as a college student, the story was very unsettling to him. He began wondering, if the New Testament story of Herod's soldiers killing boys under the age of two in Bethlehem was such a horrific act, why then is it OK when God does something similar? This really troubled him, which led him to ask his small group leaders about it. He was disappointed with the lame answers he received, answers like "I don't know, but when we get to heaven we might know." This left him even more unsettled.

He began searching online and discovered websites like the ones the eighth grader had found. His questions became more insistent. He began asking why women in church talk when it clearly says in 1 Corinthians 14:34-35 "it is shameful for a woman to speak in church." And what about the one where a woman is commanded to marry her rapist (Deuteronomy 22:28-29) or those about slavery and polygamy. On and on the list went. He said he asked his parents about these, and they weren't even aware of some of the verses he had discovered. He asked his former youth leader, and even he wasn't quite sure how to answer his questions. The people he trusted the most seemed to merely accept the authority of the Bible without really knowing much of what's in it.

He told me this so shook his foundations that he went into a strong period of doubt. The more he searched online, the worse it got as he discovered how "evil" God and the Bible really were. He eventually felt he could no longer believe and abandoned his faith.

What was most stunning about listening to his story was that he wasn't mad at the church. He had a really good experience at his church. He wasn't thinking his church was irrelevant or boring. They had great music, very lively and active programs for youth and college age. The preaching addressed felt needs about relationships, understanding who Jesus is, about salvation through the cross. The church wasn't judgmental but was kind and loving. He wasn't mad at his parents either. He knew he was loved and cared for by them.

But the church had not addressed these types of questions he now had nor were they prepared to adequately address them when he asked—so his Christian faith unraveled. I am hearing more and more stories like this.

"Don't Blame Us—It's in the Bible!"

For so long, most Christians have not had these troubling passages pointed out to them, so they are caught off guard when they encounter them for the first time. A popular tweet from someone using the name "almightygod" hits an uncomfortable cord in many of us: "To most Christians, the Bible is like a software license. Nobody actually reads it. They just scroll to the bottom and click 'I agree.'" This is perhaps truer than we care to acknowledge, which only adds to the confusion about the Bible.

Many Christians grew up reading the Bible. But more often than not, they were focused mainly on verses of encouragement or lifestyle guidance for followers of Jesus. Many positive Bible verses got memorized. You'll see comforting verses like "Be still and know that I am God" on coffee mugs with a calm nature scene, but you won't see other verses from Isaiah like, "The LORD is enraged against all nations…He has given them over to slaughter…the stench of their corpses shall rise." Imagine that written on a mug you use for sipping tea during your morning devotions or as a theme verse for your church's women's retreat.

We love and need the encouraging verses in our minds and hearts. But our ignorance of the difficult parts of the Bible is catching many Christians off guard. I spoke recently at a megachurch on this topic, and afterward four different sets of parents told me their college-age son or daughter had recently abandoned their faith. The same pattern was there—they discovered verses they never realized were in the Bible and it sent them in a downward spiral.

An atheist group has used the slogan, "The fastest way for a Christian to become an atheist is to read the Bible." The thought is that most Christians don't know what's in the Bible they carry with them to church and have in their homes. A former Christian who is now an agnostic has authored several books pointing out violent and bizarre things in the Bible. He writes:

> "We aren't trying to offend anybody, we just want people to really
> think about the most important book in the history of the world—a
> book many have never read," says Gilgamesh. "A recent Pew sur-
> vey shows an overwhelming lack of Biblical knowledge among

Christians in the U.S., with 55% unable to even name the four Gospels. And, these are the very foundation of Christianity!" When asked about the online controversy that some of the illustrations have caused, he adds, "It is no surprise that some readers are shocked to see what the Bible really says about the Great Flood, Jesus' anger issues, birth control, slavery, or women's rights. But, don't blame us—it's in the Bible!"[1]

Unicorns in the Bible?

It isn't just Christians who are being affected by the focus on what's in the Bible. Even my barber, who does not have a Christian background and doesn't know the Bible or read it, is asking me questions. He wondered whether Christians should play football since the Bible says we aren't supposed to touch the skin of a dead pig. Why do we disobey the Bible by touching pigskin when we play football? I asked him where he heard that, and he said he saw it on the Internet.

Someone else asked me how we can take the Bible seriously when there are unicorns in it. I didn't know what he meant, but he told me to do a search on the Internet. I did and found plenty of clever graphics, including the image of a unicorn with Isaiah 34:7 written underneath it: "And the unicorns shall come down with them, and the bullocks with the bulls; and their land shall be soaked with blood, and their dust made fat with fatness."

At first glance that seems crazy, but when you look below the surface you discover that *unicorn* was the word the translators of the King James Bible used for a Hebrew word they didn't know how to translate. Modern translators now translate it as "wild oxen." But these graphics use a 1611 mistranslation to support the idea that the Bible promotes the existence of unicorns. And most people don't do the homework to see if that is correct. After all, it looks like a Bible verse, so people think the Bible is not a trustworthy book but a crazy and absurd human document.

All this is shaping a different narrative of the Bible. It is no longer the "Good Book" but even an evil book that propagates myth, slavery, and violence. It is not a beautiful book about a God of redemption, forgiveness, and grace but one of a bloodthirsty God killing people and telling others to kill people, pleased with dashing babies against rocks, and allowing polygamy, rape, and hatred.

If you are a Christian who has read the whole Bible and understand the overall narrative, you know God's character as it's revealed from Genesis through Revelation. You know Bible study methods that enable you to determine how to look at author intent, original audience, historical and literary context, how specific stories fit within the whole, and whether a passage is intended to be applied directly today.

But so many don't know this.

Compassion God Becomes Scary God: Hide Your Children

Mary Poppins is a wonderful movie about a caring, magical nanny who helps a dysfunctional family. Mary is kind and loving and everyone loves her. But I saw a fascinating movie clip where someone took short scenes from *Mary Poppins* and arranged them out of context. A scene of a group of nannies being blown away as Mary looks out sternly through a window at them. A boy being sucked into a closet and the doors shutting as Mary stares at him. A girl being sucked up into a chimney. Children running in fear. The clip ends with the words "Scary Mary" and then the line "Hide your children." Someone who had never seen the whole *Mary Poppins* might assume it's a horror film.

Similarly, taking bits of the Bible out of context paints an altogether different narrative than the true one of the God of compassion who is slow to anger and abounding in love.

So What Do We Do Here?

I am very optimistic about all this, quite honestly. But we do need to pay attention and be strategic in our current times.

We need to admit that we are part of the problem. The church has focused mainly on the nice stories and nice verses in the Bible. We generally teach right through the difficult passages, not pausing long enough to explain those places where a woman is told to marry her rapist, or women are told to be silent in church, or why God would instruct Israel to kill all the Canaanites or David would kill two hundred men and cut off their foreskins to buy a wife.

Because we ignored passages such as these or didn't directly teach about them, youth and young adults are now reading them and are shocked no one ever told them they are in the Bible. And most parents and even many youth pastors don't know how to respond. I didn't until I was challenged and had to then study them for myself.

The church has also modeled a lot of teaching that didn't include showing basic Bible study methods. Because so many sermons involve reading a Scripture or two and then jumping straight to application, we have a generation that has not understood how to look at context, genre, where in the whole Bible story a verse takes place. So we in the church have been part of the problem by how many of us have approached teaching the Bible.

We need to proactively teach young people (and parents!) about these very questions. The good news is that so much of this is preventable. There are reasonable responses to the things being pointed out as "crazy" in the Bible. When someone who has been taught these responses sees a clever graphic on the Internet mocking the Bible, they can then see through that misrepresentation. When they encounter something they have not been taught about, they have more confidence to know there probably is a reasonable answer, and they may even be equipped to know how to find an answer to it.

I was with Sean McDowell when he took twenty-two Christian high school students to Berkeley for three days. He had six training meetings leading up to it, so it wasn't just done spontaneously. But he had a gay former Episcopalian priest who is now an atheist speak to the high schoolers. He shared his story and why he no longer believes in God and the Bible. Sean also had a leading atheist speak to the high schoolers about why he believes science disproves God. He had a leader of the Bay Area Atheists come in and make a case why Jesus didn't exist. The students then got to ask questions and interact with each speaker. After each speaker, there was about ninety minutes of debriefing and training. This is a great example of proactively exposing teenagers to the kinds of questions and stories that will be coming, training them in advance how to respond. What so impressed me was that the teenagers were being taught not just how to give answers but how to think. It wasn't "Here is the answer"—they were being taught how to think about beliefs and why we believe, not just the facts of belief.

We need to admit that the Bible does contain crazy sounding things, and we don't have neat and tidy answers for all of them. We have to admit there are very weird things in the Bible. We may be able to understand many of them, but some are difficult to explain. I can give some reasoning for the violent war passages and explain they don't represent an out-of-control bloodthirstiness but instead the judgment of a compassionate and just God who had warned and warned for hundreds of years and eventually could no longer tolerate the evils the people were doing (including child sacrifice and more). Any violence is difficult to comprehend, but I trust God since I know his character through the whole of the Bible.

I believe we gain credibility when we share that some things are tough to understand. And it does not then seem like a copout or a "we'll just have to wait for heaven to get that answer" when we are teaching about the many difficult things we can give solid responses for.

We need to create a culture in our churches that says that asking questions is a good thing. Youth and college age are in a time of questioning, a stage everyone goes through. The worst thing we can do is to suggest that asking questions is a bad or shameful thing or that anyone who asks questions is not a strong Christian. We should be encouraging questions and celebrating them. We can teach a series each year based on questions the youth, college age, or even adults ask. One youth group set up a blog specifically to post responses to questions youth have about the Bible, and they rally students to not be afraid to ask questions. We need to communicate to all ages that church is a safe place to ask questions and celebrate when questions are asked.

We need to pray. I don't say this lightly, but I do sense this could very well be the work of the enemy trying to confuse this next generation. If this next generation doesn't trust the Bible, then they don't trust the gospel the Bible tells us about. We need apologetics and training, absolutely. But more than ever we need to pray. It isn't just about knowledge; it is about the Holy Spirit using Scripture to transform hearts and minds. So I have been compelled to pray more than ever for this generation in this confusing time in our country when the Bible and Christianity are seen in a negative light.

A Most Important Final Word

This also means we need to model what it means to be a Christian. We can teach doctrine and apologetics, but our lives need to reflect to our children and youth and people in general what we say we believe. In this chapter I focused mainly on the knowledge part, but we must be examples of truly living as a follower of Jesus with love and kindness or our words and teaching may not be listened to. I know Christians who are very much into doctrine and theology who are also mean-spirited and argumentative. They may have great apologetic answers, but their tone is sharp rather than kind and loving. So as we teach, we need to talk with great love and compassion about those who have differing beliefs.

If our beliefs are not expressed in love and by example, we miss the greatest command of all, which is loving God and loving others.

DAN KIMBALL is on staff at Vintage Faith Church in Santa Cruz, California, overseeing the mission and teaching. He is the author of several books, including *They Like Jesus But Not the Church,* and director of the ReGeneration Project at Western Seminary. He is married to Becky, has two daughters, and loves rockabilly, punk, drumming, and comic books.

PART 2

New Methods in Apologetics

SEAN MCDOWELL

The gospel hasn't changed. It is the same today as when Jesus first declared it. *Through the death and resurrection of Jesus, God offers forgiveness and eternal life to those who believe* (John 3:16; 6:29). Paul gives strict warnings against those who proclaim a different gospel than the one first delivered by Christ (Galatians 1:8-9).

Human nature doesn't change either. Regardless of our technological innovations and intellectual progress, human beings essentially remain the same. We are still magnificent creatures who reflect the *imago dei*, and yet our hearts are fallen and bent toward rebellion and sin (Romans 3:23).

While the gospel and human nature remain the same, culture changes. Some of these changes are in seemingly small ways, such as fashion or music tastes. Other changes run deeper and have to do with worldview issues such as the perceived connection between science and faith, what it means to be human, and the purpose and nature of relationships.

This dynamic raises an important question: How do we proclaim the timeless gospel in our modern context? While there are no simple answers to this question, there are three general positions we can take:

- Assume a "not of this world" approach and abandon culture.
- Embrace an "in the world" posture and change our core convictions to fit in.
- Adopt a "middle ground" position where we hold firm to our convictions, and yet focus on being gracious, kind, and truly loving toward outsiders.

For those of us committed to the gospel, the first two are not genuine options. We cannot isolate ourselves from the world, nor can we conform to it. Even though we are not of the world, Jesus has sent us into the world to be his witnesses (John 17:15-19). In embracing the third option, we are essentially asking: How can we effectively and lovingly proclaim the gospel without compromising our core convictions?

This last question should be at the heart of what motivates our apologetic efforts today. And it is the driving question for the second section of this book, which is aptly titled "New Methods in Apologetics." The gospel does not, and will not, ever change. But if we want to be heard today, we may need to think creatively and strategically about how best to proclaim it.

Various chapters in this section tackle topics such as reaching youth with apologetics, doing apologetics in the inner city, using stories to proclaim truth, learning to ask good questions, encouraging women to get involved in apologetics, and more. The purpose of this section is not to offer apologetic answers to difficult questions, but to provide some thoughtful methods for doing apologetics in our modern culture. My prayer is that you will read these chapters carefully and apply the principles to your own life and ministry.

— 7 —

Shepherd Is a Verb
The Role of Relational Mentoring
in Communicating Truth

JEFF MYERS

In movies, the best leaders always head up the charge. If you ask Professor Linda Hill from Harvard Business School what the best leaders in real life do, though, you might be surprised at her response.

Hill's perspective on leadership was formed through a visit to Cape Town, South Africa, where she read of Nelson Mandela's boyhood memories of watching Xhosa shepherds. "A leader is like a shepherd," she wrote. "He stays behind the flock, letting the most nimble go out ahead, whereupon the others follow, not realizing all along that they are being directed from behind."[1]

Yes, there are times when leaders blow the trumpet and fling themselves headlong into battle. But shepherding leaders guide and nurture with a light touch that helps their followers conquer timidity and live out their design more fully.

Shepherd is a verb. I'm convinced that the new kind of apologist is a person who shepherds students with truth in the context of relationship, challenging them to pass on to others what they have learned (2 Timothy 2:2).

In this chapter we'll explore a simple, memorable picture of how shepherding apologists transform lives by intertwining truth and relationship. Plus we'll examine five steps that move our own churches and organizations toward preparing thoughtful, virtuous believers who shape culture based on a biblical worldview.

Some people say, "We already know relationship is important. Why do we need to talk about this?" My work with fellow educators has shown that when it comes to relationships, we don't know as much as we think we do, and we practice very little of what we know.[2] In fact, as a lifelong communication scholar, I'm not sure I fully grasped the long-term significance of truth and relationship until two years ago. It's a lesson I learned from seeing a stain on the fireplace of a dying friend.

The Stain on the Fireplace

Researchers call them the "nones." As in, what's your religious preference? "None." One-third of young people give this response in polls, a figure that has tripled in just one generation.[3] Disbelief is the fastest growing religious trend in America. Of those who faithfully attend youth group as teens, 70 percent are no longer attending in their twenties. What do you do with an army that loses seven out of ten of its troops before they even finish boot camp?

Ravi Zacharias believes we're asking for trouble by teaching a "gospel devoid of a context of social struggle."[4] That phrase haunts me. Those I'm influencing have to struggle. They have to watch *me* struggle. Growth happens when we walk with one another in our struggles.

I saw this in my own childhood. When I was in grade school, my family moved from Detroit to a small town in Kansas. During an evening prayer meeting at our tiny new church, my brother Scott and I were told, "We don't have a youth program. Why don't you just play outside?" We found some Dixie cups, masking tape, and gasoline and tried making a bomb. Of course it spilled and started a fire in the parking lot. We quickly put it out, thinking no one had noticed. But the next week, oddly, a youth program had started.

Don, a grocery store manager, volunteered to lead the boys' group, which included my brother and me and one other kid. The breadth of Don's influence on my life did not become clear until just months before he lost his battle with cancer. On my last visit to Don, his wife, Angel, walked me over to the fireplace and said, "When this fireplace was brand new, you and Scottie cooked hotdogs and some grease dripped here. Every time we see the stain, we pray for you guys."

For thirty-five years this couple had prayed for my brother and me every time they came near their fireplace. They walked with us through their struggles—and ours—in order to send us ahead in a stronger, straighter way.

I now understand what Don did for my brother and me. It's called mentoring. While mentoring is a common strategy in business, it has the potential to transform the church too. The Barna Research Group found that twentysomethings who stay in church were *twice as likely* to have a close personal friendship with an adult inside the church. Those who had an adult mentor at church, aside from the pastor, were almost *three times as likely* to stay as those who did not. [5]

Mentoring is a special kind of shepherding that involves intentionally guiding the next generation toward God's purposes. At Summit Ministries, the organization I have the privilege to lead, we are seeking to capture this mentoring mindset by picturing one of the most common structures in the universe, a DNA double helix.

The Double Helix of Truth and Relationship

Summit is serious about preparing the rising generation to intellectually pursue their faith. Yet our research has shown that Summit affects students' personal spirituality as much as their mental growth. Feelings of closeness to God, prayer life, devotional life, and willingness to share their faith rate just as high among the changes our graduates say they experience as their understanding of a Christian worldview, understanding of other worldviews, and general preparation for higher education.

The "secret sauce" to Summit, if there is one, is that in our twelve-day course, we focus on *truth* and *relationship* as two strands of a DNA double helix. Both are crucial. Truth without relationship leads to arrogance, while relationship without truth leads to apathy.

We tell our team: "Your job, every day, is to build a rung in the ladder between truth and relationship. If we miss a few details in our work but we do that, we've won." Here are some things our team is learning about weaving together personal spirituality and intellectual growth:

1. We're learning to inventory our strategies.

We encourage our team to take a good hard look at what we're doing now, not with an eye toward throwing it out and starting over, but with a focus on more consistently reaching our desired outcomes. Are the students we're walking with staying involved in church? Are they ministering to others? Are they successfully applying their faith in their daily lives? In their careers?

When the answer is no for any given student, we try to find out why. We ask what happened. You'd be surprised how much you can learn about increasing faithfulness from someone who has left the faith.

2. We're learning to develop a personal creed reflecting our convictions.

Speaking only for myself, my creed used to be, "Reach as many people as you can, as quickly as you can." It's different now. Our team shares in this new approach by telling ourselves things like this:

- Life is a relay. We win only when we pass the baton to those who come after us.

- We teach what we know, but we reproduce who we are.

- We constantly kindle our own fires of inquisitiveness. We are teachable teachers.

- When confronted with difficulty, we surrender the outcome to God and look for his redemption.

3. We're learning to generate a learning culture.

In corporate America, between 30 and 50 percent of high-potential leaders derail within the first eighteen months on the job.[6] Long-term success comes from injecting personal mentoring and coaching into the organization's DNA. David Clutterbuck and David Megginson share the values needed to make this happen:

- Everyone believes that learning is critical to individual and organizational success.

- The leaders use a non-directive coaching style with peers and subordinates.

- Those closest to implementing decisions are given freedom to take risks and set their own goals.

- Leaders view developing others and creating a learning environment as one of their major responsibilities.

- Peers coach one another to share knowledge and to pass on expertise.

- Having a mentor or coach is viewed positively, and people are encouraged to seek mentoring or coaching support.[7]

We can create a learning culture in ministry as well by growing in our ability to coach and mentor and walk alongside those we seek to influence. "We never stop learning, and we learn together" becomes our new mantra.

4. We're learning to reclaim catechism.

Josh McDowell and Sean McDowell reveal in *The Unshakable Truth* that the early church grew from twenty-five thousand believers around AD 100 to around twenty million in AD 300.[8] What explains this extraordinary growth? The short answer is *catechism*, which means to "echo toward." In catechism, mature believers *teach short* and *listen long* as converts articulate truth in their own words. Then together they find ways to apply what they've learned. Catechism helps turn knowledge into belief, which turns into virtue.

Catechism is central to every pursuit in life. In 1995, the then director of General Electric's training division noted something astonishing about the company's half-a-billion-dollar budget for formal training: "I wish I could tell you that courses are the key, but they are not. When we ask our people to write down the outstanding development experience of their lives, only about 10% cite formal training."[9] What *does* work is on-the-job learning experiences. Catechism, not curriculum.

5. We're learning to focus on moral character.

If our students become immoral know-it-alls, we've failed. Not everyone experiences the same level of success, but Dennis Moberg, a professor at Santa Clara University, thinks there are eight things we can do to form tight-knit mentoring relationships that develop moral character:

1. Protégés develop moral character when they voluntarily set goals to cultivate specific virtues that reflect their interests, emotions, and sense of self.

2. Protégés develop moral character when they are tutored by mentors about watching for and solving practical problems.

3. Protégés develop moral character when mentors help protégés become sensitive to the way their context and habits inform the way they live with character.

4. Protégés develop moral character when their learning environment enables them to function at their best.

5. Protégés develop moral character when they reflect regularly but not excessively about the relationship between their actions and "the good life."

6. Protégés develop moral character following a genuinely inspirational event.

7. Protégés develop moral character when they identify with role models who personify moral character.

8. Protégés develop moral character via social learning from the mentor.

Notice that of Moberg's eight ways of developing moral character, only one has to do with inspirational events. Apologetics conferences, classes, and sermons plant seeds, but the harvest comes through personal attention, creating a learning climate, and helping protégés set and achieve life goals.

So there you have it. Transformation begins with taking stock, establishing a personal course, forming a learning culture, reclaiming catechism, and focusing on the relationship between knowledge and moral character.

This shepherding approach to the next generation of apologists could change the world. Indeed, it already has.

Mentoring Changes History

When you think about it, life-on-life mentoring relationships in the context of social struggle, nested in the church, have always been a robust source of world-changing influence.

In the 400s, a man named Germanus mentored a young escaped slave, who became a missionary named Saint Patrick. Patrick prepared Ireland to plant the seeds of Western civilization across Europe. No Germanus, no Saint Patrick.[10]

Solomon Stoddard mentored his grandson Jonathan Edwards, who then led the Great Awakening, preparing the way for a new birth of freedom in America. What if Stoddard hadn't taken his grandson seriously?[11]

In the late 1700s a former slave trader named John Newton mentored a young politician named William Wilberforce. By the end of his life, Wilberforce had successfully led the movement to abolish slavery in Britain. If Newton had turned his back, how many might still be in chains?

James Vinter, director of the lay preachers' association at a parish church in Cambridge, saw a preaching gift in a young Charles Haddon Spurgeon, who became one of the most well-known preachers in history. What if Vinter had said, "I'll just let someone else do it"?[12]

I sometimes wish I had known twenty years ago how powerful life-on-life influence could be. As a professor, my mistake was to assume that what happened in the classroom was my greatest source of influence. I put every-thing I had into my lectures and then rushed off to work on books or speeches. My students were impressed. I felt like a rock star.

Meanwhile, there was a tradition at our college commencement ceremony that I found irksome. Our graduates were given fifteen seconds to say thank you to the professors who had helped them succeed. Some names came up over and over again. Never mine.

It's embarrassing to admit this, but I had a hard time connecting the dots. I knew influence was strongly correlated with relationship, but in my frenzy I couldn't see what I should do differently. After a hard look at my teaching strat-egy, I realized I was covering the globe but making very little impression on it.

Change didn't come all at once. But as I began looking for genuine influ-ence opportunities—visiting with students in the hall, meeting them for lunch, counseling, forming mentoring relationships—I found that my students and I were both experiencing change.

Here's my takeaway: academic training piles up kindling; personal life-on-life influence lights the match. Apologetics training is invaluable for this generation, but transformation takes place when that truth is experienced in relationship. This insight is now shaping how Summit prepares the rising gen-eration of influencers.

Jesus said, "I am the good shepherd." To lead like a shepherd is to lead like Jesus. The secret to changing lives is looking for ways to put rungs in the ladder between truth and relationship every day. It is also the secret to changing the church, and perhaps even the culture.

JEFF MYERS, PhD, is president of Summit Ministries (www.summit.org), which introduces 16-to-21-year-old students to America's top Christian thought-leaders in an intensive mentoring to prepare them to confidently stand for the truth. Jeff's recent book/film *Grow Together* shows churches how to apply what the Summit team has learned by repairing the generational gap and developing a mentoring mindset in churches. See www.growtogether.org for more information.

— 8 —

A Practical Plan to
Raise Up the Next Generation

BRETT KUNKLE

I grew up in a Christian home. I came to Christ at five and was baptized at six. My family was committed to the local church. My dad faithfully taught Sunday school, led small groups, and was even an elder. My mom was always involved in ministry as well. I grew up attending Sunday school, Royal Ambassadors, and Awana. As a teenager, I was the model youth group kid, a student leader in high school, and a ministry intern as a senior, even committing my life to full-time vocational ministry before I graduated.

Then I met Dr. David Lane.

It was my freshman year in college and the course was Philosophy 101. Dr. Lane systematically dismantled the Christianity I grew up with. In class. In front of everyone. And I was not ready. But why not? I had spent the first eighteen years of my life in the church. Wasn't that enough time to prepare me to engage the world for Christ?

Sadly, the majority of our Christian students aren't ready either. They're not prepared for the serious intellectual challenges awaiting them, let alone the barrage of moral challenges from an increasingly secular culture. It's a huge reason why we continue to hemorrhage youth from our churches.

Thank God I discovered apologetics amidst Professor Lane's intellectual assault on my Christianity. Apologetics helped rebuild my faith in Christ, and I became convinced of its absolute necessity for student discipleship. That's right, I said *necessity*. Apologetics is not optional in a post-Christian culture. It's not just for the nerdy youth group kid "who's into that kind of stuff." God is a rational God, and we are made in his image. Therefore, every student is rational by design, instinctively gathering reasons and evidence as they seek to make sense of the world around them and form a coherent set of beliefs about reality. As the church equips a new generation for the cause of Christ, we must begin with the conviction apologetics is an indispensable tool.

Now, I'm under no false pretense that if we simply give students apologetics we'll automatically secure their faith in Christ for a lifetime. Human beings are not just thinking beings; we're emotional, experiential, and volitional as well. That's why 1 Peter 3:15 (NASB)—the apologist's theme verse—begins and ends with two very important phrases. Peter starts with this reminder: "But sanctify Christ as Lord in your hearts." Apologetics should be done amidst a certain kind of life, one where we surrender more and more of ourselves to Christ. When we do this, he transforms us. A life transformed by Christ is the requisite context for making "a defense to everyone who asks you to give an account for the hope that is in you." Peter ends the verse with a picture of such an apologetic: it is gentle and respectful.

So while apologetic training is necessary in discipling the next generation, it is not sufficient alone in forming fully devoted followers of Jesus. However, this does not minimize its necessity. The mind plays a prominent role in our spiritual transformation—"be transformed by the renewing of your mind" (Romans 12:2 NASB)—and therefore, we ignore the minds of the next generation to our own peril.

Maybe you're already convinced but wondering, "How can we *effectively* equip a new generation with apologetics?" Let me share some ideas that are borne out of my own experience teaching students as a youth pastor for eleven years, as a parent for eighteen years (and counting!), and as Stand to Reason's Student Impact director for the last twelve years. I've made plenty of mistakes in all three roles, but my experience has allowed me to hone an approach that can be effective at home, at church, at youth group, or in a Christian school.

Back to the Future

Before we look forward in the formation of the next generation, let us first take a look to the past. If we can lay aside what C.S. Lewis called chronological snobbery—"the uncritical acceptance of the intellectual climate common to our own age and the assumption that whatever has gone out of date is on that account discredited"[1]—we will discover long-forgotten insights to help forge a path forward. So for a moment, I want you to lay aside modern educational models and contemporary youth ministry approaches and programs and consider an ancient model.

As our oldest daughter approached the junior-high years, my wife and I began to rethink our views on educating and discipling our kids. We were dissatisfied with things we were seeing in her life, not only academically but spiritually and morally. In that process of reevaluation, we discovered an ancient approach to education called "classical education," stretching back to the Classical Greeks and Romans and formalized in the Middle Ages. Educator Susan Wise Bauer offers a concise description of this approach:

> Classical education depends on a three-part process of training the mind. The early years of school are spent in absorbing facts, systematically laying the foundations for advanced study [Grammar Stage]. In the middle grades, students learn to think through arguments [Logic Stage]. In the high school years, they learn to express themselves [Rhetoric Stage].[2]

While not an exhaustive definition, it gets us started and highlights the three-stage pattern of classical education called the *trivium*. In the early years of elementary school, called the Grammar Stage, children's minds are like sponges. There is a natural wonder at the world around them and a corresponding love of learning.

Young children are primarily interested in the *what* questions. They want to know facts about the world, and they absorb and memorize them with ease.

Nearing the middle-school or junior-high years, a student's mind grows in its ability to analyze and think abstractly. During this phase, called the Logic Stage, students are asking the *why* questions. Many adults perceive such questioning to be a direct challenge to their authority, but often it's merely the outworking of our natural inclination to sort things out for ourselves. At this stage, students want to know if there are good reasons to believe the so-called facts they were given at younger ages and to see if those facts provide a coherent picture of the world.

As students approach high school and enter the Rhetoric Stage, they must grow in their ability to communicate. During this stage, students build on the first two stages by taking the *what* and the *why* and communicating what they've learned through writing and speaking. Research, writing papers, giving speeches, debating and the like force students to articulate what they've come to believe as true.

The medievals believed this *trivium* pattern corresponded to the universal human experience of learning. It accurately captures the manner in which young minds are best trained.[3] Thus, we should take this ancient approach to education and breathe into it new life for our modern context. Indeed, the *trivium* provides us with a three-stage approach to discipling the next generation:

Stage 1: Teach the *What*—Grammar Stage (primary focus of grades 0–4)

Stage 2: Teach the *Why*—Logic Stage (primary focus of grades 5–8)

Stage 3: Create Experiences—Rhetoric Stage (primary focus of grades 9–12)

Outlining a general approach is vital. First, it keeps us from getting lost in the details of training. Without the big picture, we may wander aimlessly, looking for the latest and greatest video series or searching for that one comprehensive curriculum package. Certainly individual tools are important, but we need to understand the larger strategy within which our tools fit and make sense. Second, it brings to light the requisite context for effective training. Apologetics is the *why*, but there must be an appropriate foundation of the *what* in place first for the *why* to secure it.

So first, we must be convinced of the necessity of apologetics, and second, we must have a larger discipleship framework in place into which we fit apologetics. Now we're ready to explore the practical how-tos.

Stage 1: Teach the *What*

Before we can teach our students how to defend what we believe, they must know what it is we actually believe. They must first engage theology, the study of God. Apologetics is properly understood as a sub-branch of theology; theology is its foundation. When should theological training begin? As soon as our kids can speak.

From the youngest of ages, we need to teach children God's attributes, Trinitarian doctrine, the deity of Christ, the meaning of the cross, the nature of Scripture, the nature of man, and the nature of the church. Grab any standard systematic theology and its table of contents will give you an overview of theological topics to teach. Of course, we need to communicate theology in an age-appropriate manner, so a child's first exposure will be basic, but it will also be foundational. Just as learning language during the Grammar Stage of classical education provides the building blocks for all future learning, learning the language of theology builds a foundation for future training in apologetics. Here are three practical steps for this stage.

1. Reading. Read, read, read. I cannot emphasize this enough. Start by reading to them. Read children's Bibles, individual biblical stories, classical stories, and any Christian children's books you can get your hands on. Read to them at home, at church, and at school. Reading is an indispensable tool in teaching theology. It's no accident God gave us his Word in written form and not on a DVD.

2. Catechism. A catechism is simply a summary of Christian doctrine. It is generally laid out in question-answer format and is a fantastic tool to build a theological foundation in our kids. My wife and I are currently working our way through a children's version titled *First Catechism*[4] with our three-year-old son and seven-year-old daughter. We ask them a catechism question—"Who made you?"—and they memorize the answer—"God." I'm astonished at my three-year-old's ability to memorize large portions of information. By having our kids memorize the catechism, we are pouring into them the raw theological material we will build upon in later years. We also teach the two- and three-year-old class at our local church and are taking them through this catechism as well.

3. Memorization. Capitalize on your kids' capabilities by having them memorize significant theological pieces. In addition to the catechism, have them memorize important passages of Scripture and the great creeds of the church. Singing praise songs and hymns is a great way to memorize theological content as well. Here is a list of ten important items to have children memorize:

1. First Catechism

2. Apostles Creed

3. Nicene Creed

4. Attributes of God

5. Ten Commandments

6. Lord's Prayer

7. Psalm 23

8. The Beatitudes

9. The Great Commandment (Matthew 22:37-39)

10. The Great Commission (Matthew 28:19-20)

Sadly, this is where much of our Christian education stops. Whether it's children, youth, or adults, we just keep teaching the *what* and never equip our people with the *why*.

I recently role-played an atheist with a group of adults at a local church in Southern California. An older gentleman began to engage my atheist character, telling me he had been a Christian for more than thirty years. He then began his defense of Christianity with the "God-said-it-I-believe-it-that-settles-it" approach, stating emphatically that the Bible was the Word of God. I simply responded, "Why do you think the Bible is the Word of God?" Silence. He had no answer. He was stuck in the *what* and could not answer the *why*.

Laying the theological foundation in stage one is just the beginning. Now we must move on to the apologetic training of stage two.

Stage 2: Teach the *Why*

Around fourth or fifth grade, a student's mind grows significantly in its capacity for abstract thought. Their ability to reason grows, and they move from merely the *what* questions to the *why* questions. Don't be surprised if they begin to question you and challenge your answers at this stage. And don't be threatened by it either. Instead, capitalize on it. They've reached the Logic Stage and are now ready for a good dose of apologetics.[5]

Here we need to give students arguments for God's existence, evidence for the resurrection of Jesus, and reasons why the Bible is not only historically reliable but also divinely inspired. In addition, we must help them overcome objections to Christianity, such as the problem of evil and suffering, moral relativism, religious pluralism, and challenges to the Bible. When we equip them with "the reason for the hope" we have in Christ, we help secure the theological foundation of stage one and strengthen their confidence that Christianity is objectively true. Here are three practical steps for this stage.

1. Ask them questions first. Don't wait for students to raise questions and challenges; be proactive and provoke their questions. Question the theological training you provided in stage one: "You believe God is all-powerful and all-loving, but how do you know he exists in the first place?" And then wait. Let them struggle to answer, and then question their answers. Struggling can create some healthy internal motivation for our students to care about the questions and seek out satisfying answers.

2. Never shut down their questions. Create a safe space for students' doubts by allowing them to ask any and all questions. And when they ask, affirm them in their questioning. According to recent research by the Fuller Youth Institute, students who were free to express their doubts during high school showed greater faith maturity in college.[6] If you shut down their questions, they won't stop questioning, they'll just do it without you.

3. Answer four key questions. The case for Christianity is a cumulative one.

That means there is no apologetic silver bullet, no single argument that establishes the entire case. Instead, we must help students identify the key components of our cumulative case and supply them with the supporting reasons and evidence. Have them answer these four key questions to establish the truthfulness of Christianity:

1. Does truth exist?

2. Does God exist?

3. Does God act (miracles)?

4. Does God speak (Scripture)?[7]

By the time a student graduates from our home or our ministry, she must move beyond merely *believing* the truth to actually *knowing* the truth. What's the difference? Philosophers generally define knowledge as justified true belief. If I know something, not only do I believe it to be true, but it's supported by adequate reasons. The theological training of stage one supplies the true beliefs of Christian orthodoxy and the apologetic training of stage two provides the reasons and justification. Together they furnish our students with knowledge of the truth.

Stage 3: Create Experiences

At the next stage, it's time to get the theological and apologetic training out of the classroom and into real life. The best way to learn something is to teach it to someone else, and the rhetoric stage forces students to do just that. Students must learn to take the *what* and the *why* of Christianity and communicate it in a coherent and reasonable manner. We need to create experiences in which students have the opportunity to articulate what they believe and why they believe it. Here are three practical examples.

1. Role-play. I love being invited to an unsuspecting youth group to role-play an atheist or Mormon. By dialoguing with my non-Christian character, students are forced to explain and defend their Christian views. Unfortunately, most Christian youth are ill-equipped to do so. What's worse is that they don't know how ill-equipped they are. After a thorough dismantling through role-play, students' eyes are opened and many are motivated to learn the *what* and the *why*. And over time, continued role-play can help students hone their ability to articulate the truth.

2. Invite guests. Don't just role-play non-Christian characters with your students, invite the real thing. After teaching your students about the Trinitarian nature of God, invite Jehovah's Witnesses into your home or youth group to discuss the topic. Teach your students about the nature of salvation and invite Mormon missionaries over for a conversation on the matter. Once you've equipped your students with arguments for God's existence, ask your atheist neighbor to discuss the topic with them. When students are forced to have real-time conversations with real-life people, their learning increases exponentially.

3. Visit another religious site. As a youth pastor, I would teach my students about other religions. I knew they would eventually encounter a friendly Hindu neighbor, a kind Muslim classmate, or some other person who held opposing beliefs, and I wanted to expose them to those ideas first. My strategy was inoculation, not isolation. So after teaching about a religion like Buddhism and offering a biblical and philosophical critique, I would arrange a field trip to the local Buddhist temple. A monk gave us a tour, explained their basic beliefs and practices, and answered students' questions. Everything the students learned in the classroom prior to the field trip came to life as they engaged a Buddhist monk in the flesh. The encounter was exciting, and it gave students an opportunity to get the theology and apologetics out of the classroom and into a real conversation. Again, they were forced to articulate the truth, and in doing so, they learned the truth in a deeper and more meaningful way.

Training Must Be Intentional

It's time to stop bemoaning the exodus of students from our churches and start doing something serious about it. The world is certainly serious about stripping students of their Christian faith. Atheists like Daniel Dennett say as much: "They will see me as just another liberal professor trying to cajole them out of some of their convictions, and they are dead right about that—that's what I am, and that's exactly what I am trying to do."[8] They're intentional out there in the world. We'd better get intentional here in the church.

This three-stage plan of training provides a practical strategy that can be implemented immediately. Take it and use it. Build on it and add your own ideas. But do not wait to start training up the next generation. Too much is at stake.

BRETT KUNKLE is the student impact director at Stand to Reason. Brett was a contributor to the *Apologetics Study Bible for Students* and wrote the *Ambassador's Guide to Mormonism*. In addition, he has developed a groundbreaking training experience that immerses participants in real-life apologetics, theology, and evangelism. Brett received his master's in philosophy of religion and ethics from Talbot School of Theology.

Interview with Dennis Rainey
SEAN MCDOWELL

In your research and work on the family, how important is apologetics training for the next generation?

It is absolutely imperative that every parent equip their sons and daughters in the basics of apologetics—the parents and the children must know how to think critically and biblically about what the culture is throwing at them and know how to winsomely defend their faith. This is going to become an increasingly important issue because of the accelerated attacks and changes that are occurring in our culture.

Never before in the history of our nation have the fundamental institutions of marriage and family been redefined to be anything other than a man and a woman in a committed covenant marriage relationship.

Never before has there been a multiple-choice approach to gender, with Facebook now offering multiple options.

Never before has there been a generation that has given up on marriage and family and chosen to cohabit as its preferred method of marriage preparation.

Never before in our nation's history have we seen a movement to silence all followers of Christ around issues of morality, marriage, and family

The result of this cultural tsunami will be a nation of confused, lost, and hopeless people. This will represent an unprecedented opportunity to share the gospel of Jesus Christ with a generation that will be looking for a harbor in the storm.

What are some practical things parents can do to teach their kids apologetics?

First, parents need to be proactively teaching the Scripture to their children. Many parents think that taking their children to Sunday school or enrolling them in Christian schools or universities is the solution. Parents need to understand that God gave children to them to train them to know and love God and be wise about their everyday choices.

Second, parents should be honest about their own journey of faith. As parents we must realize that real faith has to be hammered out on the anvil of experience. And sometimes that means children will have doubts about matters of faith. The home needs to be a safe place to discuss struggles and even failures.

Third, protect your family time at dinner. We'd use time at dinner to find out what was going on in the lives of each of our children. Many times we'd find they were facing challenges to their faith and needed some time to decompress honestly about their fears, doubts, or unbelief. We'd try to listen carefully to what our children were thinking and feeling as they confronted issues. We'd discuss the issues and then seek to train them to know how to think biblically and defend their faith.

Finally, we taught our children to defend their faith through discussions about appropriate movies. We'd watch a movie together, and afterward get some ice cream and compare the message of the film with Scripture. Our kids would roll their eyes and say, "Can't we just go to a movie without evaluating it?" To which we'd say, "We could do that, but you are going to be exposed to all kinds of messages in your lifetime and our assignment is to train you in how to think critically and biblically about what you hear, see, or experience."

What topics related to the family should apologists focus on today? Any practical advice for doing that?

I think *the* most important topic to address with your children is their worldview. This will help your children understand why conflicts can arise with our secular culture and why the way they think is going to be different from their peers in grade school all the way through college.

Specific issues that I'd encourage them to discuss and train their children to understand and be able to address biblically include:

Sexual identity and gender issues—they need to understand that the Bible clearly teaches that God, not man, made us and that he created us as male and female, in the image of God (Genesis 1:26-27).

Sexual activity was designed by God to be enjoyed in marriage, and they are accountable to God for how they protect their moral innocence. I'd want daughters to know that Mom and Dad are there to protect them, and it's why Dad will talk to young men who take them on a date (see my book *Interviewing Your Daughter's Date*).

And I'd want my sons to know that Mom and Dad are there to help equip them to know how to respond to girls who will be sexually aggressive. I'd read Proverbs 5–7 to my sons and teach them to know what to do with their sexual desires and how to protect their sexual innocence for marriage (see my book *Aggressive Girls, Clueless Boys*).

I strongly recommend that every dad take his son and every mom take her daughter through *Passport2Purity*. This will help your son or daughter develop a defense for their faith in several key issues they will face as a teen.

I also recommend that parents have numerous discussions about gender identity. Specifically, this discussion would answer your daughter's question if she asked, "What does it mean to be a girl and not a boy?" And for your son if he asked, "What does it mean to be a boy and not a girl?" In other words, what is the essence of femininity and masculinity as God designed it? (We have a variety of resources that can help at FamilyLife.com.)

DENNIS RAINEY is the president and CEO of FamilyLife, a subsidiary of Campus Crusade for Christ. He has authored or coauthored more than two dozen books and is the cohost of the nationally syndicated radio program *FamilyLife Today*.

The Multiethnic Church: God's Living Apologetic

DERWIN L. GRAY

"Congregations that want to embody the gospel to the world should have a bias towards being multiethnic."

TIMOTHY KELLER[1]

As a first-century, Second Temple Jew saturated in the Jewish Scriptures, the apostle Paul was captured by God's future vision for redeemed humanity in the new heavens and new earth. God's eternal church is a blood-bought, regenerated, reconciled, multiethnic family united in its worship of Jesus. God's eternal church is not segregated, but it is a beautiful mosaic of colors and cultures that display the *manifold* (multicolored) wisdom of God (Ephesians 3:10).

Paul knew that humanity's future was rooted in the past when God made a covenant with Abraham (Genesis 12:1-3; Ephesians 2:12). God told Abraham that all the families (people groups) of the earth would be blessed through him. Ultimately every ethnicity would be blessed by Jesus and his work, and through faith in him, they would be incorporated into his ethnically diverse family (Galatians 3:7-9; 3:24-28; Ephesians 2:8-16). This convergence of the past and future motivated Paul to be a multiethnic church planter and missionary throughout the racially hostile and divided first-century, Greco-Roman world.

Before planting Transformation Church in 2010, I was constantly asked, "Who are you trying to reach?," and I would say, "People." Then they would ask, "What kind of people?" I would say, "Sinners. White ones, Asian ones, Latino ones, and Black ones!" I would then explain that the gospel does not allow me to reach just the people I want to reach or people just like me. If Jesus died for the world, then I am compelled by his mission, not mine. I must develop ministry practices to reach the multiethnic, multiclass community in which Transformation Church finds herself situated.

The apostle Paul knew nothing of starting churches that were separated based on ethnicity or class. Preeminent New Testament scholar Scot McKnight writes,

> Paul yearned that there be no invisible people in the fellowship because he knew the power of God's grace. He knew grace was the new creation at work in the present to make one family, Jews and Gentiles, under one Lord, King Jesus. Paul's vision contrasts violently with American churches. Fully 90 percent of American churches draw 90 percent of their people from one ethnic group, and only about 8 percent of American churches can be called multiracial, multiethnic, or interracial.[2]

In an increasingly post-Christian and diverse America, it will take multiethnic local churches to reach people with the gospel. The multiethnic church is a testimony and witness to God's grace. It is also an apologetic in a racially divided America and world.

The Gospel We Preach

The gospel that we preach shapes the churches we have. In America, we are preaching a gospel that creates local churches where nearly 90 percent of the people are of the same ethnicity. Sociologists Michael O. Emerson and Christian Smith write, "Local churches are 10 times more segregated than the neighborhoods in which they sit and 20 times more segregated than nearby public schools."[3] Just about every facet of America is ethnically integrated except for Jesus's church. The one community that bears the name of God is the most segregated in America, whereas the early church was ethnically integrated with Jews and Gentiles. Theologian Christopher J.H. Wright writes in *The Mission of God: Unlocking the Bible's Grand Narrative,*

> The first major council of the church (Acts 15) was convened to consider a knot of problems caused by the success of cross-cultural church planting efforts. These had been initiated by the church of Antioch and carried out among the predominately Gentile and ethnically diverse peoples of the Roman provinces that made up what we now call Turkey. Paul and Barnabas, who had been entrusted with this initiative, were not the first to cross the barrier from Jew to Gentile with the good news of Jesus Christ. Philip (Acts 8) and Peter (Acts 10) had already done that. They were, however, the first to establish whole communities of believers from mixed Jewish and Gentile backgrounds—that is, to plant multiethnic churches.[4]

The apostle Paul along with other believers planted multiethnic churches because of the gospel.

The Gospel Paul Preached

The gospel is an announcement that there is a king named Jesus who established a kingdom through a multicolored, regenerated people called the church who are empowered by the Holy Spirit to embody heaven on earth as a foretaste of what is to come on that great day (Revelation 5:9-12). Our Western individualistic gospel is obsessed with sending people to heaven when they die, yet Jesus and the apostle Paul were more interested in building a church that would bring heaven to earth through reconciled, redeemed, Spirit-sealed people. Let's take a look at a few texts from Paul:

> There is neither Jew nor Greek, there is neither slave nor free, there is no male and female, for you are all one in Christ Jesus (Galatians 3:28).

> Here there is not Greek and Jew, circumcised and uncircumcised, barbarian, Scythian, slave, free; but Christ is all, and in all (Colossians 3:11).

> I am under obligation both to Greeks and to barbarians...For I am not ashamed of the gospel, for it is the power of God for salvation to everyone who believes, to the Jew first and also to the Greek (Romans 1:14,16).

> I have become all things to all people so that by all possible means I might save some. I do all this for the sake of the gospel, that I may share in its blessings (1 Corinthians 9:22b NIV).

Even the glorious book of Romans is about how the gospel empowers Jews and Gentiles to express God's glory by living in harmony as a diverse community of reconciliation on earth as God's fulfillment of the covenant promise he made to Abraham:

> May the God of endurance and encouragement grant you [Jews and Gentiles] to live in such harmony with one another, in accord with Christ Jesus, that together you may with one voice glorify the God and Father of our Lord Jesus Christ. Therefore welcome one another as Christ has welcomed you, for the glory of God.

> For I tell you that Christ became a servant to the circumcised to show God's truthfulness, in order to confirm the promises given to the patriarchs, and in order that the Gentiles might glorify God for his mercy. As it is written,

> "Therefore I will praise you among the Gentiles,
>   and sing to your name."

> And again it is said,

> "Rejoice, O Gentiles, with his people."

And again,

> "Praise the Lord, all you Gentiles,
>   and let all the peoples extol him."

And again Isaiah says,

> "The root of Jesse will come,
>   even he who arises to rule the Gentiles;
> in him will the Gentiles hope."

> May the God of hope fill you with all joy and peace in believing,
> so that by the power of the Holy Spirit you may abound in hope
> (Romans 15:5-13).

Pastors, church planters, and Christ-followers, if you care about the future of the church in America, you must care about learning how to partner with the Holy Spirit in creating multicolored, Jesus-exalting, missional congregations that can reach a changing America and give a foretaste of Jesus's eternal kingdom. If the church in America is not just to survive but to thrive, it must be multiethnic in the twenty-first century.

Paul planted and built multiethnic churches for the "sake of the gospel" because at the heart of the gospel that he preached was reconciliation between God and humanity and man to man.

Reconciliation

Some Jews in the first-century Greco-Roman world believed that Gentiles were created to be fuel for the fires of hell.[5] Some would not help a Gentile woman in the agony of childbirth because they would be guilty of helping her bring another Gentile into the world.[6] If a Jew married a Gentile, the Jewish family would have a funeral for its son or daughter, and the Jewish child would be dead to the parents.[7] However, this doesn't mean that the Jews totally separated themselves from Gentiles in everyday life; some types of everyday interaction would take place.

This horrible racism and ethnocentrism was not one-sided. Many Gentiles believed that Jews were less than human. For example, Cicero, the Roman philosopher, wrote, "As the Greeks say, all men are divided into two classes—Greeks and barbarians. The Greeks called any man a barbarian who could not speak Greek; and they despised him and put up the barriers against him."[8]

The first-century world was filled with racism, sexism, division, injustice, and oppression. (Sounds a lot like the twenty-first century!) The apostle Paul said that Jews and Gentiles were divided by hostility and unreconciled (Ephesians 2:14-16). But then Paul drops a gospel bomb that explodes racism and division when he says Jesus is our peace. In a world saturated with hate, racism, and division, God brought peace in the person of Jesus, and his peace is so beautiful that Jews and Gentiles, former enemies, would become a family and be a living example of God invading the world with peace. The ethnic unity of God's church is a sign to the world that his kingdom has broken through the darkness; multiethnic local churches are God's living apologetic.

> For as many of you as were baptized into Christ have put on Christ. There is neither Jew nor Greek, there is neither slave nor free, there is no male and female, for you are all one in Christ Jesus. And if you are Christ's, then you are Abraham's offspring, heirs according to promise (Galatians 3:27-29).

In Christ, ethnic, class, and gender barriers are obligated by his grace. Instead of our distinctions becoming sources of division, they become sources of blessing.

Grace from Heaven So Heaven Can Come to Earth

Paul says that it is by grace that humanity is saved through faith in Christ. This is the great gift in which no one can boast. Jesus the Messiah did it all (Ephesians 2:8-9). Typically we stop there, but Paul doesn't. He sees in high definition the bigger, greater, and more beautiful story of what our triune God is accomplishing through the epic work and achievement of Jesus through his life, death, resurrection, and ascension. In Ephesians 2:10 (NIV), Paul writes: "For we are God's handiwork, created in Christ Jesus to do good works, which God prepared in advance for us to do." What are these "good works" the apostle Paul is talking about that "God prepared in advance for us to do"? Based on Ephesians 2:11-22, these good works are the fulfillment of God's promises to Abraham in Genesis 12:1-3. Read Ephesians 2:12: "Remember that you were at that time separated from Christ, alienated from the commonwealth of Israel and strangers to the *covenants of promise*, having no hope and without God in the world" (emphasis added).

God promised Abraham that all the families (both Jew and Gentile) on earth would be blessed through him. The great blessing is Jesus—the seed of Abraham—and through Jesus, a new multicolored family called the church would be blessed in him. In Galatians 3:7-9, Paul writes, "Know then that it is those of faith who are the sons of Abraham. And the Scripture, foreseeing that God would justify the Gentiles by faith, *preached the gospel beforehand to Abraham*, saying, 'In you shall all the nations be blessed.' So then, those who are of faith are blessed along with Abraham, the man of faith."

The heartbeat of salvation is that Jesus is faithful to his covenant with Abraham, and through his life, death, resurrection, and ascension, Jesus creates a new humanity called the church where "there is no Gentile or Jew, circumcised or uncircumcised, barbarian, Scythian, slave or free, but Christ is all, and is in all" (Colossians 3:11 NIV). Instead of the local church being colorblind, it becomes color blessed.

The greater and more gloriously beautiful story of salvation by grace through faith is that God has created heavenly colonies of reconciliation and ethnic diversity on earth as it *will* be in heaven. Wright says:

> But whereas much western understanding has seen the individual as the goal, Paul sees individual Christians as signs pointing to a larger reality. He describes his own mission vividly in [2 Corinthians 5] verse 20: We implore people on the Messiah's behalf, he writes, "to be reconciled to God." He longs to see the heaven-earth event, the temple event…the new temple is to be the place to which all nations will come to worship the God of Abraham and Jacob…the reconciliation of Jews and Greeks was obviously near the heart of Paul's aim.[9]

Intrinsic to Paul's gospel was a barrier-breaking, hostility-destroying power that brought ethnically diverse people together in Christ and created a species of humanity that was no longer defined by its tribe or ethnicity but by Christ. Marinate on Paul's God-inspired words of Ephesians 2:14-16:

> For he himself is our peace, who has made us both one and has broken down in his flesh the dividing wall of hostility by abolishing the law of commandments expressed in ordinances, that he might create in himself one new man in place of the two, so making peace, and might reconcile us both to God in one body through the cross, thereby killing the hostility.

According to Paul,

1. Jesus is the peace that brings ethnically diverse people together.
2. Jesus breaks down walls that divide ethnically different people.
3. Jesus creates a new man or new human species. Before Jesus, only Jews and non-Jews existed. After Jesus, a new group of people called the church was created in him.
4. Through the cross, individual sins are forgiven, different ethnic groups are reconciled, and hostility between people has been killed.
5. As Paul writes in these verses, these four gospel realities are complete. God's people just need to walk in the good works Jesus has prepared beforehand for us to walk in (Ephesians 2:8-10).

But How?

But how can we put into practice this biblical theology so our local churches can become multiethnic heavenly colonies of reconciliation?

1. Pray and fast. The division in the American church can be broken only by prayer and fasting.

2. Local churches must be led by ethnically diverse leadership teams, as early churches were (see Acts 6 and 13).

3. Incorporate Christ-exalting diverse musical styles during weekly services.

4. Cross-cultural training and competency is a necessity.

5. Preach the gospel Paul preached.

6. Find a local church that is doing multiethnic ministry and learn from them.[10]

7. Have courage because you will need it for the spiritual warfare you will endure.

The multiethnic church is a testimony of God's grace and a living apologetic for a modern age.

> "I pray that they will all be one, just as you and I are one—as you are in me, Father, and I am in you. And may they be in us so that the world will believe you sent me" (John 17:21 NLT).

DERWIN L. GRAY is the founding and lead pastor of Transformation Church (www.TransformationChurch.tc), a multiethnic, multigenerational, mission-shaped community. TC has been recognized as one of the fastest growing churches in America. Gray is the author of *The High-Definition Leader: Building Multiethnic Churches in a Multiethnic World.*

— 10 —

Come and See:
The Value of Storytelling for Apologetics

HOLLY ORDWAY

Let me tell you a story.

Once upon a time there was an atheist. Then he read a fairytale and discussed myths. As a result, he stopped being an atheist and became a Christian.

That, in the very briefest of summary, is the story of C.S. Lewis's conversion to Christ. As a young atheist, Lewis was profoundly influenced by reading the novel *Phantastes* by the Christian author George MacDonald. *Phantastes* does not mention Christ or the Church anywhere in its pages, but it is deeply imbued with the Christian worldview. Lewis later wrote that this literary encounter was pivotal: "my imagination," he said, "was, in a certain sense, baptized; the rest of me, not unnaturally, took longer."

By 1931, Lewis had come to belief in God on a rational, philosophical level, but he found himself unable to accept the claims of Christianity; he couldn't find the doctrines *meaningful*. Then one day Lewis walked through the grounds of Magdalen College, Oxford, in conversation with his friends J.R.R. Tolkien and Hugo Dyson. They helped him to see that Christ's sacrifice is a story, just like the stories Lewis loved, but with the difference that it *also* happened in history. Doctrine became more than a dry set of propositions; Lewis realized that the two hemispheres of his life, his imagination and his reason, could be united in the Christian faith. The final barrier to belief fell. He could become a Christian as a whole person—and he did. Now he is known to millions as the author of the Chronicles of Narnia; he has a memorial in Poets' Corner of Westminster Abbey; his books have helped countless people to know Christ.

Lewis's conversion shows that stories matter—and not just for him, but for all of us.

We experience our own lives in terms of story. Birth announcements connect the new baby with the lives of the parents; later, graduation, wedding, retirement announcements flag important plot points; the obituary will be a final summing-up. Couples recount the story of how they met and fell in love. Travelers regale us with the tales of their adventures. A bad day can become a good story when the sting has passed.

We see the basic human need for story wherever we look. Skeptics tell just-so stories to explain every aspect of our lives in terms of biology. Celebrity culture allows us to have heroes and villains. On the personal level, one of the signals of our *need* for narrative is that we are dissatisfied when we feel that our lives lack purpose. Our unstated expectation is that our lives have a beginning, middle, and end that make sense; we are troubled by seemingly random events, and when tragedy strikes, we ask, "*Why* did this happen?"

The work of apologists must always be centered upon Christ in the most robust sense possible—and that includes using both argument and story, both reason and imagination. Unfortunately, Christian apologists have often tacitly accepted the modernist, scientistic focus on empirical evidence alone, and tried to convey truth as if story didn't matter, delivering a set of answers without regard for how the other person arrived at his questions or objections. Yes, we work to demolish false arguments and remove obstacles to belief, but we also work constructively to help people encounter and engage with Christ. And that includes telling a good story!

When I talk about using story and imagination in apologetics, I am most emphatically *not* talking about taking apologetics arguments and inserting them into fiction like a bitter pill hidden in a sweet treat. No! I mean something far richer and more interesting—and more effective.

To begin with, the creative impulse itself is a reflection of the image of God in each person. The great fantasy writer J.R.R. Tolkien understood this. We make stories, he said, "because we are made: and not only made, but made in the image and likeness of a Maker."

We can see the value of stories in apologetics perhaps most clearly if we look at Scripture. God is the ultimate Storyteller, both as the Author of history and as the Author of Scripture. The inspired Word of God is in large part a narrative, the story of salvation history—a drama that might be summed up in five acts: Creation, Israel, Incarnation, Church, Apocalypse. Life stories are recounted—such as those of Abraham, Moses, David. Entire books of the Bible are written in poetry. Preeminently, the Word became flesh and dwelt among us, full of grace and truth.

One of the ways that storytelling is valuable is that it makes our apologetics *incarnational*. For apologetics to be incarnational is first of all to consider the implications of the "Word made flesh" on all aspects of life. We who follow Christ do not just know *about* him, though we can know many true things about him through the use of our reason, such as the fact of his resurrection and the nature of his claim to be our only Lord and Savior. We also *know* him, directly and experientially. That kind of knowledge can't be shared directly, but it can be shown indirectly through the working of the imagination. Art, music, architecture, film, and literature all provide opportunities for people to catch a glimpse of the world as we see it in the light of Christ, to taste the goodness of God, to get a hint of something important just around the corner—something worth following up on.

Certainly that was my experience. As an adult atheist (and a hostile one!), I would never have bothered to pick up a book of Christian apologetics or theology because I was sure it was a stupid superstition. Yet the deeply meaningful world of Tolkien's *The Lord of the Rings*, and the profound depths of poetry by Gerard Manley Hopkins and others, gave me a glimpse of something beautiful and mysterious about the Christian faith. I didn't believe it was true, but

I was drawn, fearfully and reluctantly, to learn more. Eventually I began to investigate the claims of Christianity, and was convinced by rational argument that God existed, and even that Jesus of Nazareth died and rose from the dead.

However, I still struggled, unable to grasp the shocking idea that God had become incarnate. It was only in rereading the Chronicles of Narnia, and encountering once again the Christ-figure of the great lion Aslan, that I was able to connect what my reason told me with what my imagination showed me—and then to lay down my arms in surrender to Christ.

Appreciating the incarnational nature of Christianity includes realizing that God made us with bodies and emotions, as well as minds and souls, and that he placed us in the physical world that he had made—and he called all of this good, even very good. The future we look forward to is not a disembodied spirit-heaven, but rather a new heaven and a new earth, where we will have glorified, resurrected *bodies*. Thus, any fully-orbed presentation of the truth about ourselves and God's plan for us cannot be a disembodied, purely intellectual truth; it must truthfully reflect our nature as created beings.

Part of being incarnate means that it is good and right for us to have emotions and express them—as our Lord did, for example, by weeping at the tomb of Lazarus and by getting angry with the money changers in the temple. The fact that little children wanted to come to him suggests that he had a welcoming physicality and a warm personality that they instinctively trusted and found attractive. He wasn't just a walking dictionary of Christian theology.

Literature and film offer a mode of doing apologetics incarnationally, putting meaningful flesh on bare-bones concepts like justice, faith, sin, or love, and showing that truth is never merely a private affair, but also shapes how we relate with others. In a good story, we relate to the characters as if they were real people, feeling sympathy or dislike for them, experiencing nervousness, sorrow, or joy at the plot twists that involve them. We reflect on whether their actions were right or wrong, wise or foolish, and wonder what we might do in their situation, whether it's President Bartlet making a decision of state on *The West Wing*, or Elizabeth Bennet forming an opinion about Mr. Darcy in *Pride and Prejudice*.

Stories allow us to present truth in such a way that it impacts the whole person: emotions and intellect, relationships and self-knowledge.

To be sure, literature's power of evoking emotion is in itself neutral; the question is, to what end is it oriented? Authors can use the power of language and storytelling to make evil things seem harmless or even appealing. (Consider pornography or the manipulation of desires by advertising.) But any good thing can be twisted; this does not remove its proper use. For the apologist, the point is that emotional response to the images we see and the language we hear and read is an innate part of being human; people are not, never will be, and indeed cannot be purely rational and unaffected by emotion. If they were, they would have ceased to be fully human. In a rightly ordered human being, rational understanding is accompanied by appropriate emotional response: St. Paul directs us to rejoice with those who rejoice and weep with those who weep.

Furthermore, being incarnate means that we are creatures who live in the flow of time, and are thus naturally predisposed to absorb truth in the form of narrative. When our Lord tells us that we must become like little children to enter the kingdom of heaven, perhaps he is also reminding us of the goodness of the child's instinctive cry, "Tell me a story!" The story of Christ, for instance, involves expectation of his birth, then the actual event of his nativity (in dangerous circumstances), his childhood, his public ministry, his passion and death, his resurrection and ascension. The Church calendar enables us each year to relive this drama and in a sense to reenact it, moving through it sequentially, in time, rather than stepping outside it as if we were more than human, turning it into an abstract system of propositions that only Mr. Spock would really value. The power of story allows the apologist to transform abstract truth into something that the reader or listener can engage with.

The Gospel is the greatest story ever told—but as apologists, are we telling it for all it's worth? We've all seen movie posters and book covers that give us a vivid image and a tagline for the story—hinting at the *Adventure! Romance! Suspense!* that awaits us. The tagline is not the story itself: it's intended to draw us in, so that we'll enter the movie theater or sit down with the book.

All too often, though, we allow the Gospel to remain as a movie poster or a book cover that has some adjectives and abstract nouns attached—salvation, redemption, hope—without immersing people in the flesh-and-blood drama of it. If we move beyond using individual verses and passages as proof texts and present them as part of the grand narrative of salvation history, we can better help people experience the fullness of what Scripture has to say, rather than reducing Scripture to a mere reference footnote. The Gospels don't merely recount that Jesus rose from the dead: they dramatize it. We meet the distraught Mary Magdalene at the empty tomb, and the bewildered and downcast disciples trudging along the road to Emmaus, before they—and we—encounter the risen Lord.

The stories of Christians through the past two thousand years provide another form of apologetics. Consider St. Paul and St. Peter, St. Thomas Aquinas and St. Francis of Assisi, William Wilberforce and Mother Teresa, and so many more. We could simply talk about missionary zeal and solid doctrine, loving God with mind as well as heart, and respecting the dignity of all people—but these ideas have much more meaning when they are embodied in the stories of real men and women. St. Paul's shipwrecks and hairsbreadth escapes from death, St. Thomas's quiet work writing millions of words of philosophy and theology (and a few wonderful hymns), Wilberforce's decades-long anti-slavery campaign, or Mother Teresa's tireless care for the poor in the slums of Calcutta, are the sorts of stories that make people sit up and take notice. Examples of conspicuous holiness and goodness (even by secular standards) may help people to wonder: What motivated that person? How could I gain some of that joy, some of that strength?

Stories remind us of the complexity of life and something of the mystery of Christian faith. Consider the parable of the prodigal son, told by the master storyteller himself. Here is the story of a young man who thinks there's a much more exciting life ahead for him than being at home. He squanders his inheritance and finds himself in a faraway country, hungry and lonely, all too aware that he doesn't deserve any help. Ashamed, he trudges back, hoping to get a menial job—only to find his dad running out to embrace him, even to give him a party!

Yes, the parable is "about" God's love and mercy—but these words are embodied in the story. It is in the particulars of this sore-hearted, sore-footed young man, who can scarcely believe that his father is really taking him back into his home, that we encounter the *meaning* of conversion, repentance, forgiveness. Most importantly, the reader can imagine himself or herself into the story—and the more vividly realized the world of the story, the more likely it is that the reader will *want* to inhabit that story and experience it imaginatively...and perhaps begin to ask, "Could it possibly be true?"

Storytelling matters for apologetics because a story is, ultimately, a reflection of what it means to be a Christian. Our faith is an adventure: "The road goes ever on and on," says Bilbo Baggins in *The Hobbit*. As Christian apologists, we do not merely show that there *is* a road, we invite people to join us on it, headed toward the heavenly Jerusalem to meet our Lord and King. "Come and see," we say. "Join us in this story."

HOLLY ORDWAY is professor of English and director of the MA in apologetics at Houston Baptist University, and the author of *Not God's Type: An Atheist Academic Lays Down Her Arms* (Ignatius Press, 2014). She holds a PhD in English literature from the University of Massachusetts Amherst; her academic work focuses on imaginative apologetics and on the writings of C.S. Lewis, J.R.R. Tolkien, and Charles Williams.

— 11 —

Using Hollywood Blockbusters to Share Your Faith

LENNY ESPOSITO

'll never forget the first time I saw *Star Wars*. I was young enough to see it on the big screen and lucky enough to have no expectations. The theater darkened and John Williams's majestic theme burst forth. Then, a rebel ship appeared with lasers blazing, fleeing for its life. It was quickly followed by the ominous Imperial Star Destroyer that didn't simply fly into the frame; *it consumed the screen*! This ship never ended. The experience still resonates with me today.

Star Wars didn't impact one generation. It continues to influence culture even decades later. Films have that kind of power. They are the modern equivalent to the traveler who visits the local village and weaves a tale of exotic places and heroic exploits. We get a new perspective on the world and we become the heroes we see on the screen. Movies whisk us away from our problems and our dreary lives. The storyteller has always had this power, but now the power is enhanced by computer-generated graphics and multimillion dollar budgets.

Movies will influence people in ways they never even realize. Take "The *Sideways* Effect." The 2004 film centered on two friends touring California's wine country, where the main character gives an eloquent speech about his preference for one type of wine, pinot noir, and his disdain for merlot. In the year following its release, sales of pinot noir jumped 16 percent while merlot sales shrank 2 percent. The wine industry dubbed this "The *Sideways* Effect."[1] This is how effective powerful storytelling is in transmitting new ideas.

Using Story to Communicate Truth

Jesus knew the power of story. He continually used storytelling to more easily communicate difficult concepts, both to his disciples and to his challengers. Jesus relied on parables so much that "he did not speak to them without a parable" (Mark 4:34). Jesus's parables would use the familiar experiences of that culture, and then draw a spiritual lesson from them. Like Jesus, we need to use examples to help us illustrate our points. Our apologetic can be more effective by drawing on the shared experience of popular films to share spiritual truth.

Movies are not only shared across our culture, they're highly relatable and they can present clear pictures of complex ideas. Movies have the added benefit of being enjoyable to watch. While your nonbelieving friends or family may balk at the idea of attending a Bible study, most wouldn't mind watching the latest blockbuster. And with any good film, people get excited to talk about it afterward. That gives you the advantage. Using movies in your apologetic offers you a nonthreatening way to witness to friends or family using a powerful medium with relatable examples that they'll remember for a long time. Here are just three examples of how you can use Hollywood blockbusters in your apologetic.

The Need to Hold On to What's Real

The idea that truth is relative is rampant today. How often have you heard someone say in response to your beliefs, "Well, I'm glad that you find meaning in your beliefs, but that's your truth, not mine"? This is frustrating, primarily because truth isn't something one can pick and choose. God either exists or he doesn't. Yet, people continue to think that the statement "God exists" is more like one's preference for a particular soft drink rather than a fact like the earth revolves around the sun. But both statements make claims about reality. Truth cannot be like preferences; it's true whether we like it or not.

The Matrix—Choosing the Difficult Path

The Matrix (1999) offers a great example of why knowing the truth outstrips our need for comfort and conformity. In *The Matrix* the computers control the world, keeping people alive in cocoons while drawing energy off their body heat. People don't realize they are imprisoned; they are fed a virtual reality world by the machines, but all their experiences are simulations.

One such prisoner is Neo (Keanu Reeves), a nothing-special hacker who is told by rebels who have themselves been set free that his life is an illusion. They offer Neo a way to escape and discover a greater reality than he dares to imagine. Without even knowing what awaits him, Neo agrees and discovers the hideous truth: the real world is dead. Freed people survive underground on sloppy porridge and shabby clothes. Yet, Neo chooses to live in the real world, seeking to overthrow the simulation. Neo sees the value in reality.

Neo's counterpoint is Cypher (Joe Pantoliano), one of the film's villains who had escaped the Matrix years before. He's sick of his uncomfortable existence, so he arranges a meeting with Matrix sentries at an expensive virtual restaurant and asks to be placed back into the machine. He declares, "You know I know that this steak doesn't exist. I know that when I put it in my mouth, the Matrix is telling my brain that it is juicy and delicious. And after nine years do you know what I've realized?...Ignorance is bliss."

We naturally recoil at Cypher's decision because we recognize the value in having true beliefs. Even if it makes you uncomfortable or forces you to live in a way that you don't like, there's value in holding to what's real. To seek self-delusion for comfort is cowardice. Cypher's actions demonstrate as much.

The Matrix makes a compelling argument for seeking out the truth. Either Christianity is true or it isn't. The person who dismisses claims of reality by stating "That's true for you but not for me" makes the same mistake as Cypher, choosing comfort over what may be a difficult truth. Investigating the truth claims of Christianity is valuable, whether or not they currently make sense to you. For Neo, abandoning what he thought was true and embracing a new paradigm wasn't easy, but it's noble. We should strive to be a Neo, not a Cypher.

The Need for Justice and the Problem of Evil

The search for justice runs through all storytelling. We watch some nefarious villain executing his evil ploy and we hang on the edge of our seats hoping our hero will be victorious. There's something fundamental in the human spirit that wants to see good triumph.

This desire for justice is what attracts us to the adventure quest, like Peter Jackson's adaptation of J.R.R. Tolkien's *The Lord of the Rings*. There, Frodo Baggins is given a ring that holds the power of the evil Sauron, who seeks to wield it and rule Middle Earth. Because he bears this ring, Frodo assumes the dangerous responsibility of finding the path to destroy it. Frodo never asked for this assignment; circumstances thrust it upon him. Yet, he knows the quest is vital even if he may lose his life in the process.

In one poignant scene, Frodo is feeling the weight of his choice and laments to Gandalf about the evil Gollum, who is threatening their quest:

> *Frodo*: It's a pity Bilbo didn't kill him when he had the chance!
>
> *Gandalf*: Pity? It was pity that stayed Bilbo's hand. Many that live deserve death, and some that die deserve life. Can you give it to them, Frodo? Do not be too eager to deal out death in judgment. Even the very wise cannot see all ends. My heart tells me that Gollum has some part to play yet, for good or ill before this is over. The pity of Bilbo may rule the fate of many.
>
> *Frodo*: I wish the Ring had never come to me. I wish none of this had happened.
>
> *Gandalf*: So do all who live to see such times, but that is not for them to decide. All we have to decide is what to do with the time that is given to us. There are other forces at work in this world, Frodo, besides the will of evil. Bilbo was meant to find the Ring, in which case you also were meant to have it. And that is an encouraging thought.

In Frodo's complaint, we see a particular instance of the problem of evil. You may have heard someone complain about how a loving God could allow so much evil in the world. Frodo believes the world would be better if Gollum had been killed. It's easy to make the charge that there's too much evil in the world, but we don't know how the story of this world plays out. However, fans know that Gandalf is right. Gollum's existence does figure into the ultimate salvation of Middle Earth.

Evil Gollum must exist in order for Frodo's quest to succeed and a greater evil vanquished. The Roman executioner's cruelty must also exist for the sacrifice of Jesus to succeed. It isn't a contradiction to say God exists and is in control even if evil hasn't been eliminated. We just haven't gotten to the end of the story.

Forrest Gump and Jesus's Resurrection

Forrest Gump tells the story of its title character, played by Tom Hanks. The film places Gump in key historical events and highlights popular trends of the sixties and seventies. It amazed viewers in its use of editing techniques, showing Gump next to John Lennon and shaking President Kennedy's hand. The chain of Bubba Gump Shrimp Company restaurants that exist today were inspired by the film.

Yet, even with the convincing editing tricks and the interweaving of real history, no one would mistake *Forrest Gump* as a documentary. If Watergate or Vietnam happened, is it reasonable to believe Gump must also have existed? No. Elements of fiction are obvious in the film, and there are too many people alive today who were alive in the sixties who could correct the misconception. If a group of Americans sought to honor Gump for service to his country or contributions to society, they would be rightly looked at as detached from reality.

Yet, this is the very same scenario certain atheists want us to believe happened at Christianity's inception. They claim the Gospel stories are copies of dying-and-rising-god myths of deities like Horus or Dionysus that were afterward embellished with historical details. As Earl Doherty puts it, "By the time another half century had passed, almost everyone who followed the religion of these storytellers accepted their work as an account of actual historical events and a real historical man."[2]

Such charges have become more common, especially with the debut of the YouTube video *Zeitgeist*. However, it's a very oversimplified view that has tremendous problems. One is the strong monotheism among faithful Jews in Jesus's day. How does Doherty account for Jews like Peter who so strictly followed Jewish laws that he balked at eating non-kosher food?[3] Would he follow pagan myth stories just wrapped in a Jewish cover? It's highly unlikely and less believable.

The conversion of the apostle Paul is an even bigger problem. Paul, by his own account, was a zealous Pharisee who hunted down and killed Christians because he thought they were blaspheming the God of Israel.[4] Why would such a man believe in pagan dying-and-rising-god myths, especially when they were spun by the very enemies he sought to kill? Would an al-Qaeda operative watch *Forrest Gump* with anything but skepticism, even if he didn't know it was supposed to be fiction? That's what the Jesus-mythers would have us believe.

The distance between the events portrayed in *Forrest Gump* is also the same as that between Jesus's resurrection and the Gospel accounts.[5] It's hardly enough time for such fables to become believable. Even a gap of fifty years, like the one that exists between the sixties and today, is not enough time to convince any reasonable person that *Forrest Gump* tells a true tale of an American hero.

In order to believe that Jesus is a myth, one must indulge in a tale more fantastic than Hollywood. Because of Paul's conversion and his early recording of Jesus's death and resurrection, the Jesus-mythers are on extremely flimsy ground.

The Opportunities Are Endless

In this chapter, I've just briefly outlined three apologetic arguments and how to use film to communicate your point effectively. But these are just examples. Many other films offer good illustrations for discussing concepts like sin, salvation, the wickedness that exists within all persons, or the need for a savior. It's incumbent upon you to be a thoughtful viewer and ask yourself, "How can I use the ideas in this film to clarify the Christian worldview to someone else?"

Then invite someone to the movies. Use the power of storytelling to tell the greatest story in history in one of the most effective ways possible.

LENNY ESPOSITO, author and speaker, has been spreading convincing Christianity across the globe for twenty years. A pioneer in online apologetics with his popular www.ComeReason.org website and podcast, Lenny has also contributed to books such as the award-winning *Apologetics Study Bible for Students* and *True Reason: Confronting the Irrationality of the New Atheism*. His articles have appeared in the *Los Angeles Times* and the *Southern California Christian Times*.

— 12 —

The Urban Apologist

CHRISTOPHER BROOKS

*"Walk in wisdom toward outsiders, making the best use of the
time. Let your speech always be gracious, seasoned with salt, so
that you may know how you ought to answer each person."*

COLOSSIANS 4:5-6

Recently I was invited by a major evangelical organization to participate in a panel discussion on the topic, "What's Next for the Church." I was excited to accept this invitation primarily because I am a lover of diverse and difficult questions and the people who ask them. Experience has proven that it is at the intersection of tough questions and their practically and theologically sound answers that transformation happens.

This conference had a reputation of bringing together people who are passionate about the major issues of our time and genuinely in pursuit of well-reasoned answers. My fellow presenters did an excellent job sharing what they believed to be the major trends facing twenty-first-century followers of Christ. Their topics ranged from the theological to the social, from postmodernism to religious persecution and from human sexuality to human trafficking. Without question these are the issues ministries that desire to influence culture and maintain their evangelistic effectiveness must embrace with both scholarly and pragmatic vigilance.

However, as timely and relevant as these topics were, of far greater importance was the composition of the audience that sat before us. This was a multicultural, multilinguistic, and mixed-gender group of leaders who longed for answers that were contextualized and relevant to meet the needs of their mission fields.

When the time came for me to speak, I could not overlook the beautiful multiethnic mosaic that existed within this audience. I am sure that my observations concerning the theme sounded more like an announcement of sorts, or a breaking newsflash. The report of racial diversity and multiculturalism is vital information for church leaders who desire to shape the evangelical agenda. To ignore it was no longer an option. Evangelicalism is rapidly changing and so is the profile of its typical leader and the composition of our congregations. Similar to the global South we in the US are now seeing massive amounts of racial diversity. The long predicted demographic shift to a majority minority America was now upon us.

For example, Jen Manuel Krogstad of the Pew Research Center reported in July 2014 on the current trend of minorities in US classrooms. In her study Krogstad states, "Fueled in part by Hispanic population growth, there may be more minorities in classrooms when school starts this fall (among them blacks, Asians and Hispanics) than white students nationwide in K-12 public schools, according to U.S. Department of Education projections. In 2014, some 50.3% of students are projected to be minorities."[1]

This trend is also true for local churches in many sections of our nation. What's next for the church is the recognition that the urbanization of Christianity in America had brought with it a tidal wave of ethnic minorities whose insights, questions, and concerns radically transform the ministry of the local church and the world of apologetics in wonderful and formidable ways.

Defining Apologetics in a New Way

At its core, apologetics is the art and science of defending the faith. However, practically understood, the work of the apologist is simply to answer with integrity, clarity, and compassion the questions critics are asking about the gospel

(1 Peter 3:15). The context of this passage implies a lifestyle on the part of the apologist that engenders and welcomes questions from their audience. The encouragement of Peter seems to be that we avoid the telemarketer approach of simply enduring questions solely for the sake of closing the deal. Rather, Peter calls us to anticipate and patiently answer the questions of our unbelieving friends, family members, and neighbors in an uncompromising and yet humble manner. Affirming this perspective of apologetics is crucial and carries with it some very significant implications. When Christians view apologetics as the skill of effectively answering the skeptic's objections concerning the gospel, the most important effect is the realization that different questioners bring different assumptions and apprehensions to the table.

Put plainly, ethnic minorities are asking new questions of the gospel that today's apologist must take seriously. A different cultural perspective drives these new questions. By culture I mean the shared history, concerns, aspirations, and character qualities of a group of people. Culture is often expressed through food, music, and literature. It is here that we encounter the heartbeat and critiques of a particular group. Behind every question is a questioner who brings their unique heritage, experiences, and worldview. It is impossible to separate the cultural conditioning of the questioner from their questions. This requires that today's apologist must be part anthropologist, part sociologist, and part theologian. Apologists and thought leaders such as Carl Ellis Jr., Anthony Bradley, Ravi Zacharias, and Russell Moore are excellent examples of this multi-disciplinary approach.

Practicing Apologetics in a New Way

It is also good for apologists to be sensitive to their own cultural conditioning. I recognize, as an apologist, that I bring certain assumptions to the conversation. Being raised in the African-American community has afforded me the privilege of experiencing the ethos and beauty of black life firsthand. From the music of Motown to the conversational back and forth in barbershops over current events, I have heard apologetic discourse from the time of my youth. This rich dialogue forever marks me.

However, I have also seen the brokenness and disappointment among many within my community over the perceived failure of the church to adequately address the central issues that plague our families. In addition, for nearly twenty years now, I have taken on a pastoral concern for the unchurched and the underrepresented in our urban centers. I have done my best to listen with an attentive ear to the burdens and doubts of my people and that of other minorities. My book, *Urban Apologetics: Why the Gospel Is Good News for the City*, attempts to take up these challenges to the gospel and to equip apologists with the tools needed to compassionately, creatively, and competently provide a well-reasoned, biblical response.

Apologetics in the City

Involvement in both apologetics and inner-city ministry has created within me a passion to see urban Christians develop a love for apologetics and to see apologists develop a love for urban Christians. When we begin to take seriously the unique critiques of ethnic minorities to the gospel, we discover that their concerns are shaping culture in significant ways.

Take for example, the Black Lives Matter movement, a crusade that began in the aftermath of the death of Trayvon Martin and has become the rallying cry for tens of thousands, often but not exclusively ethnic minorities in inner cities. Launched by three very creative and intelligent women, Alicia Garza, Patrisse Cullors, and Opal Tometi, this slogan has saturated social media. But Black Lives Matter is far more than a mere mantra; at its heart it is a postmodern appraisal of the existing social structure, including the church. The founders of the movement are also lesbians who are heavily influenced by liberation ideology. An examination of their website reveals a convergence of some of the most influential currents sweeping through our culture today. They have successfully molded a campaign that brings together the core themes of Occupy Wall Street, Black Liberation Theology, and the LGBTQ movements. The following is a direct quote from the founders concerning their mission:

> Black Lives Matter affirms the lives of Black queer and trans folks, disabled folks, black-undocumented folks, folks with records, women and all Black lives along the gender spectrum. It centers

those that have been marginalized within Black liberation movements. It is a tactic to (re)build the Black liberation movement.[2]

Embedded in this compelling mission statement are several diverse and difficult questions, which the church should take up with critical thinking and compassion. I want to draw out several of these questions and place them into three categories of objections to the gospel that are representative of what urban apologists will face as they attempt to influence people for Christ. Again, it is at the intersection of these questions and our ability to answer them with scriptural and social clarity that transformation and salvation are discovered.

Questions Behind Black Lives Matter

The first question is one of personhood: "Do individuals of African-American descent qualify as people, with all the social rights afforded to people? Do their lives truly matter as much as other persons' lives?" This is a deep philosophical and theological question and has historical grounds. Pope John Paul II is arguably the most noted theologian to take up the philosophical questions of personalism. Cardinal Avery Dulles suggests, in his article for *The Catholic Review*, that the heart of John Paul's theology was the mystery of the human person.[3]

In recent time Anthony Bradley, associate professor of theology at the King's College in New York, has done an excellent job addressing personalism as well. In a series of lectures for the Carl F.H. Henry Center for Theological Understanding, Dr. Bradley challenged his audience with the following charge:

> In Christian personalism, there is an inherent sense of worth and dignity in all humans because we are made in the image and likeness of God. We are endowed with intellect and reason, making observations about the world around us through our senses…Personalism calls us to love and care for others simply because they are people. Variations of this theory influenced Dr. Martin Luther King Jr. and his thinking about social justice; Pope John Paul II and his opposition to the Soviet Union and his ethics of abortion and euthanasia; and even Francis Schaeffer and his creation of L'Abri.

The plight of blacks in America has been a quest to be seen as fully human persons. Dating as far back as the founding documents of our nation, article 1, section 2, clause 3 of the US Constitution declares that slaves are to be counted as only three-fifths of a person when considering representation of states in Congress. Those who are familiar with the images and scenes from the civil rights movement of the sixties will readily remember that slogan "I am a man," which black male protesters often carried at rallies.

Many within today's Black Lives Matter movement believe that the church has done a very poor job affirming the personhood of blacks and have in many cases articulated a narrative that dehumanizes minorities. This scorn for the church has produced a quest to find alternative narratives in competitors to Christianity such as the Moorish Science Temple, the Nation of Gods and Earths, Black Hebrew Israelites, Islam, and for some a total rejection of religion altogether and an embrace of black humanism.

Religious Objections to the Gospel

I call this first category of questions the religious objections to the gospel. The urban apologist has to be well versed in the beliefs of nontraditional religious options prevalent in minority communities and how they attempt to answer the major existential questions such as personhood. If we are going to see the gospel penetrate minority communities, we must be able to show not only how Jesus compares to Muhammad or Buddha, but also how Christ stands in contradistinction to the teachings of Yosef Ben-Jochannan (Dr. Ben), Louis Farrakhan, and Noble Drew Ali, just to name a few. It is also wise for urban apologists to familiarize themselves with leading figures in humanist movements, such as the enormously popular atheist and astrophysicist Neil deGrasse Tyson, who has over 2.5 million Twitter followers.

The wonderful news is that Christ affirms the personhood of all people, making a special emphasis to bestow value on those viewed as subhuman in the eyes of many in his culture. The seminal example of this is the story of the Good Samaritan found in Luke 10:25-37. Jesus makes no mistake when he places this mix-breed Samaritan as the main character of the narrative and challenges his Jewish listeners to see these minorities with neighborly sympathy and equal humanity.

Admittedly, many within the Christian tradition have failed to live up to these teachings. Nevertheless, this is the consistent message of the gospel and this is what our Lord commands us to model. Although we cannot deny the sinfulness of some within our faith, we should point people to the clear message and modeling of our Savior. Our ability to provide the gospel's response to the question of personhood in an incarnational manner to a hurting and dehumanized community will bring healing and win us an audience for the gospel.

The Ethical Objections to the Gospel

The second category of questions that arise from the Black Lives Matter mission statement is what I call the ethical objections to the gospel. One can clearly see emerging from this group a worldview that flows from a place of pain and hurt. Black Lives Matter is appealing primarily to those who feel morally condemned, in particular in the area of homosexuality. Their woundedness creates a suspicion about God himself. Implicit within the heart of most gay-affirming movements is the assumption that the God of the Bible and those who espouse the values of Scripture are immoral. This is sad because the misconception they have of God and the teachings of Scripture keeps them from coming to the source of the very healing they are searching for, namely Christ. The urban apologist must be prepared to defend the morality of God and explain why the ethics of Jesus are not just right in a divine command sense, but how they are also loving, protective, and virtuous.

We cannot deny that the Bible disapproves of same-gender sexual behavior, just as it equally denounces pornography and all sex outside of the marriage covenant. What we must present to our gay friends and family members are a broader set of questions by which we frame all sexual ethics. The seminal question should be, "Is there anything right or wrong when it comes to sexual behavior?" All reasonably minded people will affirm that human sexuality is far too powerful a force to not have some parameter placed upon it.

Once this truth is established, we can then move to the next question:

"Who has authority to determine what is right and what is wrong?" No doubt this will provoke a rigorous discussion, but most ethicists agree that the answer boils down to one or two options—either we determine what is right or wrong on a personal and individual basis or we must look to a higher authority than personal preference.

The problem with the first option is that you and I are prone to coming to radically different conclusions concerning our ethical views. We could never build a coherent moral system if morality is based solely upon individuality. This leads us to the alternative offered by Scripture that we need to look to a higher moral agency. Jesus is the only one qualified to provide us with ethical guidance because he is morally perfect.

In addition to this reasoning on ethics we must faithfully communicate that God is compassionate and sympathetic to our temptations and struggles. Christ offers to transform our hearts and provide us with the grace needed to live virtuous lives.

Social Justice Objections to the Gospel

The final category of questions that can be drawn from the quote from Black Lives Matter, which represents the broader social consciences of many ethnic minorities, is what I call the social justice objections to the gospel. These questions have to deal with the need to reform societal structures and systems that so often lead to the abuse, mistreatment, and marginalization of people groups who do not have the privilege of being born in the major population of our country. Sadly, Christianity is often seen as one of the prime culprits in the creation and protection of systems that tend toward racism and oppression.

The urban apologist must be able to honestly dissect these concerns, validating only those that are evidentially true and correcting the misunderstanding and fallacies that are at the core of those that are false or emotionally subjective. This requires wisdom and skill to walk the tightrope of expressing compassion without compromise. Arguably the greatest obstacles to effectively addressing this category of questions are the political differences between the evangelical church and ethnic minority communities. We must be sure to remind ourselves that the call of apologetics is not the defense of our public policy position but the protection of the gospel. Our effectiveness in reaching minority communities for Christ will be found, in large part, in our willingness to address issues in a nonpartisan manner, which exalts the gospel above all else.

Of additional importance is the marriage between the salvation of the soul and the reformation of the cultural. No longer can we fall into the false dichotomy of the mission of the church being either evangelism or social change. We must embrace the fact that the gospel calls us to both proclaim Jesus and to bring the reforming light of the gospel to the dark areas of our society. We must do our best to eradicate evil wherever it exists and to preserve the beauty and good that is present in our communities.

The church should be known as lovers of all people and protectors of those who are marginalized. Our presence in cities should produce greater flourishing for all people as a result of our commitment to living out the implications of the common grace of God in society. When we fail to live up to this vision, we must repent and confess our failures to God and the watching world.

As urban apologists we must never lose faith that God will bring salvation and transformation to the people in our communities if we embrace the diverse and difficult questions they are asking of the gospel and provide them with compassionate and credible answers from Scripture. This is the glorious task of the new kind of apologist.

CHRISTOPHER BROOKS is the senior pastor of Evangel Ministries, a thriving 1600-member church in the heart of Detroit, and the author of *Kingdom Dreaming* and *Urban Apologetics*. He hosts *Equipped for Life* (www.equippedforlife.tv), aired daily on the Salem Network. He was appointed campus dean of Moody Theological Seminary's Michigan campus in 2013.

— 13 —

Intuitional Apologetics:
Using Our Deepest Intuitions
to Point Toward God

TERRY GLASPEY

'll never forget the first time I visited the Grand Canyon. Standing there before this awe-inspiring natural phenomenon, I found myself speechless. I could find no words for the thoughts and feelings stirring inside me. Wonder. Amazement. Awe. The beauty, the majestic natural power of what I saw moved me in an unexpected way, and I felt uplifted at the same time that I felt small and humbled—a tiny being standing before this immensity. And had I not already believed in God, this might have been the moment when I would have first entertained the possibility.

Sure, you could have regaled me with the facts about how large this rift in the earth was, unfolding its jaw-dropping dimensions; you could have described the way the sun played upon the walls of the canyon in an ever-changing riot of color and texture; you could have given me a detailed explanation for the geologic processes that brought it into being; but you still could not account for how I felt at that moment, and how I was instinctively drawn toward some explanation much deeper than all these facts and statistics.

I imagine that you have had similar experiences, whether while viewing the vast expanse of a star-strewn night sky, listening to a Bach concerto, experiencing a painting by Van Gogh or Rembrandt, standing in hushed silence in a cathedral, strolling quietly through a forest and bending your ear toward the sound of birdsong and the rustling of leaves, or maybe even walking through the city just after a rainstorm, hearing the sizzle of tires on the wet street. God has made human beings to respond to beauty and wonder and the mysteries of life.

In this essay I'd like to explore how certain common human experiences might be understood and embraced as an oft-neglected tool in the apologetic task. In the framework of this essay, I can begin to suggest only some of the ways we might engage the experience of these moments of transcendence in helping people along the road toward faith.

Traditional Apologetics and the Modern Challenge

When we think about the apologetic task, we usually think of creating arguments that might convince someone who doesn't believe that the Christian worldview is compelling, much less rational or reasonable. This task is an important one, for one's questions may keep them from fully embracing faith if those questions are ignored or minimized or answered in inadequate and unconvincing ways. Not for a moment do I want to suggest that *intuitional apologetics* can somehow replace this kind of intellectual engagement. But I do propose that we consider expanding our understanding of apologetics to go beyond the realm of argumentation—and into the realm of reflection on transcendent experiences.

No one needs to be told that the apologetic task has become more urgent, yet much more difficult. It seems harder to convince the intelligent nonbeliever than it was in times past. Our arguments struggle to find footing on the rocky terrain of their unbelief. And the number of people who self-identify as atheists and agnostics seems to be on the rise. Is this because their arguments have become stronger and more difficult to refute? Hardly. The arguments are mostly variations on those that have been made since the Enlightenment. If anything, perhaps their success is due to the fact that they have found better ways to market their unbelief, and they are helped in their crusade by those Christians who embrace a simultaneously belligerent and anti-intellectual stance.

Most apologists would likely agree that the reason it is so difficult to communicate Christian truths these days is that the cultural assumptions about the nature of God, humanity, and truth have undergone great changes. The vast majority of people have not carefully considered the arguments on both sides and made an informed decision about their worldview and perspectives on life. Instead, they have responded in the same way they might catch a cold—they breathe in the germs of prevailing assumptions from the cultural air around them, and this determines their belief system.

With this being the case, the difficulty we face is that conscious thinking isn't necessarily the primary problem. It isn't so much that people are unconvinced because the arguments for faith don't make sense to them, but rather that a religious perspective of any kind is not so much seen as irrational as it is seen as inconceivable. For many people it is almost impossible to even entertain the *possibility* of faith.

Sociologist Peter Berger has argued that the underlying problem in communicating about faith in our postmodern world is that our story doesn't seem *plausible* to our friends and neighbors. If this is indeed the case, then it is easy to understand why our task feels so daunting. It may do little good to build careful rational arguments when the whole Christian worldview seems implausible.

There is an important rational component to overturning such a prejudice against belief. But I'd like to suggest another approach that might—for some individuals—be an effective preamble to any sort of direct intellectual engagement. Perhaps there is a need for encouraging a sort of pre-rational apologetics that focuses not so much on changing the way someone thinks about a particular question, but rather the way they perceive of the universe, themselves, and the spiritual realm. The job of this kind of apologetics is to open people's hearts and minds to the possibility that existence may be different from what they have perceived. It works toward a new way of seeing: that *the materialistic assumptions they cling to might not be an adequate explanation for the world as they actually experience it.* It recognizes that sometimes the biggest hurdle is getting nonbelievers to seriously entertain the possibility that the gospel *might* be true. By reflecting more deeply on certain kinds of transcendent experiences that seem to point beyond this world, we might help people begin to doubt their doubting and wedge open the door for serious consideration of spiritual truths. This task is what I am calling *intuitional apologetics.*

Intuition, Revelation, and Transcendence

Intuition is variously defined as a "natural ability or power that makes it possible to know something without any proof or evidence; a feeling that guides a person to act a certain way without fully understanding why" (*Merriam-Webster*) or "the ability to acquire knowledge without inference or the use of reason" (*Wikipedia*). The implication is that there are truths we "know" at a deeper level than the level of cognition...or that we might be able to at least entertain as possible truths. They are the things we know "in our bones" or "in our blood." With intuitional apologetics, we help people to realize that there are deeper truths residing beneath the surface of our consciousness that might be teased out by reflecting on some of these transcendent human experiences.

The work of intuitional apologetics is predicated on the theological notion of general revelation, which suggests that we can discover something true about God by exploring the world he created—both the world outside us and the world inside us. Alongside God's revelation in history and Scripture is a secondary and less specific revelation about him. That is why Thomas Aquinas referred to nature and the Bible as "God's Two Books." This understanding of general revelation reminds us that there are traces of God all around us if we will only pay attention to them. God's fingerprints are all over his created world, and the psalmist suggests that they speak of his glory with revelational knowledge (Psalm 19:1-4). In Romans 1:20 Paul writes that God might be "perceived" in "the things that have been made."

Therefore, the task of intuitional apologetics is akin to the job of the midwife. We help bring to full fruition the deeper meanings of people's transcendent experiences. We assist them in awakening to the reality of a bigger world—one filled with more meaning, purpose, love, and grace than they might ever have imagined. We provide clues or point to the clues that already exist. We help them imagine a world richer than their own experience, a world suffused with a deeper spiritual reality. In our day, we may need to awaken people to the spiritual before we can direct them to the redemptive.

The life of every human being is filled with what the songwriter Bruce Cockburn has called "rumors of glory." These are hints and guesses and pointers toward mystery, not-quite-focused intuitions and inklings that something bigger than material reality stands beside and behind our everyday existence. They tug at us, gently demanding attention like a beloved pet that always seems to be underfoot. We cannot entirely elude them, as they often rise unbidden. They nag at the human heart and mind, provoking the question of whether there might be something more to life than meets the eye.

The strategy of intuitional apologetics is twofold. *First*, to help people awaken these intuitions by introducing them to moments of transcendent experience, either through the use of the arts or the beauties of nature, or through asking questions that evoke contemplation on the great mysteries of our human experience.

Second, we exegete the deeper meanings of these experiences, unpacking them in search of their deeper meanings—not merely as a philosophical exercise, but in a manner that draws together the heart and the mind. We demonstrate how their transcendent experiences fit both within their own personal story and in the bigger story of redemption. We help them see that transcendent moments can be sacred moments, pointers toward a connection with God.

These transcendent moments are as individual as the person experiencing them, but also universal in that such experiences are common to every human being. The question becomes what to make of them, and this is where intuitional apologetics finds its place in the apologetics task.

Rumors of Glory

So, what kinds of experiences am I talking about here? The following list merely suggests some possibilities, many of them overlapping in various ways, but all fruitful for helping prepare people to see that the materialist explanation of life is woefully inadequate in the face of these mysterious moments.

1. Contemplation of the beauty of the natural world. The Psalms remind us that God can be glimpsed in his creation, so the created world points beyond itself. The best scientific explanations do not suffice to grasp the glories of God's world. If we stop with the wonder of nature, we end in pantheism. But nature can be revelatory about the power, majesty, and beauty of the One who made it.

2. Contemplation of human creativity. Not only is it astonishing and inexplicable that a human being would be capable of some of the magnificent works of art, literature, music, or film to which we might introduce someone (William F. Buckley once said that the music of Bach might be the single greatest evidence of God's existence), but the best art evokes reflections and questions upon some of life's most urgent issues. Great art helps us see through the eyes and experiences of another, and the most skilled Christian artists can help overcome prejudices against faith by helping their audience to see in a new way. Their goal is not necessarily to have all the answers in place (which is the artistic weakness of many of today's mediocre religious films and novels) as to provoke questions and call upon their audience to wrestle with the big questions for themselves. And the wise Christian artist is not content with religious subject matter, but through their art they bring all of life and experience under the umbrella of faith. Their imagination is freed to soar, challenging, inspiring, discomforting, and provoking their readers, listeners, and viewers. In our times, artists and apologists can work together to evoke questions and propose possible answers.

3. Contemplation on the mystery of love. No human experience so transcends the mind and depends upon the heart as the experience of deep love for another person. What is it about love that takes us outside ourselves and allows us to be more giving and less self-absorbed? Does anyone really believe that falling in love is only a matter of chemicals surging through the bloodstream, or is it a clue to something more and a preview of an even deeper divine love?

4. Contemplation on the experience of awe and wonder. Rudolf Otto, in his classic book *The Idea of the Holy,* suggested that the root of a lot of religious belief was in the experience of the mixture of awe and fear we feel in the face of the overwhelmingly Other. He used the term *numinous* to describe this sensation. When we feel awe we realize how small, contingent, needy, and unworthy we are in the face of something grand and wondrous. One thinks of how well C.S. Lewis evoked such a feeling in his depiction of the great lion, Aslan, in the Chronicles of Narnia. As is the case in his books, so it is in life. When we have such an experience, our natural response is something akin to worship and adoration of something greater than ourselves.

5. *Contemplation on the sense of the sacred.* Sometimes we have experiences that need a different category to describe them than anything in our world. A place can sometimes seem invested with a sense of the sacred, as though it stands apart from anything we know, and it feels as though it is a point of intersection between this world and the spiritual world. Sometimes a work of art seems too lovely and glorious to account for in common human terms. Other times a moment seems invested with a significance beyond description. Such intimations of the sacred are another pointer, another intuition of something more.

6. *Contemplation on the experience of birth or death.* Just last year I stood beside my father as he struggled with his final breaths. A long battle with Parkinson's disease had laid waste to his body and adversely affected his mind. When he drew his last shuddering breath and died, it was a transcendent moment for the loved ones who had gathered around him. One moment he was there, and the next moment—mysteriously—he was gone. Something important had happened that even led one of my agnostic relatives to remark that it felt like he had gone to "another place." If you have ever been present at a birth or a death, you will likely remember them as moments when you sense your own mortality and, however dimly, grasp something of the mysterious wonder of living.

These are just a few of the clues we might follow that have the capacity to lead the heart and mind toward God and his redemptive love. When we pursue intuitional apologetics we can help people come awake to the reality of these experiences and gently guide them toward the deeper meanings within the experience so that it is not somehow explained away. The intuitional apologist can help make explicit what was once only inherent.

Intuitional Apologetics and Traditional Apologetics

Intuitional apologetics can work hand in hand with traditional apologetics in that it is essentially preparatory to the task of exploring the reasonableness of the big theological truths. It takes into consideration what a nonbeliever accepts and experiences and uses that to coax him toward what he does not yet accept. It may have to be content with wedging the door ajar, preparing a heart and mind for a more fully realized explanation that can only become convincing when it is first seen as plausible. We must be patient in allowing the transcendent the time to do its work.

Ultimately, intuitional apologetics offers the promise of using a means of knowledge other than the purely rational or historical or evidential. It uses, like the parables of Jesus, a more indirect means of communication. And it is a different method of communication. Traditionally doctrines are transformed into ideologies, truth statements that can be debated and fought about. At its best, intuitional apologetics relies more on imagination, finding ways to evoke important questions that ultimately will be up to the hearer to grapple with. It recognizes the mystery and complexity of life and knows that one must often pass through such complexity to reach a position of faith. But it can, in the end, be a very effective way of moving the conversation toward the place where more traditional apologetics might be deployed.

In the world of apologetics, the gates of rational knowledge beckon us with great promise. They are thrown wide open, though perhaps not as many enter as we might wish. Nearby are many rarely opened doors, covered with the dust of neglect. These partially obscured, ivy-covered entryways remain largely unguarded, suffering from disregard and lack of use, but if we turn the key in their lock, they fall open to unimaginable vistas. These doors bear such names as "beauty," "wonder," "art," "imagination," and "awe." Our culture tends to treat such things as diversions, distractions, or ephemeral experiences. But we know better. We can show the spiritual seeker that they are so much more—pointers toward deeper truths and "rumors of glory."

TERRY GLASPEY is a writer and researcher who specializes in issues related to the intersection of art, theology, spirituality, and creativity. He is the author of several books, including *75 Masterpieces Every Christian Should Know: The Fascinating Stories Behind Great Works of Art, Literature, Music, and Film; Not a Tame Lion: The Spiritual Legacy of C.S. Lewis;* and *The Prayers of Jane Austen.* You can learn more at terry glaspey.com.

Interview with Gavin MacFarland
SEAN MCDOWELL

What role did apologetics play in your conversion to Christianity?

There was a time a few years ago when I told my wife that I didn't think the God of the Bible existed. In fact, I was 99.9 percent sure that I could not be convinced otherwise. I spent a lot of time reading books, discussing theology with friends, and even allowing a group of high-school students to ask me questions about my beliefs. I was confident that I had been intellectually honest with my dismissal of Christianity.

Looking back, I think that I always knew, deep down, that my belief system stood on shaky ground. I had attended a debate between Christopher Hitchens and William Lane Craig, and came away certain that Craig had the stronger arguments. Yet I was still unwilling to fully accept the implications of what he had said.

I started to revisit old debates with some longtime friends, and their arguments took on a new sense of clarity. However, it was not until my personal life hit rock bottom that I fully opened my heart to God and the Bible. Last year I did a Bible study through our church, and I opened up about being a new believer. I told them my story of packing up my family and moving to Bend, Oregon, with no job and no real plan. My son's teacher attends our church and our next-door neighbors do as well. Perhaps it was a divine plan?

What I learned as I reflect on the past two years is that the intellectual arguments for God needed to come at a time when I was spiritually ready for them. If my life had not taken the negative turn that it did, I do not know if I would be here today as a believer. I reread C.S. Lewis's *Mere Christianity*, and the arguments made so much sense that I could not understand how I had dismissed them before.

What arguments have you found persuasive on your way to becoming a believer?

Currently, I am most convinced by the Kalam Cosmological Argument as well as the idea of objective moral truth. My Christian friends have debated with me for twenty years about these ideas, and even though there have been some contentious interactions, I have always known that there was never malice behind any of their words.

Not long ago, I was reading an old email exchange between you and my dad where you had been discussing some theology and philosophy. In one of my dad's posts, he mentions the idea of trusting his intuition. It sounds reasonable. However, when I think about this more critically, I have to ask if it is, in fact, reasonable to trust our intuitions. I am skeptical that an evolutionary model of thinking can lead us to the conclusion that our intuitions are true. I do not believe naturalism can make any legitimate claims to truth.

What are some helpful things, and unhelpful things, Christians did during your journey?

Pastor Eugene Cho talks about the need for Christians to focus on building relationships first and foremost before moving too quickly to evangelism. Too often, I believe, in the excitement and challenge of discussing our faith with nonbelievers, this step is overlooked.

The tricky thing about relationships is that they don't always look or feel the same to the participants. I often felt that many of my Christian friends were more motivated to convert me than they were to get to know me. I don't know if that is accurate, but that's how it felt at the time.

Similarly, I don't know that Christians are always aware of how they are perceived by their non-Christian friends (not that this is unique to Christians). One example of this that I often see today is a comment that goes something like this: "Wow, you should feel really good about XYZ school because a lot of strong Christians work there." The not-so-subtle message is that students are safer and teachers are better than if the teachers were not Christians.

So, in sum, my suggestion is for apologists to build genuine relationships with people and to care for them as human beings, whether or not they ever convert to Christianity. If you truly love people for who they are, have an open mind to learn from nonbelievers, look for natural opportunities to talk about spiritual things, and have a long-term view, you might be amazed at how God can use you to be a part of someone's life transformation. I am living proof of this.

GAVIN MACFARLAND, a former skeptic, is a National Certified Counselor. He lives with his wife and three kids in Bend, Oregon.

— 14 —

Why We Should Love Questions More than Answers

MATTHEW ANDERSON

Everybody's looking for answers." So says Ulysses Everett McGill, a cynical "Dapper Dan man" who has escaped prison and is making his way home in the Coen brothers' film *O Brother, Where Art Thou?* A modified retelling of Homer's *The Odyssey, O Brother* humorously depicts the irrepressible searching that is at the center of the human experience. Like Ulysses, we are all looking for an intellectual home, for answers deep enough that we can happily live within them.

But questions are the means by which we travel.

When the rich young ruler comes to Jesus in Mark 10, he asks a question that his entire world hangs on: "Good Teacher," he says, "what must I do to inherit eternal life?" Such a question begins a path: it provides a direction and a focus to Jesus's thoughts. The terms of the question frame the conversation, and while Jesus accepts the invitation to talk, he deftly challenges the conversation's basis: "Why do you call me good?" he responds. Still, the young man is what we might call "a seeker." He wants something, even if he is not quite sure what it is.

For people burdened to say and defend the goodness and truthfulness of

Christianity, it is tempting to hurriedly skip past the questions in our rush to demonstrate our answers. Such an impulse makes sense. Christianity, after all, has the most profound answers to offer the world's most difficult questions. But if the work of apologetics involves more than building up the faithful, its primary orientation should be toward helping those who are already traveling to arrive. It is *persuasion* that apologetics hopes for, not only defenses or justifications of the Christian position as true or reasonable. We should point the way home rather than shout from the balcony of our bedrooms about how good looking it is.

We have to care about the means of travel, not just the intellectual destination. We have to attend to the questions if we are going to help people find answers.

Listening to Questions

In the exchange in Mark 10, Jesus clearly demonstrates that he listens closely to people's questions. He could pass over what the rich young ruler called him, and treat it instead as irrelevant to the conversation. But instead he sees the question as an opportunity to pose one of his own. His careful listening allows him to hear the presuppositions the rich young ruler has adopted, and to draw attention to them. The rich young ruler's question reveals what he thinks more than he realizes when he asks it. He believes that "eternal life" is worth pursuing and thinks there is something he can do in order to attain it. Those presuppositions may be true or false, but they are at least worth talking about.

A question reveals more than what a person thinks, though; it also exposes the person's attitude. The question of whether we think all the evil in the world is compatible with believing in God may indicate a cheeky dismissiveness of the Christian faith, a lofty superiority, or an earnest and heartfelt confusion over how Christians could affirm such a thing. Questions, like all forms of speech, give us a tiny glimpse into the character of the person we are talking with.

But perhaps most importantly, questions are windows into what people *want,* at least when they are earnestly posed. The question is an expression of desire. It shows us where a person would go if they only knew how to get there.

"Is it permissible for humans to seek immortality through technology?"

By posing such a question, the questioner indicates *what kind* of answer would satisfy them. To respond that the resurrection was a historical event would be to leave them still hungry and wanting more (not to mention annoyed by our obtuseness). It may be the case that they are asking a question that does not have an answer, or that they are pursuing a question that would need to be reformed in order to make progress. But the questioner shows their hand, so to speak, about what they want within the conversation.

The Importance of Having Good Questions

Like many Christians, apologetics was the soil in which my intellectual engagement with the faith first took root. The lack of confidence that I felt when people questioned me moved me to find answers: I hated feeling as though I didn't have anything to say and did everything in my power to fix it. And like many Christians, I fell prey to the great spiritual danger of that pursuit. By framing my intellectual life in opposition to those who disagreed with me, I succumbed to a hard-nosed pride that refused to acknowledge the gravity of the challenges others made against the faith.

If we want to be sympathetic with those who are searching, it is important to search ourselves. We must be Christians first and apologists second, which means our intellectual lives must be primarily shaped by seeking to understand the faith we live within rather than debating, disputing, or *even* persuading those who do not believe it.

But seeking understanding ourselves is not something different from the work of apologetics; it is, instead, its life-giving spring. The adage that *what we win people with is what we will win them to* has bearing here. If our Christian lives are more characterized by the giving of answers than by seeking for understanding, then the faith we pass on will be similarly stunted. And as we feel the force of questions ourselves and search out answers to them, we will be able to invite others in to journey alongside us.

Persuading others is best done when it is organically and immediately connected to our own development in the faith itself. If persuasion is tied to discipleship, then it demands displaying a life of faith so that others can discern its intrinsic power and attractiveness. Somewhat paradoxically, the method of answering the objections and questions from skeptics actually risks undermining their discipleship if they *become* Christians, as it can convey that having a satisfactory resolution to every question is a necessary criterion to believe. But who among apologists has achieved such a blessed state? The whole joy of Christianity is that it provides answers that keep the questions alive, deepening them and renewing them so that its adherents can go on seeking deeper understandings of the world forever.

There are other apologetic benefits to having our own questions. For one, Christians who unrelentingly pursue their own questions make it clear that Christianity is an intellectually fruitful religion. Christianity demands faithful obedience, yes, but such obedience introduces new questions that could never be asked before. And those questions allow us to reconsider not just Christianity itself, but the whole world anew in their light.

Consider the doctrine of the Incarnation, which is one of those great paradoxes that Christianity rests upon. The claim that God and man are together in the person of Jesus Christ is an infinitely renewable intellectual resource. It is possible to dismiss the doctrine as incoherent, but doing so means we lose out, if nothing else, on a good deal of intellectual fun. Doctrines are more than theological Sudoku; they are something more than rationalistic puzzles for cloistered academics to pass the time with. But the world is an infinitely complex and interesting place to live, and Christianity has a dogmatic order that fits it.

The Importance of Asking Good Questions

"What if it were discovered that fetal tissue is a delicacy," Stanley Hauerwas is purported to have once asked. "Could you eat it?" Though Hauerwas is hardly known as an apologist for the Christian faith, his question is as effective a bit of rhetoric as any I know. He has a point: the possibility that fetal tissue might be a delicacy strikes at fundamental intuitions about the nature of the human person, intuitions that we may not even realize we have until after we have heard the question. Hauerwas could have made that point as an assertion, as a *reductio,* and quitted the field as an intellectual victor. But the question grips us in a way that a reductio does not. By taking up lodging, a question demands that *we* supply the answer. If a statement attempts to declare the truth to us, a question leads us to it and invites us to see for ourselves.

Apologists should be more familiar with questions than any other tool in their rhetorical toolbox. They should have the well-worn familiarity of a favorite hammer. While it's true that to someone with a hammer, everything is a nail, if the aim of apologetics is persuasion, then we need our interlocutors to *speak.* And questions are invitations to conversations. An apologist who only has answers is playing chess without a queen.

The criterion for asking a good question depends in large part upon the aims of the speaker. If the point is to persuade, a good question might introduce tension, as Hauerwas's question does. If the goal is to understand or to help someone else understand, then the question might be more straightforward. ("What do you mean by that?") If the purpose is to highlight the speaker's presuppositions, a question might turn itself back on the speaker. ("Why do you call me good?")

But whatever the purpose, a question that is genuinely asked is necessarily an invitation to a conversation. If the aim of the apologist is *persuasion,* rather than simply trading arguments like baseball cards, then he has to know how his interlocutor thinks. A question places the burden on the other person to speak, and in speaking, to reveal themselves to us. An apologetic approach that deploys questions freely is more akin to discipleship than traditional conceptions of the task. By drawing others deeper into conversations, we learn how they see the world and the roadblocks between them and the Christian faith.

Asking questions does not need to entail a conversational free-for-all, though. Questions are signposts that tacitly direct the conversational path. Asking "Why do you call me good?" directs the young man's attention to a previously unnoticed feature of his own thought. It shows the young man where to look, but it does not necessarily dictate what he shall see. By drawing people's attention toward certain features of the world, we enable them to draw their own conclusions (which we might hope are the same as our conclusions) without telling them what to think. Giving them an answer might be faster and easier, but questioning respects their freedom while still giving us an active role in the conversation.

Asking good questions is harder than it might seem. It is easy for questions to become interrogations or inquisitions rather than invitations to a dialogue. The point of using questions is not to put people or their opinions on the stand and to play judge and jury. That mentality introduces an inequality to the conversation, establishing one person as superior to the other. Instead, the point of questions is to understand what the other person is saying and to help the other person understand what they are saying. If Christianity is true, then it is the only religion that will finally and completely make sense. Using questions effectively opens up that possibility without introducing a rhetorical climate of opposition or disagreement.

A Closing Word

How can apologetics become a life-giving practice, a renewable source of joy and renewal and hope for churches? Unless we learn to love the life of questioning as much as we love the answers, apologetics will grow moribund. Though questioning well can be learned, it is not a technique; there is no checklist that can be followed on the path to using or listening to questions well. Like all the practices of the Christian life, questioning can be properly gained only through imitation and repetition, by cultivating an attentiveness to its inner dynamics and adopting it as a mode of life. Listening to questions, having questions, and asking questions—unless these are genuine overflows of our interest in and love for one another, they are little more than manipulative rhetorical tactics that dehumanize those we are talking with.

Turning questioning into a central practice of apologetics may also deprofessionalize the field and invite many new Christians into it who otherwise might be daunted by its difficulty. Learning to master arguments is hard, but questions are among our most widely used forms of speech. Apologetics is not a special vocation to which God uniquely calls some; it is the life of the Christian in its outward mode. And that mode means listening, questioning, and learning alongside those who are—with Ulysses—looking for answers.

MATTHEW LEE ANDERSON is pursuing a DPhil in Christian ethics at Oxford University. He is the lead writer at Mere Orthodoxy and the author of *The End of Our Exploring: A Book about Questioning and the Confidence of Faith*.

— 15 —

Why More Women Should Study Apologetics

MARY JO SHARP

I had just finished a talk on conversational apologetics when I noticed four women off to the side of the platform, apparently wanting to discuss the topic further. As soon as I gave them the word, the anxious questioning unfolded.

"What do I say to my son?" one woman began. "He was an active church member in junior high and high school. After a year in college, he's now proclaiming himself an atheist."

"My spouse is doubting that God exists," the second woman said. "He thinks the church may be a cult. How should I respond?"

"Well, my teenager won't even pull her earphones out to listen to me, let alone have any kind of reasonable conversation," the third said. "What do I do? I'm worried about the influence of culture on her mind."

The fourth spoke mournfully. "My son died of leukemia at three years old. How can I still believe there is a God?"

While these questions, on their own, present a considerable challenge, the questions are never presented within a cultural vacuum. The current culture creates more confusion in our questions, not to mention answers, because of society's predominantly negative and pervasive caricature of Christianity. Current sound bites we grapple with include:

- Christianity is harmful to people.
- Christians are ignorant and intolerant, or at least on the fringe of society.
- God is dead, an outdated ideology of superstitious cultures.
- Science is the torchbearer of truth.

On top of all these obfuscations, a woman must also grapple with conflicting messages about her identity: an object reducible to sexual pleasure, a homemaker, a nurturer, a breadwinner, an intellectual, a nonintellectual, a person of power, a person who is weak, a person whose worth is found in the beauty of her youth, a person of intrinsic worth, someone to target with the fashion market, and so on. It is a difficult task, at best, to pull away from all this confusion to focus on basic things like the foundations of Christian belief.

I find that the women I speak with are excited about answering difficult questions, but they are intellectually bogged down by the confusion of our society. The digital age inundates us with so much information that it can stifle our motivation to even try to sift the wheat from the chaff. To encourage more women to get involved in apologetics study, we should first establish that there is a need to answer these hard questions. As a lighthouse warns incoming ships of dangerous obstacles, those of us who are equipped can shine through a foggy existence. Women will either begin to follow a path toward answers or risk a bitter shipwreck against the culture's untruths.

Answer Doubt

A friend once caught me off guard by asking, "Why would a woman want to attend a session on apologetics?" Actually, it had never occurred to me that my gender would be a factor in whether or not I should seek and discover answers to foundational questions about belief in God. Why wouldn't a woman who had been given a rational mind, as made in the image of God, want to know what she believes and why she believes it? After all, I had come into the field of apologetics through my own doubt about God's existence. And yet, the question was laid out before me.

I began to understand that apologetics was a relatively new[1] area of the Christian faith. Women's ministries generally did not have materials for this kind of study. So I had to think of what would communicate the purpose of this mostly unknown field to the souls in those ministries. I found my answer through my own story, beginning with answering doubt.

Doubt is common to the human experience. We do not have all the answers, no matter what the field of inquiry. This is certainly true in the Christian faith as well. Dr. Gary Habermas states, "Doubt, manifested in many forms from the assurance of one's salvation to factual questioning, is certainly one of the most frequent and painful problems which plague Christians."[2]

Further, doubts can arise for many reasons other than not just having knowledge. First, when our life experience does not match up to what we perceive our life should be, we can view this as a failure by God to live up to those expectations. Our reaction may be to distrust God or to question his very existence.

Second, we may have a brush with great evil or may be concerned about evil in general when we see so much of it daily. One of my friends began questioning God's existence after his wife suddenly died, leaving him to raise four beautiful girls by himself. An audience member, mentioned previously, asked me how she could continue to believe in God when her three-year-old son died of leukemia.

Third, we are exposed to so many bad arguments due to the age of the Internet. Just as we can access more knowledge more quickly than ever before, we are also exposed to more bad philosophy and illogical statements than ever before. As C.S. Lewis stated in *The Weight of Glory*, "Good philosophy must exist, if for no other reason, because bad philosophy needs to be answered."[3] It's not so much that we get argued out of faith or have doubts based in well-reasoned arguments; we just sort of fall away due to the unanswered influence of bad philosophy.

Fourth, a lack of intentional living in the presence of God due, in part, to a profound split in our minds and lives between the sacred and secular has caused us to live as secular people while trying to maintain that we believe in the sacredness of all life. We cannot merely *affirm* belief in God as a rational proposition; we must also *practice* belief in God in our everyday lives in the big as well as small things. Otherwise, we effectively live as atheists, as if there is no God.

So if we step away from belief in God, we might say that life with or without God isn't much different, and that belief can fuel doubt into a raging fire. If we never intentionally put forth any effort to know the reality of God in our lives, it is no wonder that our lack of experiencing God would lead to doubts about his existence.

These reasons for doubts, along with many more, have been gleaned over years of conversations with women. While there are many reasons why someone may experience doubt, a crucial element of having doubt is how one handles it. This is the difficulty I see for women. We have so many confusing messages in our society about what a woman is supposed to be and what she is supposed to focus on that she can forget her most important role is as a disciple of the Lord Jesus Christ. All other relationships and roles should be secondary to her primary role as a child of God. When her relationship with God is no longer the priority, she can begin to fall away through the busyness of distractions. As C.S. Lewis stated,

> [M]ake sure that, if you have once accepted Christianity, then some of its main doctrines shall be deliberately held before your mind for some time every day. That is why daily prayers and religious reading and church-going are necessary parts of the Christian life. We have to be continually reminded of what we believe. Neither this belief nor any other will automatically remain alive in the mind. It must be fed.[4]

Yet, in order for women to bring their doubts to the table, they must have a safe environment—free from ridicule, suspicion, or rejection—in which to do so. They must have a loving, encouraging Christian community that focuses on identifying as a disciple of Jesus. While many Christian communities and churches encourage women to focus on many good things, such as being a wife, mother, leader, friend, church-goer, or career woman, some have forgotten that truly only "one thing is necessary."[5] A woman's identity should be grounded in her relationship to God. Her faith can be damaged when her identity is reduced to the roles placed upon her. When that happens, she has no time to sit at the feet of the wisest and best Teacher, to grow in knowledge and faith, and to be empowered to boldly proclaim the truth.

When we focus on building safe communities within our churches for answering doubts and encourage women to bring their questions about God to our churches, we will begin to build up their confidence in what they believe.

Build Confidence

While we looked previously at what causes doubts, it is worth mentioning a few more influences that tear down confidence in God. Women are constantly barraged with imagery and sound bites from our culture that attack the Christian worldview. Some of the most infective sound bites emanate from the new atheist movement.

- "Faith is believing what you know ain't so."[6]
- "Faith is a lack of critical thinking."[7]
- "Religion is about turning untested belief into unshakeable truth through the power of institutions and the passage of time."[8]
- "Surely there must come a time when we will acknowledge the obvious: theology is now little more than a branch of human ignorance. Indeed, it is ignorance with wings."[9]

In addition to these, some of our beloved television shows and movies portray Christianity as intellectually bankrupt and Christians as ignorant, racist, or bigoted. *Doctor Who* from the British Broadcasting Corporation (BBC) in the United Kingdom and *The Big Bang Theory* from the CBS Corporation in the US disparage the Christian faith in multiple episodes as anti-intellectual. Christian philosopher J.P. Moreland, in arguing why we needed to teach a defense of the faith, noted, "television, movies, and the media present a secularized version of society," including a view that the cultural and educational elite are largely secular and the uneducated are largely evangelical.[10] Our media reflects cultural idioms of our day, such as statements inferring that smart people are skeptical or that science is the only way to know truth.

Further, we have the problem of Christians who do not take personal responsibility to grow in the knowledge of God, especially with regard to answering the cultural attacks of our day. Whether knowingly or not, Christians can hurt others through their lack of discernment and lack of thoughtfulness. More specifically, I've experienced a tendency within evangelical Christianity to be reactive to culture rather than proactive through the intentional cultivation of spiritual growth in God. So Christian women are left to react to an antagonistic culture rather than being taught how to be godly leaders, empowered by the Spirit, to change culture. Because of exposure to cultural influences, women can slip into thinking that their beliefs are unfounded or irrational. It is especially so if the church is not providing any thoughtful means by which to combat ideas contrary to belief in God or if we are not purposefully analyzing what we see and hear.

Christian women can lose confidence in their belief in God not because of good arguments but because of a lack of attention to the life of the mind. As J. Gresham Machen stated, "One cannot reasonably trust a God whom one holds with the mind to be either non-existent or untrustworthy."[11] However, apologetics can serve as a confidence-builder for belief in God through focus on developing a rigorous Christian thought life. As Christian women begin to see a positive case for belief in God, as well as begin to answer the cultural idioms and objections against belief in God, they can see Christianity as an intellectually defensible worldview. We must remember, "It is very difficult to believe something one takes to be absurd or with no intellectual support whatever."[12]

As women grow confident in their belief in God, they will also trust and rely on God more. As they put more trust in God, that's when we begin to see changed lives.

Change Lives

Over the years, when I've discussed apologetics with other women, they tend to put apologetics into a category of strictly intellectual inquiry. I'm asked, "How could arguments possibly relate to my spiritual life?" However, the study of apologetics is not strictly an intellectual endeavor; it's also a part of being transformed into Christlikeness. For a woman to know what she believes and why she believes it can have a tremendous impact on her life. How so? The truth we are investigating is the truth about a person we are in relationship with, the person of Jesus Christ. Our engagement in apologetics always goes back to relationship with Christ. As I grow in my relationship with Christ, I am growing in my spiritual life.

Further, according to *The Dragonfly Effect,* a book on social movements, there are three basic human needs for establishing self-worth: competence, autonomy, and relatedness.[13] Apologetics serves all three needs by providing women with competency in handling the doctrines and arguments of their faith, giving women autonomy to discuss these beliefs in any situation, and providing a means of communicating with the community in the search for truth. All three of these effects of apologetics have the potential to change people's lives. As women become more confident in handling their faith, they will become emboldened in sharing their faith. In my experience, people generally do not discuss topics in which they do not perceive they are competent. Yet discussions on belief in God with people in my community have been some of the most fruitful means of growing in my faith.

In conclusion, let's return to the questions those women asked me at the end of my session on apologetics. Though the scenario I described is a combination of questions from multiple conferences, it accurately represents real questions I receive at any women's ministry event. The reason more women should study apologetics is to answer the difficult questions they are holding on to right now. Doubts and difficulties about faith in God will not resolve on their own, they must be thoughtfully discussed. Left unattended, these doubts and difficulties can keep women from trusting God with all their heart, soul, and mind.

I have further found that though Christian women are already engaged in the cultural battle for truth, as evidenced by their questions, some don't seem to recognize it. So we, as the church, have the responsibility to help Christian women recognize that apologetics serves as a great help for women in such a confusing culture by answering doubt, building confidence, and changing lives.

MARY JO SHARP is an assistant professor of apologetics at Houston Baptist University. She is the author of LifeWay Christian Resources apologetics-based Bible studies, *Why Do You Believe That? A Faith Conversation* and *Living in Truth: Confident Conversation in a Conflicted Culture.* Mary Jo is the founder and director of Confident Christianity apologetics ministry (www.confidentchristianity.com).

PART 3

New Issues in Apologetics

SEAN MCDOWELL

Young people have a lot of questions today. If you spend time with students, and if they sense you are a thoughtful person who cares, you will discover they have some of the same questions people have always asked: *Why is there evil? Does God exist? Where do I go when I die?*

And yet in each generation there are unique questions brought on by the circumstances of the day. This is true today. There are a few issues that continue to persist, and we need to address them in a fresh manner. And there are also questions arising today for the first time.

For instance, how do we address other religions? Christianity arose in a pluralistic culture, and yet with travel, global communications, and changing demographics, we find ourselves asking this question differently than before. And specifically, how are Christians to reach out to Muslims? Islam is the fastest growing religion in the world, and much of this growth is in Western societies. We need to be prepared to lovingly reach out to our Muslim neighbors.

Questions related to the Bible and the historical Jesus have been around since the inception of the church, and yet today there are new challenges and issues that cannot be ignored. The skepticism, confusion, and doubt of our broader culture have seeped their way into the church. In their respective chapters, Jonathan Morrow and Michael Licona tackle two of the most pressing questions against the Bible and provide a road map for how to best present the case for Jesus today.

There are also some fresh questions today that we need to have the courage to tackle head-on. For instance, the sexual revolution has raised new issues related to gender and sexuality. How can we best speak the truth about sex in our increasingly broken culture? It would be easy to ignore some of these issues, and yet as Martin Luther observed, "If you preach the gospel with the exception of the issues that deal with your time, you aren't preaching the gospel."

In this section, you will find some ideas about how to speak apologetically into some of the pressing issues of our day, such as economics, race, politics, transgenderism, religious liberty, and more. Many apologists have ignored these issues, and so you will find some fresh material to help you address them.

My prayer is that this section will give you the confidence and training to become a new kind of apologist. The world needs Jesus more than ever before. And we must have the courage to speak truth, and yet with compassion, understanding, and humility.

— 16 —

A Christian Political Apologetic: Why, What, and How

JENNIFER A. MARSHALL

In the spring of 2015 the state of Indiana adopted a religious freedom policy mirroring laws passed by Congress and nineteen other states over the course of the prior twenty years. But this time, a firestorm of protest upended two decades of support. Opponents succeeded in mischaracterizing the religious liberty law as "antigay" and "a license to discriminate." They claimed it would lead to horrible things—like emergency responders refusing to help gays and lesbians.

Never mind that, in all its history, the law had never once been used in the shameful ways that opponents suggested. The facts were lost in the chaos: the policy—developed with broad support from liberals and conservatives alike—simply makes the government prove that it has a very serious reason for violating someone's religious liberty.

We live in the midst of an increasingly pluralistic culture, where competing worldviews on basic issues collide more and more frequently. These include clashes over issues on which, until recently, we took consensus for granted—like religious liberty and marriage. The dignity of human life made in the image of God, male and female, is no longer accepted but openly contested, for example.

Political debates increasingly touch the core of biblical teaching about human existence. Christians must be equipped to speak and to act consistent with biblical truth. As these issues are debated, it's not a matter of whether or not there will be a Christian public witness. The question is whether that testimony will be silence, snap reactions, or thoughtful responses based on serious biblical reflection. Christians need a sound political apologetic—a framework for why, what, and how to engage in politics for the glory of God and the good of our neighbors.

Why Engage

Maybe it's the complexity of issues, like what on earth to do about the national debt or North Korea. Or perhaps it's the petty bickering between parties, or doubts about whether the political process makes any difference anyway. Whatever the reason, many believers keep their distance from politics.

But disengaging isn't the answer. For the Christian, citizenship is about stewardship.

That's especially true in a country where our most important governing document begins with "We the People." That means *we* have a lot of responsibility. In a free society, citizenship requires us to think through many decisions deeply and personally. Outsourcing our opinions on issues isn't an option.

Good stewardship in this case requires at least a basic understanding of civics (think *Schoolhouse Rock*'s "I'm Just a Bill") and general issues of debate. But a Christian's reflection on politics ought to go beyond an eleventh-grade government curriculum. A biblical worldview should shape our diagnosis of the problems politics seeks to address and our vision of how to resolve them.

What we call politics is one part of a much larger human quest to order our lives together. That's a process that takes place from the family room to the boardroom to the congressional hearing room. Each of these forums—and many others—has its own authority structure, and each has a part to play as we figure out how to meet everyday needs and solve problems. As all of these players interact, politics is about harmonizing diverse interests and building consensus on what's worth pursuing as a society. Those who serve the Creator and Lord of the universe ought to approach all these arenas with a coherent biblical worldview.

What to Engage

A biblical worldview shapes how we size up and sort out the problems politics tries to solve. Government is always dealing with questions about the common good, justice, morality, and the nature and purpose of human beings. Where will it look for understanding of these profound concepts?

A Christian worldview has a wealth of resources to offer in response, if we make the effort to mine it. The Bible teaches that individuals are created in the image of God, male and female, made for each other, more than material beings. The Bible also gives insight into the nature of authority and the roles and responsibilities of various institutions—like family, church, and government. A biblical worldview has quite a bit to say about justice, and one way to summarize it is right relationships among institutions and individuals. Scripture also makes clear the existence of transcendent truth and morality. These ideas about individuals in community and the persistence of the moral order should make a difference in a Christian's convictions about the common good.

The Bible makes clear that human beings are made for relationships and that human flourishing has a lot to do with that. We can think of this relational capacity in four dimensions: a person's relationship with God, self, others, and the material world.[1] Brokenness in any of these areas hinders human flourishing and often leads to further relational breakdown.

Scripture is clear that each of us is responsible to strive for the flourishing, or *shalom*, of our neighbors in all these relational dimensions. As we pursue *shalom*, we should be thinking in these relational terms. The first cultural task God gave human beings was to care for creation and to order human community in a way that reflects his design for human flourishing. God has ordained the institutions of family, church, and government with distinct roles and responsibilities that serve the needs of individuals and communities.

Scripture presents the family centered on the marriage union of a man and a woman as the primary institution—the basic unit and first community—in human society. The family is responsible for the material, relational, emotional, and spiritual needs of each of its members. A day in the life of a parent might include playing the role of teacher, cook, driver, nurse, janitor, counselor, and law enforcement to children. Thinking about a parent wearing all those hats gives a good picture of how the family provides its members with accountability and comprehensive care through intimate, loving, permanent relationships.

The church is the earthly expression of Christ's spiritual kingdom. The church embodies and points toward that kingdom, which has begun but not yet reached its fullness. The church transcends this earthly existence, and at the same time, the church is an institution in public life. Picture an old New England town where the church—with its steeple pointing heavenward—is right on the main town square, present in that common space alongside the village hall, shops, and homes. That image serves as a reminder of God's transcendent authority over human beings and above the state, while interacting with them. A part of everyday life, the church speaks to and serves spiritual purposes that go beyond the material aspects of human existence. Because of that, the church is equipped to meet a broad range of needs for the individual, the family, and community.

As it testifies to God's moral law—especially about the dignity of human beings made in the image of God—the church is a powerful public witness. One of the greatest examples of a leader who understood this dimension of the church's role was German pastor Dietrich Bonhoeffer. He was executed seventy years ago in a Nazi concentration camp for his opposition to and his call for the church to resist Hitler's murderous regime, which represented an appalling abuse of the authority placed in the hands of human government.

God has ordained government as one way that he shows grace to all people. Government should recognize the God-given dignity of human beings and respect the roles and responsibilities of family and church. Government is to keep the peace through the rule of law and to use force to punish those who break it. The role of government is to maintain justice and peace in society so other institutions, especially the family and the church, can do what they are designed to do.

These basics about the role of family, the role of the church, and the nature of *shalom* are all part of a framework Christians need in order to be able to pursue their callings as citizens. Christians should seek public policy that respects these roles and that is structured with incentives that reflect the reality of human nature.

What would this look like? Take poverty as an example. Scripture is clear that we should care for our neighbors in need. Taking the time to learn about poverty in America will reveal that need frequently shows up where family isn't around as a first line of support. A child born outside of marriage is more than five times more likely to experience poverty than a child born and raised in a home with a married mother and father.

If relational breakdown is part of what leads to poverty, we should make every effort to prevent it. Churches have enormous potential to take on this challenge. The relational capital that rests in congregations can be harnessed to serve neighbors suffering from the collapse of this most intimate relationship—and to prevent the vicious cycle from repeating in the next generation. If Christians were to catch the Bible's extraordinary vision of marriage, we would have no shortage of creative ideas to help rebuild a culture that supports the permanent union of a man to his wife and any children they bring into the world.

But prevention is only part of the picture when fighting poverty. Intervention is sometimes required in the case of serious need. In these instances, it's important that public assistance work in harmony with the way people are made. The Bible emphasizes that work is an important part of what we are designed to do. When government provides aid that discourages work for those who are able, it ignores this reality of human nature and disserves the people it is intended to help. Instead, assistance should be designed to provide for basic needs while pointing a person on a path toward work.

Perhaps the most challenging Christian worldview elements to apply to politics today are its confessions about truth and morality. The Bible teaches that truth exists, and there is a created reality. That means, for example, that even if a legislature or court says otherwise, the created truth about marriage, the union of a man and a woman, will not change. Even if policy asserts that gender is a social construct rather than a biological reality, that does not change the truth of Genesis 1 and 2 that we are created male and female, and that male and female are created for one another. As Christians, we must speak and act in accord with these truths, regardless what the laws of the land may say.

The Bible also testifies to a transcendent moral order: right and wrong rest in the unchanging character of God. It is not a shifting standard, and majority opinion or congressional votes can't change it. By contrast, relativism tends to descend to an exploitive system of "might makes right."

Christian ethics shine a light that exposes error, injustice, and corruption in society. Every age has its ethical blind spots that need to be illuminated by the truth of God's Word. In generations past, these included the racism of slavery and shameful Jim Crow laws that did not do justice to human dignity. Today many disregard the dignity of unborn human life fearfully and wonderfully made by God. Witness to these biblical ethical principles is needed for the good of all our neighbors.

How to Engage

How we engage in politics is as important as the stands we take. Our words and actions related to public policy should reflect our goal: seeking the flourishing of all our neighbors and recognizing that we live in community with them. On the other hand, civility shouldn't be confused with timidity. We must be willing to name evil and raise objections to wrong ideas and actions—even if it comes with a potential cost to our reputation or job. Speaking the truth, in love, with discernment should be our goal.

But should Christians bring their faith into political debates? In recent years, many Christians seem to have accepted the secularist claim that to argue publicly from a point of view that can be traced back to the Bible is forcing one's religion on others.

Secularists say that they offer the only genuinely neutral perspective. But Christians should not accept this myth of neutrality. Everyone argues from fundamental beliefs, whether they acknowledge them or not. Secularists charge that taking a stand on issues like abortion or marriage is "imposing your morality" on others. If that's true, then they are guilty of their own charge. Every public policy makes moral judgments about what is good, from smoking bans to military spending decisions to the definition of marriage. Even voting is an exercise in expressing a worldview.

Christians should enter the public square with a biblically shaped perspective. To apply a Christian worldview to questions of public policy is not exercising self-interest. It is simply serving our neighbor by testifying to the way God has made the world.

After all, we serve the God who defines the common good. The first cultural task God gave human beings was to order society and care for creation in a way that reflects his design for human flourishing.

Applying that charge in our American public policy context today—where we have the freedom to shape our laws through debate and elections—means seeking consensus that reflects that design. We use reason to persuade, recognizing that competing worldviews sometimes may cloud the capacity to reason together. In spite of that, we can engage confidently on the basis of our beliefs with those who oppose us, appealing to their best interests and the longing we know that God has placed in the hearts of all human beings—a longing for the transcendent, for fulfillment, for wholeness (Ecclesiastes 3:11).

Sorting Out Our Lives Together

If Christian apologetics is about giving the reason for our hope, no sector or subject needs it more than politics. The sin of cynicism runs rampant in the practice of politics and discussions about it. For the Christian, stewardship—not cynicism—is our calling as citizens.

Politics brings together fallen human beings with transcendent longings to sort out our lives on earth together. Christians are called not just to engage in but to ennoble that endeavor. With a biblical understanding of the nature and purpose of human beings and the role of God-ordained institutions, Christians are equipped to pursue human flourishing in its fullest sense.

Sitting on the sidelines is not an option. Some are called to equip Christians for citizenship through preaching and teaching; others are called to work directly in the political process. All of us are called to basic stewardship of our roles as citizens. To inform that lifelong calling, we need a Christian political apologetic that provides a framework for why, what, and how to engage in public life for the glory of God and the good of our neighbors.

JENNIFER A. MARSHALL is vice president for the Institute for Family, Community, and Opportunity at The Heritage Foundation and a fellow at the Institute of Theology and Public of Reformed Theological Seminary in Washington, DC.

— 17 —

An Assessment of the Present State of Historical Jesus Studies

MICHAEL LICONA

A few years ago, I boarded a plane for a very long flight. I had a new book I had saved for the trip and was very much looking forward to reading it. Shortly after I took my seat, an elderly man, probably in his eighties, took his seat next to me. I smiled thinking, *He's going to fall asleep and I'm going to get in a lot of reading.*

I was mistaken. Just after I began reading, my fellow passenger leaned over and looked very deliberately at the pages of my book. I smiled and showed him the cover. It was a book on the historicity of the resurrection of Jesus. He chuckled and said, "Well, I guess we don't have to think seriously about that, since it has now been proven that Jesus never even existed!" He then sat up straight, as though our conversation had ended and now it was time to find something else to do. Hit and run? Not a chance, my new friend.

"Why do you think Jesus never existed?" I asked. This led to a short conversation on Jesus's existence. It did not take long for him to concede that Jesus had, in fact, existed. But he maintained that "resurrections are impossible. There is no evidence for the resurrection of Jesus and it certainly could never be proved."

Perhaps you have had a similar discussion with someone and wished you had known how to reply. In what follows, I am going to discuss three key areas that will both inform and equip you to engage in intelligent discussions about Jesus with others.

Current State of Historical Jesus Studies

Our first matter is to define what is meant by the "historical Jesus." Although scholars have not agreed on a definition, most would at least be satisfied with the following definition as a means to enter a discussion: When the data has been sifted, sorted, and assessed, the historical Jesus is the Jesus historians can prove with reasonable certainty and apart from faith.

It is important to observe that the historical Jesus is not the real Jesus who walked and taught in Judea and Galilee, but is the Jesus known through the results of historical investigation. The real Jesus was much more than the historical Jesus, just as a corpse in a grave was once much more than the minimal information described on the tombstone. And then there is the Jesus in the Gospels. This third Jesus is also a partial representative of the real Jesus who had many more elements to his personality and many more things that he said and did than could ever be reported in a Gospel with a length of less than twenty-five thousand words.

It is very important to understand these distinctions and many often fail here. In theory, these three Jesuses are not necessarily in conflict. For example, if historical investigation were some day to prove that the real Jesus did not claim to be the Son of God, the real Jesus and the historical Jesus would be in conflict with the Jesus in the Gospels, since the Jesus in the Gospels claimed to be the Son of God. On the other hand, the inability of historical investigation to determine whether Jesus was born of a virgin does not place the historical Jesus in conflict with the Jesus in the Gospels or the real Jesus, since the former will always be an incomplete figure. Accordingly, if historians cannot prove Jesus performed *Event X*, it is a misstep to conclude on that basis that it did not occur. To do so would be quite naive, since numerous events that actually occurred in the distant past cannot be verified.

How do historians arrive at conclusions regarding Jesus? There are several approaches and various tools used within each approach. The most common approach at present is to recognize that Jesus was a Jewish itinerant preacher who lived in first-century Palestine in a culture that was both Jewish and Greco-Roman. This provides historians with a background knowledge that helps them obtain a more accurate understanding of what Jesus taught and the impact it may have had on those who heard him. They then apply what are referred to as *criteria of authenticity* to the words and deeds of Jesus as preserved in the Gospels. These criteria reflect commonsense principles. If two or more sources that are independent of one another provide similar reports of the same event, we can have more confidence that the event had occurred than if only one source had reported it. This is called *the criterion of multiple attestation.* For example, the Gospel of Mark and Paul's letters are independent of one another. So, when both report that Jesus was buried, we have multiple attestation of the event.

If a source that is unsympathetic or even hostile toward the Christian faith provides a report that agrees with the Christian reports, we can have more confidence that the event had occurred, since the unsympathetic or hostile source would not have the bias carried by the authors of the Christian reports. This is called *the criterion of unsympathetic sources.* For example, Tacitus referred to Christianity as an evil and mischievous superstition (*Annals* 15.44). This identifies him as an unsympathetic source. So, when he reports Jesus's execution by Pontius Pilate, a report entirely compatible with what we find in the Gospels, historians can have more confidence that the event had occurred.

If a report in the Gospels provides data that would have been embarrassing to the early Christian movement, we can have more confidence that the event had occurred, since it is unlikely that the author would have invented content likely to detract from the cause for which he wrote. This is called *the criterion of embarrassment.* For example, Mark reports that Peter rebuked Jesus and that Jesus in turn rebuked Peter, calling him "Satan" (Mark 8:31-33). Since Peter was a leader of the Jerusalem church, it seems unlikely that the early Christians would have invented and preserved a tradition that casts him in such an unfavorable manner.

Historians prefer to have reports that are from eyewitnesses or from a source whose report was written close to the event it purports to describe. This is called *the criterion of early attestation.* For example, almost all scholars agree that Paul has preserved an oral tradition in 1 Corinthians 15:3-7 that goes back to the earliest days of the Christian church and that the content of these verses, although not necessarily the creedal form in which the content appears, very probably goes back to the Jerusalem apostles.

It would be nice if historians could climb into a time machine, return to the past, and verify their conclusions. Since that is not possible, historians can establish matters with only varying degrees of certainty. And it is entirely possible that a lack of data could lead historians to arrive at a false conclusion. This is not only the state of affairs when historians investigate biblical events but also with every other purported event in antiquity. Accordingly, the fulfillment of one or more of the criteria of authenticity in relation to specific reports about Jesus may be said to establish their authenticity with "reasonable" but not "absolute" certainty.

Historians who investigate nonreligious matters have strenuously debated the nature of history for several decades. Understanding the many challenges to knowing the past faced by historians, some have claimed that the past cannot be known and that historians merely create their own narratives of the past based on their subjective interpretations of the data. These are known as *postmodern* historians. Although the debate concerning the nature of history continues, the majority of historians have come to reject postmodern approaches to history and embrace realism, the view that the past can be known to a degree. Of course, historical descriptions of the past will never be exhaustive, will vary in their accuracy, and can be established with only varying degrees of certainty.

Therefore, when speaking of Jesus, it is unreasonable to demand absolute certainty. This is important because many of the skeptics we encounter outside the academic world, and even some skeptics within it, have an approach that, in essence, says, "As long as there is an alternate explanation to the biblical account that cannot be absolutely disproved, the biblical account should not be taken seriously." Such an approach suggests those holding this view have a sophomoric understanding of how the practice of history works. A competent historian embraces what he or she concludes is the *most probable* explanation of the available data, since there is little of the distant past that can be established with such certainty that no room remains for an extremely unlikely alternative.

The Jesus Mythers

During the past twenty years or so, a number of books and articles have appeared on the Internet arguing that Jesus is a myth who never existed. Viewing the biographical information of their authors reveals that only a handful have any academic credentials. Unfortunately, most people reading the literature written by "mythers" (as they are commonly referred to) are not accustomed to critical thinking by comparing sources. For them, Earl Doherty and Dee Murdock (aka Acharya S) are as credible as John Meier and N.T. Wright. Yet they are unaware that neither Doherty nor Murdock ever went beyond earning a bachelor's degree while Meier and Wright earned doctorates in relevant fields and teach New Testament studies at prestigious universities.

I am not claiming the lack of academic credentials on the part of Doherty and Murdock prohibits them from having good arguments and, therefore, they should be ignored. However, it is true that they do not have the training and experience in the proper fields. As a result, they often make egregious errors and silly proposals that sound credible only to the naive.[1] Mythers are often guilty of twisting data, providing false claims, appealing to other sources who are also not scholars, requiring an unreasonable burden of proof before acknowledging the existence of Jesus while being unaware that the scenarios they have proposed in order to address the data border on unbridled fantasy. Readers should understand that publishing on the World Wide Web does not make one a world-class scholar, since the only credential one must have to publish on the Internet is to breathe.

It is noteworthy that one could count on one hand all the scholars in the fields of history and biblical studies who have been persuaded by the arguments of mythers. This is not because the majority of historians and biblical scholars are Christians (I seriously doubt that is the case). It is also noteworthy that even some atheist and agnostic scholars have blasted mythers for their poor arguments and treatment of the data.[2] Scholars simply refuse to give them much attention and regard them to be as absurd as holocaust deniers.

Discussing the Historical Jesus with Others

With the advent of the Internet in the nineties, an explosion of information became available to the public. Christians are far more likely to hear arguments from their skeptical family members, colleagues at work, and neighbors that are more sophisticated than what they may have heard before the Internet. Moreover, our culture has changed. People are easily offended and many regard truth as relative. Everyone has their own truth and thinks it is morally wrong to offend others by telling them you think they are mistaken.

The apostle Paul adjusted his approach to relate better to his particular audience.[3] We should do no less. We must be more careful than ever to be winsome in our interactions with nonbelievers. We can be respectful of those we disagree with and make an effort to listen to them while they present their views in the same manner we would like for them to listen to us while we present ours. We should not overstate our case but temper it. Instead of saying "The historical evidence proves that Jesus rose from the dead," say "The historical evidence strongly suggests Jesus rose from the dead." Instead of saying, "I know that I know Christianity is true," say "In view of the evidence I've examined as well as the answers to prayer I have personally witnessed, I'm convinced Christianity is true."

Remember the words of the apostles Peter and Paul. Peter wrote, "But set apart Christ as Lord in your hearts, always prepared to give a defense to everyone who asks you to give an account concerning the hope in you" (1 Peter 3:15, author's translation). Paul similarly wrote, "Your speech should always be gracious, seasoned with salt, so that you may know how to answer each person" (Colossians 4:6, author's translation).

It is important to recognize that presenting good arguments to a skeptic will not ensure he or she will be convinced by them. Their objections to following Christ may be intellectual (e.g., they are not persuaded by the evidence), emotional (e.g., their Muslim or Jewish family would disown them or they had a poor experience with one or more Christians or their father), or volitional (e.g., they do not want to believe because of pride or it may require them to alter their behavior).

It is their responsibility to make a proper decision. It is our responsibility to share the message of hope through Christ "with gentleness and respect" and "with grace," as Peter and Paul taught. The gospel message is already offensive to some. We need not make it more offensive by presenting it in a manner that lacks gentleness, respect, and grace. When we combine more knowledge with a heart that deeply cares for our nonbelieving friends, we will be pleasantly surprised to find ourselves engaged in dialogues that are far more enjoyable and effective than we may ever have imagined.

MIKE LICONA, PhD, is associate professor of theology at Houston Baptist University. He is the author of numerous books, including *The Resurrection of Jesus*, *Paul Meets Muhammad*, and coauthor with Gary Habermas of *The Case for the Resurrection of Jesus*. Mike has spoken on more than seventy university campuses and has appeared on dozens of radio and television programs. His website is www.Ris enJesus.com.

— 18 —

How to Question the Bible in a Post-Christian Culture

JONATHAN MORROW

The Bible is the most influential book in human history. It has shaped cultures, empires, politics, law, education, healthcare, literature, human rights, and science—just to name a few. The Bible has been translated into more languages than any other book and is the bestselling book of all time...period.

But what are we supposed to do with it in the twenty-first century? And even more importantly, can it still be trusted as the Word of God? Confusion, doubt, and skepticism about the Bible are becoming as common inside the church as they are in our broader culture.

Our Culture No Longer "Speaks Bible"

There was a time when "the Bible says so" would settle the matter. We no longer live in that world. The Bible may be special and have sentimental value, but it is no longer considered unique, authoritative, and true. This is an opportunity to engage and encourage both skeptics and a new generation of Christians to take the Bible seriously again. As the cultural pressure increases, the nominal Christian middle where people play church will evaporate. And that is actually a really good thing.

As Christians living at this unique cultural moment, we need to recognize that the rules of engagement have changed. Most people do not share basic Christian assumptions about God, truth, morality, and authority. The appropriate response is not for us to abandon our commitment to the authority of the Bible. That would be a failure of courage and a lack of faithfulness on our part. But our tactics do need to change because for many the Bible is no longer the answer, it is the question.[1]

It's OK to Question the Bible...Really!

All of us have questions about the Bible. What we have to figure out is what we will do with those questions. Will we keep them hidden and allow unanswered questions to slowly erode our confidence that God has spoken? Or will we courageously question the Bible in a way that actually builds our faith?

The first hurdle is getting over the idea that good Christians shouldn't ask the hard questions. It's easy to fall into the trap of seeing this as a lack of faith. And then there is the fear of what everyone else may think if they find out.

Questioning the Bible can be downright scary. If we dig underneath "because the Bible says so," what will we find? Have we based our lives on a bunch of fairy tales?

As I read the Bible I find people asking the hard questions. My favorite example is Luke who was one of the earliest biographers of Jesus. In a way, Luke was questioning the Bible even before there was a Bible. He investigated everything carefully. He interviewed eyewitnesses. He cross-examined the evidence (Luke 1:1-4). Why? So that he and others might know the truth. And knowing the truth is powerful because it sets people free for life.

There's no doubt that questions can be messy. But life is messy. Deep down we all long for a real-world faith that's rooted in reality. When we know why we believe, it frees us up to live out the truth with confidence. And that's what our world desperately needs.

We need to give ourselves—and our skeptical friends and family—permission to ask the hard questions. I've got good news for you. What we believe is actually true! On the other side of those challenging questions is a stronger faith because it has had to overcome resistance.

Two Challenges to the Bible Christians Must Engage

Certain questions about the Bible have captured the general public's attention and imagination more than others. This means you are much more likely to encounter these challenges on Facebook, in the classroom, on the evening news, at work, or on the History channel. This is no time to be caught off guard; we need to be prepared (1 Peter 3:15).

Challenge 1: Christianity was invented and then imposed on everyone else by the political winners hundreds of years after the death of Jesus.

Was Christianity invented? Religious studies professor Bart Ehrman pulls no punches when he declares:

> Christianity as we have come to know it did not, in any event, spring into being overnight. It emerged over a long period of time, through a period of struggles, debates, and conflicts over competing views, doctrines, perspectives, canons, and rules. The ultimate emergence of the Christian religion represents a human invention…arguably the greatest invention in the history of Western civilization. [2]

There are a lot of claims being made in this paragraph, but here are three truths that will help us better engage the difficult questions people have about the origins of Christianity and the Bible. [3]

1. Start at the beginning. The dominant narrative today is that the version of Christianity and the books we now have in our Bible weren't selected until the fourth century. Did you know that the first list containing all twenty-seven books in our New Testament doesn't show up until Athanasius writes an Easter letter to the churches in AD 367? (In case you are wondering, that is technically true.) So if the date of Jesus's crucifixion was AD 30, then that is 337 years earlier than Athanasius's letter. How can we be confident that the core message of Christianity wasn't changed, misremembered, or deliberately distorted along the way?

Don't start in the fourth century and work your way backward—this will be seen as arbitrary and begging the question. Instead, begin in the first century and work your way forward. What you want to establish is that the core of Christianity was established from the beginning in the death, deity, and resurrection of Jesus of Nazareth (1 Corinthians 15; Galatians 1–2). The earliest and best historical sources we have show that there "never was a time, when the message of Jesus' resurrection was not an integral part of the earliest apostolic proclamation."[4] This core theology of authentic Christianity was reliably passed down from generation to generation (1 Corinthians 15:3-5). If books were consistent with this core theology, not forgeries, and sourced from first-century eyewitnesses authorized by Jesus, then they were accepted as Scripture. This process was not arbitrary or ad hoc. We are simply relying on the best source material available to us to answer the question of what the *earliest* Christians believed.

2. Tell the fully human story. As Christians we can and should tell the divine story of the Bible. We recognize that its ultimate source and inspiration is God (2 Timothy 3:16-17). But in a culture where people do not recognize divine authority, we also need to be equipped to tell the fully human story. In telling this story, we need to avoid two extremes. First, we must avoid the overly sanitized version that maintains there never were any disagreements in the early church about what was and wasn't Bible. The other extreme to avoid is the exaggerated version, which maintains that no one knew what Christianity was and everything was up for grabs.

We need to adopt a more nuanced approach and affirm that God would have employed normal historical processes in the composition of these books through human authors and their acceptance as authoritative Scripture. Communication in the Mediterranean world takes time, and they had to work that out together. History is messy because humans are involved. The primary question early church leaders wrestled with in the second through fourth centuries was how wide to draw the circle of orthodoxy, not whether or not there was orthodoxy. By the time you reach Irenaeus in AD 180, about twenty-two of the twenty-seven books now contained in our New Testament were *already* functioning as Scripture. The trajectory from Jesus himself had already been established, received by, and delivered from the beginning.

3. Earliest Christianity was predominantly Jewish. This point is highly significant because the worldview of Jesus of Nazareth and his followers was rooted in monotheism and the Hebrew Scriptures (what we refer to today as the Old Testament). Recognizing this fact adds another layer of theological protection from Gnostic writings and so-called lost Gospels composed in the second through fourth centuries. Even a cursory read of these Gnostic writings reveals they were clearly at odds with Jewish monotheism rooted in the Hebrew Scriptures. Essential Jewish beliefs central to Jesus's teachings would be that there is only one God and that creation as originally intended by God was good. Gnostic writings reject these core claims, and therefore we know they do not represent earliest Christianity. That is why they were rejected.

Challenge 2: Much of the Bible is morally outdated at best and evil at worst.

A lot recorded in the Bible—especially in the Old Testament—is shocking, confusing, and makes the modern reader uncomfortable. Many Christians simply pretend it's not there. However, that tactic will no longer work because the so-called New Atheists, such as Richard Dawkins, are shouting it from the rooftops:

> The God of the Old Testament is arguably the most unpleasant character in all fiction: jealous and proud of it; a petty, unjust, unforgiving control-freak; a vindictive, bloodthirsty ethnic cleanser; a misogynistic, homophobic, racist, infanticidal, genocidal, filicidal, pestilential, megalomaniacal, sadomasochistic, capriciously malevolent bully.[5]

Those are some pretty heavy accusations to be making about the Almighty. And to be fair, these are emotionally challenging questions we shouldn't brush aside. But at the same time there are reasonable answers to these objections.

Here are three truths that will help us better engage the difficult moral questions critics and believers alike ask of the Bible.

1. The world is not the way it's supposed to be. There are only a few chapters in the entire Bible *not* affected by sin, rebellion, and brokenness—Genesis 1–2 and Revelation 20–22. Why point this out? Because many people—Christians included—read the broken parts and mistake them for God's ideal. God's ideal in creation can best be expressed in the Hebrew word *shalom*, which carries the idea of universal human flourishing, joy, and delight. In light of that, it is essential that we understand a critical principle of interpretation as we engage all of these strange and violent Old Testament passages: *Israel as described in the Old Testament is not God's ideal society.* To use an analogy from the computer industry, they were God's people version 1.0 because they were a work in progress (just as you and I are).

From the Christian perspective, all of humanity is made in God's image—that is God's ideal. When sin entered and perverted the good world God created, that ideal was violated, and the ancient world was from then on perpetually plagued by war and poverty. It was within the volatile kill-or-be-killed world of the ancient Near East that God *began* the process of restoration and redemption through the people of Israel (who would have been just like everyone else in that culture were it not for God's grace and revelation). Having this principle in mind helps us better understand the context of these strange and often controversial passages.

2. The Bible doesn't necessarily endorse everything it accurately records. Just because something is recorded or discussed in the Bible doesn't mean it reflects God's ideal. For example, the Bible accurately records lies and adultery. But it does not follow from this that God approves of lying and adultery (just look at the Ten Commandments). The Bible is more sophisticated and complex than we give it credit for. And when it is read in a culture tutored in the fine art of sound bites and slogans, that can often result in an interpretive train wreck.

Let's take just one example. Does God think slavery is a good idea? The short answer is no. How do we know? The creational norm expressed in Genesis 1 and 2 that humans are made in the image of God and possess intrinsic value and are worthy of respect and dignity. So what about all those laws and commands that deal with slavery? They should be understood in light of God's creational ideal as well as the reality of a broken world full of war and poverty with humans possessing free will making real choices embedded in various cultures where progress toward recovering an ideal takes time. Life in a fallen world is messy. But one day God has promised to renew all things. Until that day when all brokenness is made whole, we walk in hope rooted in the reality of the resurrection of Jesus (1 Corinthians 15:58).

3. *The command to destroy the Canaanites was about judgment not genocide.* In stark contrast to the way this objection is often framed, the conquest of the land of Canaan "is repeatedly portrayed as God acting in judgment on a wicked and degraded society and culture—as God would do again and again in Old Testament history, *including against Israel itself.*"[6] God had given the Canaanites 430 years to change their ways, but their wickedness finally reached the tipping point for God to judge (Exodus 15:6). In the biblical narrative, the actions of the Israelites are "never placed in the category of oppression but of divine punishment operating through human agency."[7] God as the Creator of life has the authority to take life, and during this unique occasion of judgment, that prerogative was temporarily extended to the people of Israel since Yahweh was their king. While Israel carried out this judgment against a specific people—the Canaanites—their actions were *not* motivated by racial superiority or hatred. Therefore the language of ethnic cleansing and genocide is inaccurate. Idolatry, not ethnicity, is the issue here. Judgment not genocide.[8]

Two Ways to Question the Bible...What Do You Ultimately Want?

Everyone has questions about the Bible, and it is important to be honest about those questions. But people also need to be honest about what their goal is in asking these questions. Whether they are your questions or you are walking with someone as they question, here is a framework that I have found helpful as I have had conversations with people who were questioning the Bible.

There are really just two paths to take here. If you want truth, you will find it in the end because Christianity has nothing to fear from the truth. Make a short list of the most important questions you are wrestling with, invite some other mature Christians into the process, and investigate. God is big enough for that. However, if you are using your questions to create space between you and the God of the Bible because you don't want submit to an authority...that is a different path altogether. I can't answer that question for you because I don't know your heart. You are certainly free to take this path, but if space is what you ultimately want, then you will get it because you can always create space by asking another question.

But please keep this in mind. Just because you can ask another question doesn't mean there isn't a reasonable answer to your question. If in your heart of hearts you just want space, then your will can find a back door to accomplish this with enough effort.

As counterintuitive as it may sound, I actually want people to question the Bible in this post-Christian space we now live in. Not because I want them to become skeptics. I want them to take the Bible seriously enough to question it because I want them to press through the flimsy slogans to find the bedrock of truth and the confident faith that flows from the knowledge of the truth. If you are honest with yourself in this moment, what are you ultimately after? Truth or space?

Exploring Questions That Matter

How we view the Bible is no small matter. A lot is at stake. The God of the universe may actually have spoken. Let this idea sink in: *If Christianity is true, then there are authoritative answers to life's biggest questions.* Who am I? Do I matter? What happens when I die? How should I live? It is no wonder then that Paul celebrates when people take God's Word seriously. It makes all the difference:

> For this reason we also constantly thank God that when you received the word of God which you heard from us, you accepted it not as the word of men, but for what it really is, the word of God, which also performs its work in you who believe (1 Thessalonians 2:13 NASB).

JONATHAN MORROW (DMin) is the author of several books, including *Questioning the Bible* and *Is God Just a Human Invention?* As the founder of Think Christianly, Jonathan speaks nationally and is passionate about seeing a new generation of Christ-followers understand what they believe and why they believe it. He is also a director at Impact 360 Institute. Connect with him at thinkchristianly.org and follow on Twitter: @Jonathan_Morrow.

Interview with Hemant Mehta
SEAN MCDOWELL

What is your experience like with most Christians when they discover you're an atheist?

Some Christians are a bit taken aback when they find out I'm an atheist, but it's usually because they have false preconceived notions about me. They think I'm immoral or itching for a debate or looking down at them. But because I'm very public about my atheism, I've had some positive feedback too. I've been invited by Christian schools (plural!) to speak to students in order to help dispel those stereotypes. I've had Christian students ask me questions about my beliefs out of genuine curiosity. Overall, my interactions with Christians—in person—have been pretty positive. I don't think I invite much anger to begin with.

What bad impressions do you often see Christians, and in particular apologists, giving?

The biggest frustration with apologists is that they consistently misrepresent what people like me think. They assume we have no rebuttals to their arguments. They assume we've never thought about these questions before. They assume certain Bible verses will magically change our thinking. You'd think they had never spoken to atheists before, despite claiming to be experts on us. It's like a virgin writing a sex-advice column. You can tell they've never really done it.

What are the most convincing arguments you have heard for believing in God? What are the least?

If I ever heard a convincing argument, then I'd be a Christian by now. But I haven't. I think the least effective arguments are the ones that are ostensibly based in science (like Intelligent Design or Irreducible Complexity)...because the scientists who work in those fields have debunked those theories repeatedly. Also, anything based in the Bible. First, we've read it; it's not new information. We've already dismissed it for a variety of reasons. Second, you can't convince people of the truth of the Bible by pointing to the Bible. If a Muslim tried the same arguments on you—"The Qur'an is true because it says so in the Qur'an"—you would dismiss it. It's not a good technique.

HEMANT MEHTA is the editor of *Friendly Atheist*, appears on the *Atheist Voice* channel on YouTube, and cohosts the uniquely named *Friendly Atheist* podcast. He is the author of three books, including *I Sold My Soul on eBay* and *The Young Atheist's Survival Guide*.

— 19 —

Entrepreneurs: An Economic Apologetic for the Faith

JAY W. RICHARDS

What does economics have to do with apologetics? It might not be obvious at first glance, but the answer is: quite a lot. To see this, however, we need to think about different kinds of apologetics.

Apologetics is the rational defense of the faith and can be divided into positive and negative forms. Positive apologetics includes arguments for God's existence, for the reliability of Scripture, and the historicity of Christ's resurrection. In negative apologetics, the apologist responds to objections to the faith, such as the problem of evil and the claim that miracles are impossible.

But there is another, less direct way to do apologetics, and that is to show the fruitfulness of the Christian worldview in other intellectual endeavors, such as science, politics, architecture, literature, music, art, or economics. I could give dozens of examples of books on science—from cosmology and physics to biology and geology—that have an apologetic thrust, and I can think of at least six books on art and aesthetics along the same lines.

Used in this way, a concept drawn from theology functions much like a hypothesis functions in the historical sciences. In fields such as archeology, geology, evolutionary biology, and cosmology, one of the ways scientists test hypotheses is by comparing them with the live alternatives to find which one has the most explanatory power. This doesn't "prove" the hypothesis in a deductive sense, but it does justify the scientist in concluding that the hypothesis is more likely to be true than the known alternatives.

In the same way, if Christian claims are true, if, say, a transcendent and perfectly loving God created everything for a purpose, then this truth should cast light on absolutely everything for the simple reason that it applies to everything. The Dutch theologian and statesman Abraham Kuyper suggested this when he said, "There is not a square inch in the whole domain of our human existence over which Christ, who is Sovereign over all, does not cry, 'Mine!'"

Beyond this, however, Christian theology should have apologetic value when it helps explain other fields. In this way, every Christian involved in the life of the mind should see him or herself as at least a part-time apologist. "I believe in Christianity as I believe that the sun has risen," said C.S. Lewis, "not only because I see it, but because by it I see everything else."[1] If theology allows us to explain something in economics that economists might otherwise miss or misconstrue, then that's a point for theology, even if by itself it doesn't constitute a proof. Rather than arguing from the facts of biology to the existence of God, the apologist treats a concept drawn from theology as a hypothesis or heuristic, and attempts to show that the theological concept explains some fact in another field better than the alternatives.

How to Think About Economics

A number of books integrate theology and economics, including some written by yours truly. Unfortunately, there is almost no literature on apologetics and economics. Budding apologists should see this as an opportunity to break new ground: the harvest is plentiful but the laborers are few!

As in any mature field, economics has built up its own set of empirical discoveries and theoretical insights, developed over time as a result of reflecting on and interacting with economic matters. Think of economics not just as an academic discipline but also as a domain of human existence that involves trading, buying, selling, innovating, creating, risking, competing, and cooperating for goods, services, and information. As such, the economic realm looms large in the daily life of every human being on the planet, and to a large degree determines how much freedom each of us has to pursue God's call on our lives. That's why the apologetic use of economics may have not just apologetic value but practical value as well.

Apologetics and economics is an enormous subject that I can't even outline here, so I'd like to give one brief example—a hand gesture really—of how Christian theology casts light on economics, by considering those risk-taking creative agents at the center of all dynamic economies: entrepreneurs.

How Theology Casts Light on the Role of Entrepreneurs

Entrepreneurship is a hot topic these days because we are all aware of tech entrepreneurs who have done so much to change the world in the last forty years—Bill Gates of Microsoft, Steve Jobs of Apple, Larry Page and Sergei Brin of Google, Mark Zuckerburg of Facebook, and so on. The majority of new jobs comes from new, small businesses started by budding entrepreneurs. This is all the more astonishing because most new business ventures fail in their first year.

Nevertheless, for decades, if not centuries, the formal discipline of economics has had a problem with entrepreneurs. Why is that? I suspect it's because entrepreneurs defy the predictable methods that are thought to be a hallmark of good science. If an economist aspires to be a scientist rather than a speculative anthropologist, he will want access to repeatable empirical data for testing his theories. Humans do act in regular ways, at least in the aggregate, so economists can predict what will happen to local gas prices if, say, a hurricane devastates Florida, wipes out dozens of gas stations, and prevents gasoline transport. (The price of gasoline in Florida will go up.) The perennial temptation for the economist is to assume that all things economic can be captured in this way. Entrepreneurs cannot be so captured, and as a result, economists tend to ignore them or explain them away.

Economists do talk about entrepreneurs, of course, but their talk is usually reductive. Israel Kirzner, the contemporary economist who has concentrated the most on the subject, describes entrepreneurs as "arbitrageurs" who exploit some "information asymmetry" in the market. In plain English: A clever entrepreneur finds that he can profit by buying milk for fifty cents a gallon from farmers in Iowa and selling it for three dollars a gallon in Manhattan. While this operation might benefit the Iowa dairy farmer, the New Yorker, and the middleman, it's not an inspiring story of creativity. More to the point, it vastly underplays the real innovation we see in the work of many entrepreneurs.

Better is the thought of Joseph Schumpeter, the first preeminent modern economist to study the entrepreneur. In the first half of the twentieth century, Schumpeter developed a theory called "creative destruction." "The problem that is usually visualized," he wrote, "is how capitalism administers existing structures, whereas the relevant problem is how it creates and destroys them." Innovations in an economy involve the recombination of existing materials. The innovation might be a chemical company that produces a new material for the construction industry. Or the innovation might be the recombination of existing goods and services. In either case, the successful recombinations displace their less successful competitors and spread through the economy. At some point, competitors adopt the innovation, which reduces profit margins and inspires the search for new acts of creative destruction.

For some contemporary thinkers, the entrepreneur disappears altogether, replaced by an impersonal entity that has acquired the characteristics of agency. "Good ideas may not want to be free, but they do want to connect, fuse, recombine," writes Steven Johnson.[2] "They want to reinvent themselves by crossing conceptual borders. They want to complete each other as much as they want to compete." Johnson is referring not to *people* competing and cooperating in a marketplace, but to ideas themselves. For Johnson, ideas function like genes in Richard Dawkins's account of evolution: there are no people per se, only gene-carriers. This is the reduction to the absurd of this approach to the entrepreneur and suggests that Johnson and others like him lack some essential tool in their explanatory toolkit.

Despite the name, innovation for Schumpeter, Johnson, and others is a Darwinian process and not a creative one. Charles Darwin proposed that living things were largely the result of natural selection sifting random variations, rather than divine acts of creation. Thinkers such as Schumpeter and others apply Darwin's idea to the entrepreneur. This is not completely misguided. There are similarities between the way fit organisms and better businesses succeed in the struggle for survival. The problem with such theories is that the entrepreneur is shoehorned into a limited preexisting theory, drawn in this case from biology. What is needed is a theory that fully accounts for what we know about real entrepreneurs.

Entrepreneurs: Born or Made?

The scholarly and even not-so-scholarly economic world is stuck on the horns of a false dilemma. The common debate is whether entrepreneurs are born or made. Does nature simply give some people the entrepreneurial edge or can entrepreneurial virtues be nurtured? Does biology or the environment have the upper hand?

Both nature and nurture surely play a role, as they do in almost any other endeavor. Nobody doubts that theoretical physics can be taught, for instance, just as no one doubts that a rare few are naturally gifted for doing theoretical physics. Even the most gifted pianist or basketball player or gymnast or theoretical physicist will become great only by mastering the requisite skills. Years of grueling study and practice precede mastery, even for prodigies like Mozart. Yet individual success also rests on factors not under the control of the individual, as Malcolm Gladwell shows in *Outliers*.[3] Cultural quirks, family background, and lucky timing often play a crucial role. Any full explanation will include both these facts.

But even when reconciled, limiting the options to reductive accounts of nature and nurture leaves out the main ingredient: the human person. Theorists may imagine that each of us is the sum of our biology and upbringing, but this contradicts what they know about themselves, what we all know about ourselves. We are shaped by our heredity, upbringing, and education, but we also build on and transcend these influences through our choices.

If your mother criticized you incessantly as a child, you may be critical as well. But that doesn't mean you can't develop the virtue of forgiveness. Perhaps your genes cause you to be scatterbrained. That doesn't prevent you from developing routine countermeasures so you won't lose your keys (this one I know from experience).

Each of us possesses the power to freely choose between alternatives. We perceive this capacity in ourselves as directly and surely as we perceive anything, and we attribute the same powers to other human beings. If you want to be the skeptic and doubt it, go ahead, but in so doing, you'll drop into a skeptical abyss. If we're wrong about something we all perceive directly and introspectively, and can't help but presuppose about both ourselves and others, why have any confidence in our beliefs drawn from history or physics or cosmology?

Setting aside that skeptical cul-de-sac, let's assume for the sake of argument that we do have the capacity to make some free choices. If so, then human beings at least sometimes make choices that no one could have predicted beforehand even if armed with a complete account of the hereditary and environmental factors that shaped who they are. This is the nature of a free act. The creative labors of the entrepreneur are chock-full of free acts. Yet this basic truth about entrepreneurs is rarely described with much clarity *in economics*.

So here we have a problem that emerges from the study of economics itself: the perplexing variable called the entrepreneur. And it is here that theology has an explanatory role to play. We can't paint a realistic picture of the entrepreneur without a view of the human person rich enough to account for what we know about enterprise.

We know that entrepreneurs harness resources—heredity, education, experience, family background, cultural context, physical resources, virtues, even spiritual inspiration—to create new value that did not exist before. Such value-creation is impossible to predict in detail beforehand. Think about it: if anyone could describe in detail a unique innovation that would emerge in 2017, he would already know to bring that innovation about. A key characteristic of entrepreneurial innovation is that it is unpredictable. Even entrepreneurs in the very act of creating value often have little idea of how their creations will be used by others.[4] The Christian tradition has a concept that accounts for these facts: *the imago dei*, human beings—male and female—made in the image of God.

In the opening chapter of Genesis, we see God exercising perfect freedom, sovereignty, and creativity over everything else. He speaks the world into existence without effort or resistance. And then he creates human beings "in his own image" and commands them to "be fruitful and multiply and fill the earth and subdue it." The text suggests that, to be made in the image of God is, in some derivative way, to participate in such creative freedom. The medieval theologian Thomas Aquinas wrote that God "grants, even to creatures...the dignity of causality."[5] Anyone who views the human person in this way should not be surprised by the creative feats of entrepreneurs. Put another way, the concept of the *imago dei* explains entrepreneurial creativity better than the reductive approaches preferred by so many economic thinkers.

I'm not saying that we can prove that man is made in the image of God simply by studying entrepreneurs. I am suggesting that if we take the concept of the *imago dei* as a hypothesis or heuristic, we will have a much easier time explaining what we observe about entrepreneurial innovation. We might also make predictions about what to expect if this view of the human person is true.

According to the doctrine, human beings are neither ethereal angels nor mere beasts. We are not reducible to nature, nurture, or the combination thereof. We're a hybrid of the material and immaterial, bearing the image of a Creator. We exist at the intersection of the material and the spiritual. This hypothesis or heuristic captures what should be clear from our experience but is often missed. It allows us to avoid the simplistic accounts of entrepreneurs so common in the literature. It provides us a way to account for the full repertoire of entrepreneurial virtues, whether they be material, intellectual, or spiritual.

It should also lead us to expect what we are now witnessing in high-tech information economies: over time, the matter in a material resource matters less than the mind that transforms it—manure into fertilizer, oil into gasoline and kerosene, sand into computer chips and fiber optic cables, light into lasers.[6] For this reason, nonreligious economist Julian Simon, anticipating my argument, once said that man is the "ultimate resource."[7] This is perhaps the greatest truth of economics. And it is devilishly hard to explain without recourse to a view of the human person drawn from theology. That's an apologetic point in favor of Christian belief.

JAY W. RICHARDS, PhD, is author of many books including the *New York Times* bestsellers *Infiltrated* and *Indivisible*. Richards is an assistant research professor in the School of Business and Economics at The Catholic University of America, executive editor of *The Stream*, and a senior fellow at the Discovery Institute. He lives with his family in the Washington, DC, area.

— 20 —

Telling the Truth About Sex in a Broken Culture

JOHN STONESTREET

Though the Christian *message* of sex and marriage has gone largely unchanged, our *methods* in teaching this message have evolved indeed. For example, as a youth grouper, I vividly remember what I'll call "the fear method." "If you have sex before you're married," we were often told, "you'll get a disease, or maybe get pregnant!" The seemingly daily discovery of a new STD made this approach quite effective, especially the scariest of them all: AIDS. When Ervin "Magic" Johnson announced he had contracted the HIV virus, that scared me and my friends pure for at least six weeks.

The obvious consequences to risky sexual behavior aside, the fear approach was (and still is) a bad idea for at least a couple of reasons. First, it's utilitarian. Premarital sex is presented as wrong because of its potentially negative consequences. Today, however, most of those consequences have been eliminated or at least mitigated. Magic Johnson didn't die of AIDS, as everyone expected, and medical advances now enable the infected to live mostly normal lives.

And what of that other consequence? Given the ready availability of free birth control and the legalization (and even subsidizing) of abortion on demand, we can largely avoid pregnancy as well. The inherent connection between sex and babies is dismissed these days, a fact that brings up the second problem with the fear approach.

Fear of consequences does nothing to teach the God-given purpose and design of sex. Also, we often got the impression that an out-of-wedlock pregnancy was like contracting syphilis. And it's worth mentioning, if folks are taught to fear sex, some actually will, even after they're married. It's difficult to transition from "this is bad" to "this is good," even with a ring on.

By the time I was in college, the fear approach had been largely supplanted by another approach: the rally. Large church-sponsored events, at times stadium-sized, featured cool speakers and hip musicians challenging Christians to make their commitments before God to stay pure until and during marriage, in direct competition with entertainers selling an opposite message. But Christians couldn't really compete with Madonna or free pornography and, like most emotionally charged events, found that it's easier to motivate people to make promises than it is to help them keep them. The overall effectiveness of purity pledges is highly disputed,[1] and rumor has it that hotels see a spike in porn consumption when hosting Christian men's conferences.[2]

Today, the favored approach seems to be what one of my friends has labeled "Princess Theology." In this view, chastity guarantees a marital happy ending. Stay pure, students are told, and God will write your love story. Save sex for marriage, and God guarantees "your best sex now" with prince charming (or princess charming). It's a sort of sexual prosperity gospel only, in this version, the divine genie is more of a cosmic Dr. Ruth than a cosmic Donald Trump.

Statistics do, of course, tell us that married couples have the most satisfying sex lives, but it's neither a money-back guarantee nor a divine wedding gift. What those statistics reveal is the emotional and physical security provided by marriage. In fact, there are three reasons Christian leaders should never perpetuate Princess Theology.

First, *the Bible never promises it*. Christians rightly believe that God is sovereign over our lives and human history, and in this sense he does write our love stories. However, we mustn't forget that God wrote Hosea's love story too, and many biblical stories with a beautiful beginning did not have terrific endings. Israel's patriarchs come to mind.

Second, *human nature cannot deliver it*. Biblical stories clearly reveal, and universal human experience confirms, that no one is a prince charming. Marriage involves two people, and one spouse's purity does not guarantee the other's. In fact, we risk teaching husbands and wives to approach their spouse in a demanding, selfish way as if, since they played by the rules, God owes them a perfect spouse. But what of potential life challenges that interfere with sexual happiness, such as illness or disability? What of sexual addictions or frigidity? What of infidelity or abandonment? These situations happen.

Third, *our current culture cannot sustain it*. We live in a time where the average age that women first marry is older than the average age they have their first child.[3] Nearly one in four females and one in six males will be sexually abused by age eighteen.[4] Average first exposure to pornography by Internet users is estimated to be at age eight,[5] and rates of porn addiction are at epidemic levels.

In this sexually broken environment, how many young adults can we reasonably expect to emerge unscathed? The old youth group line, "Be a virgin, marry a virgin," is unhelpful. To what are we referring? A technical virgin? Someone who has never made a sexual mistake of any kind? In that economy, how many marriageable candidates would be left? And what does this say of the restoring work of the gospel?

Admittedly, my descriptions of Christian sex education are overgeneralizations and, at times, exaggerations, but I'm trying to make a larger point: *we need to rethink how we communicate biblical sexuality both inside and outside the church.* Living and communicating a genuinely biblical view of sexuality is a powerful apologetic today. We never operate in a cultural vacuum. Our culture has undergone more than a moral slip into debauched activities. It's undergone a worldview shift. Our gut-level understanding of sex, relationships, love, and marriage has changed dramatically in the following ways.

How Sexuality Is Experienced

It wasn't easy to find sexually explicit material when I was a teenager. Maybe a friend could sneak his dad's *Playboy* or maybe we could sneak a peek at a convenience store. Today, however, there is unlimited and immediate *access* to sexually explicit material of all kinds. The Internet, smartphones, social media, and mainstream entertainment virtually ensure that we are all consistently exposed to various forms of sexual brokenness. As Josh McDowell once told me, the question for parents isn't whether our children will see pornography but when. And, of course, things once taboo are now fodder for sitcom jokes, pop music lyrics, or heartwarming family-friendly movies.

Further, the kind of sexual brokenness we experience in our culture is *predatory*. One mother told me how shocked she was when her nine-year-old asked, "What's a pervert?" When she asked him where he heard that word, he told her it was from an online popup ad that interrupted his homework. Not knowing what it meant, he clicked on the ad and was exposed to pornography for the first time. He wasn't looking for it; it was looking for him.

In light of all of this, churches should assume that because most of us have encountered sexuality early and often in a society committed to tolerance and resistant to moral judgments of any kind, we have had very few years of sexual innocence. Not only do we have little control over what sexually explicit images we encounter, we do not choose what definitions, philosophies, and arguments about sexuality we encounter. We live in a sexually pluralistic society.

How Sexuality Is Understood

An old Chinese proverb says that if you would like to know what water is, you shouldn't ask the fish. Cultural norms powerfully shape our gut-level ideas about the world and ourselves. Thus, it is crucial to understand which gut-level assumptions about sexuality our culture is catechizing into our thinking.

Sexuality has been radically *privatized*. It used to be that privacy ended at the bedroom door, and care was given to which views, attitudes, and behavior about sex were allowed in the public square. Today, however, pornography, medical technology, and public policies advance as if there are no levels of public accountability. The student center of Shippensburg University (PA) offers vending machines for soda, snacks, and Plan B (the "morning after" pill). Following suit, the Federal Drug Administration decided in 2013 that Plan B should be available over the counter in pharmacies, without a prescription, *to girls of any age*. Apparently, both the university and the feds believe that not even doctors should have opinions about a patient's sexual behavior, even if it's risky and involves a minor.

Gone are the days when red-faced males had to face convenience store clerks with their pornography purchases. We now surf the Internet alone on hand-held devices. When British Prime Minister David Cameron proposed, to counter the predatory behavior of online pornography, that the default setting for Internet providers be to block sexually explicit websites *unless the user specifically requested access*, he was made out by many to be an enemy of free speech. Apparently, many think unrestricted access to pornography is a basic human right.

Our sexual activities are best kept to ourselves, but it's a mistake to think that sex is purely private. There are public consequences: for others, for family units, for societies, and for nations. We once thought citizens accountable for the consequences of their sexual activities, but no longer. Whereas the government historically regulated against certain sexual behavior it deemed dangerous and damaging (though not always done well), it now sees its role as ensuring unfettered sexual freedoms. And whereas marriage was long thought to be the best institution for protecting and, in a very real sense, regulating sex, that hasn't been the case for quite some time. Instead, the government is expected to expand the natural limits of marriage more and more so as to officially express approval of our autonomous sexual choices.

At the root of these changes and shifting legal policies is the cultural shift I mentioned earlier. The recent song "Take Me to Church" by the band Hozier proclaims that objects of our sexual desires are more properly understood as objects of adoration and that the bedroom is an altar where we will find salvation. Sex is "the good life" to be pursued without restrictions or accountability. At root, this song reveals a culture that has embraced a new vision of life or, we might even say, a new religion.

"A culture," as Rod Dreher observed, "requires a *cultus*—a sense of sacred order, a cosmology that roots...moral demands within a metaphysical framework."[6] Cosmology is another term for worldview and consists of commitments about God, authority, human nature, and morality. Ours is a culture that considers God optional, authority self-determined, and morality relative. More importantly, human identity is reduced to sexual preferences and inclinations. To deny someone their sexual freedom is tantamount to denying their dignity. The church must understand that, given this cultural framework, biblical sexuality is not even taken seriously. Instead it is dismissed as unbelievable from the start.

It may seem hopeless to think that the Bible's life-giving vision of sexuality can gain any traction in these cultural waters. But it's not. Bad ideas have bad consequences. We may soon rediscover, like generations before us, that the biblical vision is attractive amidst the chaos of sexual brokenness. In the meantime, here are some important things apologists today can do.

We Can Clarify the Beautiful and Holistic Biblical Vision of Human Sexuality

Before we determine what to do with something, we must know what that something is and what it is for. Biblical sexual norms are nonsensical outside of the biblical understanding of what sex is. So we must start again to clarify and explain God's design. Here are three suggestions for doing this.

First, churches must disciple their own. It is not enough to teach correct values and appropriate behavior. We must ground these values and behaviors, over and over again, in the biblical worldview of human identity as first and foremost bearers of God's image, and in the biblical worldview of sexuality as God's great gift that enables spouses to bear God's image in a new way as one, in order to fulfill his purposes. This is the *why* that makes sense of the *what*.

Second, we must continuously counter the wrong definitions of love, human dignity, freedom, and marriage that are continuously being communicated by our culture, and we must consistently propose the biblical definitions of these concepts that are so much richer and truer. Words have meaning, and unless

Christians are clear on definitions, our efforts will be futile. Our best seminars and books will only be moral window dressing on a wrong and damaging worldview.

We Can Offer Hope and Healing for the Sexually Broken, Including Ourselves

Paul told the church at Corinth, "Every other sin a person commits is outside the body, but the sexually immoral person sins against his own body" (1 Corinthians 6:18). Many churches and Christian leaders are falling for the very real temptation to assimilate to ever-changing sexual norms. The impulse is understandable: stay relevant or alienate people from the gospel.

But this is a "devil's bargain."[7] We may feel, as I often do, that love and truth are incompatible when it comes to heated issues like sexual orientation, marriage, divorce, and gender identity. However, only the gospel promises forgiveness of sin and reconciliation with God, ourselves, and others. By caving where the Bible is clear, we stand in the way of sinners finding what they need most.

This forgiveness is for all of "us" as much as it is for "them." A sexually broken culture produces sexually broken Christians too. We need forgiveness as much as anyone.

We Can Embody Sexual Wholeness as the Better Alternative that It Is

Sexual brokenness is exhausting and unsustainable for both individuals and entire cultures. Sex, properly ordered, is life-giving in all kinds of ways. When not properly ordered, it dehumanizes and victimizes. There is, and will be, no shortage of victims of our sexual hubris.

Let's remember that we are not the first Christians located in a culture hell-bent on sexually exhausting itself. The earliest Christians found themselves in a world even worse than ours. Though the dominant myth is that puritanical Christians ruined all the pagan sexual fun, the truth is far different. As Rod Dreher explains,

> In fact, Paul's teachings on sexual purity and marriage were adopted as liberating in the pornographic, sexually exploitive Greco-Roman

culture of the time—exploitive especially of slaves and women, whose value to pagan males lay chiefly in their ability to produce children and provide sexual pleasure. Christianity, as articulated by Paul, worked a cultural revolution, restraining and channeling male eros, elevating the status of both women and of the human body, and infusing marriage—and marital sexuality—with love.[8]

This should give us hope. One of the church's callings is to offer good gifts to the world. Sex, properly understood and properly ordered, is one of God's best gifts. Potentially, this could be one of our best tools for pointing the world to the Giver of the gift. Let's get on with it. Great opportunities await us.

JOHN STONESTREET is a speaker and fellow with the Chuck Colson Center for Christian Worldview and cohost of the national radio commentary *BreakPoint*. He has coauthored three books: *Making Sense of Your World: A Biblical Worldview; Same-Sex Marriage: A Thoughtful Approach to God's Design for Marriage;* and *Restoring All Things: God's Audacious Plan to Change the World through Everyday People.*

— 21 —

Being Authentically Christian on the LGBT Issue

GLENN T. STANTON

How do we handle the gay and lesbian issue in the church today in fidelity to Christ? Even those taking accommodating views hold they are being faithful to Jesus, even as they take up a sexual ethic completely contrary to what Christ taught. It takes more than simply believing we are. We must recognize some essential truths.

We must all ask, "How do I represent Christ faithfully without just signing him up for my position because I think I'm right?" There are some basic things to consider.

Always Live in Grace and Truth

John 1:14 tells us that Jesus came to us from the Father, "full of grace and truth." *Full* is a definitive word. Any modifier like *very* or *pretty much* is superfluous. Jesus not only exemplifies both grace and truth, but he was FULL of them. They are what he was.

And as such, Christianity is the only religion or belief system in the world that has the balance of these two virtues and in equal measure. Truth without grace is abusive and arrogant. Grace without truth is mushy sentimentalism. Neither are what they are intended to be without the balance of the other. Thus, we must always deal with this issue—as with all others—in both grace and truth. And this rule of thumb serves as a generally reliable guide: As much as possible, always deal with the *person* in grace and the *issue* itself in truth.

Some situations require us to show more grace than truth and others demand more truth than grace. Good parenting demands this shift in balance all the time, doesn't it? So does the rest of life. But we cannot regularly sacrifice one for the sake of the other.

Make Friends

It is very helpful in navigating this issue in the spirit of Christ to seek out and develop authentic friendships with at least one same-sex identified person outside of your own family. And if you have such people in your family, certainly be gracious to them in that spirit. (But don't let that one family member fulfill your obligation.) Developing such friendships helps us get to know those we are engaging and disagreeing with, rather than just interacting with faceless stereotypes or caricatures. And they will benefit in the same way in interacting with you. It's hard to demonize the person we have gotten to know well. We don't have to agree with our friends, and it is not a sign of true friendship that we must. But developing these friendships helps us disagree in a more intelligent and civil way. And that's a good thing that everyone can use more of.

It also drives us to ask ourselves whether we are being honest with the issue itself. I like to imagine one of my LGBT friends standing right by me as I write or speak on this topic. This encourages me to check what I say and make sure it's true and fair. The criteria is not "Would they agree with me?" but "Would they think that what I said was generally accurate?" Many times they don't think what I say here or there is fair, but the check such an exercise forces upon me is helpful and makes me a sharper advocate for my beliefs.

As you work to make such friends, always seek to be friends for friendship's sake. Imagine someone wanting to be your friend with ulterior motives, especially if that is signing them up for your religion. Let them know you care about them for who they are. As your friendship develops, the topic of your beliefs will naturally come up, and that will provide the natural opportunity to tell them what Christ means and has done in your life. Remember, the most powerful apologetic tool is genuine love.

Learn a Theology of Sexuality

The LGBT issue for the church is not about same-sex sexuality. It's not about the gay lobby. It is truly all about the authority and integrity of divine Scriptures and the lordship and teaching of Jesus himself. These two things are what really matter, and any effort to challenge them must be resisted. Understand that our work in this area is an effort to understand, hold to, live by, and teach a biblical theology and ethic of human sexuality. This serves as our "center of the room," and any discussion about any other part of the room must take its direction and conviction from this center. What is a Christian theology or ethic on sexuality? We must first answer that question and know it well.

Learn a Christian Anthropology

Related to a biblical theology of sexuality, we have to learn and hold to a biblical anthropology—an understanding of what it truly means to be human. In fact, this must come before and lays the foundation for understanding a thoroughly Christian theology of sexuality. We must ask, "What is man?" Why is humanity created in the equal duality of male and female? Do both of them in their uniqueness bear the very image of God in the world? Why was it not good for the man to be alone? Hint: *It was more than just loneliness.* How do we image the Trinity in our humanity and sex-distinct duality?

What did the Fall do to us? Francis Schaeffer handles this better than anyone I know from a theological anthropology. See his book *Genesis in Space and Time* (end of chapter 5) on the four separations the Fall created in mankind. These impact every part of our experience with God, ourselves, others, and the earth.

In a book I coauthored with Leon Wirth, *The Family Project: How God's Design Reveals His Best for You*, we address the four primary verses that should inform a robust Christian anthropology. They are Genesis 1:26-27; 2:18; 3:22;

and Revelation 21:2-6. And all of these must be understood in light of the Incarnation, explained in John 1:1-18. We describe in the book how all this ties together to create a genuinely Christian anthropology that a Christian theology of sexuality must rest upon.

Know What Jesus Said About Homosexuality

Most advocates seeking to rewrite Scripture on the issue of homosexuality will tell us with great delight: "Jesus never said anything about homosexuality," and therefore neither should we...that is if we are opposed to it.

These people know better, or you hope they do. An argument from silence is no argument at all. Do you know why I never tip a waitress? Because Jesus never said anything about it. Can you find any hole in my reasoning?

Jesus indeed spoke of homosexuality in his exchange with the Pharisees in the beginning of Matthew 19 and Mark 10. He tells his inquisitors that Genesis 1 and 2 are what we must consult whenever we consider marriage and sexual unions. (And not surprisingly, these Bible revisionists always steer clear of the divine teleology of humanity explained in these chapters.) It all has to do with God creating us male and female and the man is to leave all other important relationships and cleave to his wife. And in that union, they uniquely become one flesh. No other human relationship is held up this way. Clearly, Jesus is telling us that the union of husband and wife is the only sexual union honored and permitted by God. All others—heterosexual, homosexual, or otherwise—are contrary to God's will and design.

Need to Apologize for Mistreatment?

Christians should always be in a place of humility and willingness to admit and repent of any ill-treatment toward others. And for it to be authentic, it must be based on specific behavior. With our loved ones, we cannot just generally apologize for some unspecific wrong treatment. Our apology, as much as possible, must be about particular offenses so we let those we have hurt know we realize how we have done so. This is essential.

With this, many Christians will say, "The church has much to apologize to the gay community for." While that spirit of humility is virtuous, it is not authentic to take on unwarranted guilt. Such an apology should, as much as possible, point to genuine instances and make amends for them.

But having dealt with this issue for over two decades in the public square, interacting at great length and depth with both LGBT advocates and Christians, I find that it's the rare Christian who treats gay or lesbian-identified individuals unkindly. They will disagree. They will sometimes demonstrate nervousness in such interactions. They might unintentionally say things our friends on the other side of the issue might take as insulting or ham-handed, as is the case between those who live in different social groups. Civil people can and should work through such faux pas, correcting each other when it happens.

But I do find that Christians are generally very welcoming and gracious to those in the LGBT community. And I'm very happy to see this. In fact, many of my friends on the other side of this issue admit they are generally treated with more kindness by my Christian friends than I am by their LGBT friends. This is also true when we debate at very liberal or Christian schools. The Christians tend to be very civil and polite while this is not so true on many leading secular campuses.

So we must apologize for our genuine mistreatment of others, but we should not assume or necessarily believe the rhetoric that the Christians are the mean, abusive ones. I do not find that to be true.

Don't Accept the "Born That Way" Falsehood

In the larger societal debate, it is taken as absolute dogma that people are gay or lesbian because they are born that way. Problem is, there is no data whatsoever that either indicates or proves this. In their official statement regarding how sexual orientation develops, the American Psychiatric Association admits:

> There is no consensus among scientists about the exact reasons that an individual develops a heterosexual, bisexual, gay or lesbian orientation. Although much research has examined the possible genetic, hormonal, developmental, social and cultural influences on sexual orientation, no findings have emerged that permit scientists to

conclude that sexual orientation is determined by any particular factor or factors.[1]

Most scholars of various ideological positions realize that our sexuality is a complex thing, and nearly all agree the development of homosexual attraction likely results from the interplay of many things between nurture and nature. In fact, radical feminist and lesbian provocateur Camille Paglia explains as correctly as she does bluntly,

> No one is "born gay." The idea is ridiculous, but it is symptomatic of our overpoliticized climate that such assertions are given instant credence by gay activists and their media partisans. I think what gay men are remembering is that they were born different.[2]

But just as sure, it is not a choice, as we typically think about choice. This either/or dichotomy that's been created around this question is wrong because it is too simplistic. Our psychosexual nature is a tad more complex.

This point is important because it is used to frame this debate in its discriminatory subplot: If people are born this way, how can anyone say it's wrong to oppose anything that is so central to who they are? But none of the exhaustive and advanced research conducted so far gives any indication this is "just how someone is" as is ethnicity, gender, or race.

On top of this, don't we diminish someone's humanity when we define them by just one factor, including their sexuality? People are far more than that.

Don't Accept the "Jim Crow" Accusation

It is not uncommon to hear the charge against people who defend natural marriage and a Christian sexual ethic that we are just like those who would have denied African-Americans their basic rights a few decades ago. That we are on the wrong side of history, behind the slow arc of justice. Such a comparison is abhorrent.

Racism is a full-bred social and human evil. Full stop.

Holding the conviction that marriage is about a man and woman, about providing children the opportunity to be loved and raised by their married mother and father is a universal social good.

Are we to believe that saying a man cannot marry another man is equal to telling black citizens they cannot sit on this bus, cannot take a meal at that lunch counter, cannot use this bathroom or water fountain, are not allowed in this part of town, or can't stay the night in this hotel? That they don't have the right to vote?

The comparison is not only ridiculous, it is nothing short of vile. Not only should we not believe it, we should never let it stand because it is both false and terribly manipulative. And most African-Americans know it's an affront to the seriousness of the many long decades of injustice they suffered and overcame. The comparison is insulting.

Don't Accept that Male and Female Are Optional for the Family

If we are to accept the same-sex family as socially virtuous, we have to accept the premise that male and female, husbands and wives, mothers and fathers are merely optional for the family, like vanilla or chocolate ice cream. Their value lies only in one's preference for them. Otherwise, who needs them?

This is a very radical and novel view of humanity and what it means to be human as gender-distinct beings. This ideology's effects will not be small and should not be tolerated.

Don't Assume LGBT Identified Friends Don't Want Something Better

Many people, regardless of their story, seem from all appearances to be happy and content with their lives. But nearly every story of an adult coming to Christ starts that way. "I seemed happy and altogether, but I was a mess deep down inside." All people are broken and seeking something more for their lives. This is no less true of our banker friend, our Korean neighbors, the person we carpool to work with, or the lesbian woman whose son is on your boys' soccer team. We must never shrink from sharing the great hope and transformation Jesus has given to us because we can never tell what such watering will do for that seed in their soul.

GLENN T. STANTON is the director of global family formation studies at Focus on the Family as well as a fellow at the Institute of Marriage and Family Canada in Ottawa. He is the author of nine books on various aspects of marriage, gender, and sexuality as well as a contributor to many others. His most recent books are *The Ring Makes All the Difference* and *Loving My (LGBT) Neighbor*.

— 22 —

Transgender: Truth and Compassion

ALAN SHLEMON

Imagine a woman tells you, "I'm transgender. You can call me Michael." It's obvious she's female, but she's asking you to call her by a man's name. What do you do?

Many people today reject the notion that gender is a fixed trait based on one's biological sex. Rather, they believe gender is a social construction. As feminist and social theorist Simone de Beauvoir wrote, "One is not born, but rather becomes, woman."[1] Anatomy, therefore, is not destiny. One can choose what gender one wants to be.

Though this sounds counterintuitive, the culture is buying it. They are sympathetic to the plight of transgender people. They believe "Michael" is a man trapped in a woman's body and they're willing to accommodate the transgender perception.

Recently, a woman complained to the management of a fitness gym after she was startled to see a man in the women's locker room. The public relations department responded by saying, "Guests may use all gym facilities based on their sincere self-reported gender identity."[2] In other words, if you're a man but believe you're a woman, you can use the women's locker room. Concerned by the gym's policy, the woman warned other women at the gym about the transgender person. Management asked her to stop. When she refused, the gym cancelled her membership.

That's why it's not surprising *Time* magazine called transgender the next civil rights movement.[3] They predict a cultural shift as significant as that toward African-Americans and (though not parallel) homosexuals.

Christians, then, face another great challenge. The culture thinks they're backward-thinking on moral issues, bigoted about homosexuality, and probably biased against transgender people. We need to move forward with truth and grace, the way Jesus did.

That requires becoming a new kind of apologist. We can't simply know what Scripture says because most of our culture rejects biblical authority. Instead, science is king in today's world. Apologists need to be savvy enough to know the truth revealed in Scripture (special revelation) and in science (general revelation). Both sources of knowledge come from God and, as a result, conform to each other.

As you learn the truth about transgender people from both Scripture and science, it will cause you to have compassion for them. Because Jesus had vast knowledge of those around him, he knew they were lost and hurting. That's what led him to act out of compassion.

Following in the footsteps of Christ, the new kind of apologist integrates both truth and compassion in his response. Knowing the truth entails knowing what Scripture says, what science says, and understanding the experience of transgender people. If we are steeped in this truth, it will transform us to have compassion and affect how we treat transgender people.

Know the Truth

Although Scripture is largely silent about transgender, it does speak directly to the broader question of the created order, gender, and sexual behavior. It turns out we have a biblical grounding for the gender roles we intuitively know to be true.

In the beginning, God followed a pattern of creating and separating. He created the universe and separated the heavens from the earth. He created the light and separated it from the night. He created the waters and separated it from the ground. He created creatures and separated humans from animals.

When God made humanity, he made two sexes: male and female. Though separate, they come together to create something more whole than by themselves. That's why God ordained a man to leave his parents and join his wife in a one-flesh union (Genesis 2:24). By following the gender role that correlates with your biological sex, a man and a woman can begin a family, the fundamental unit of society.

There's no scriptural indication that a person's perceived gender should differ from his biological sex. Anatomy is intended to denote gender identity.

Though gender complementarity is explicitly taught in Scripture, it's also evident from science. Even a non-Christian is hard pressed to deny the obvious anatomical and physiological reality. Men and women are, by virtue of their anatomy, a physiological complement to one another. The male and female sex organs not only *fit* together, they *function* together. Their shape, size, fluids, tissue type—everything about their anatomy and physiology—tells us they are made to work together. As a result, men and women sexually function together.

What evidence do we have that humans are made for heterosexual sex? When a couple engages in a conjugal act, *they can create another human being*. In fact, the sex organ is the only body part that *requires another human being of the opposite sex* to fulfill its ultimate function. Sperm and egg never actualize their full potential until they unite. The only way that's possible is through male-female sex. That can't happen unless we affirm that biology denotes gender identity. Then, male-female complementarity can achieve its purpose.

What Is Transgender?

In order to understand the transgender person, it's critical to understand the relationship between biology and gender identity. Your biological sex is a *physical* trait that's determined at conception. Gender identity is a *nonphysical* trait that develops from birth through young adulthood. It's the part of your personality that contains your beliefs about whether you are male or female. A person has both a conscious and subconscious gender identity.

In most cases, your gender identity follows your biological sex. A boy usually develops a conscious and a subconscious gender identity that's male. A girl usually develops a female gender identity. When gender identity matches biology, this results in heterosexuality.

It's possible, though, for a person to develop a gender identity that's different from his or her biological sex. Male homosexuals have a conscious gender identity that's male, but most (though not all) have a subconscious gender identity that's female.

A man who is transgender, similar to a homosexual, has a female subconscious gender identity. What sets him apart is that he also has a female conscious gender identity. That's why (unlike a homosexual man) he might say he feels like a woman trapped in a man's body. The converse would be true with a female transgender person. The reality is more nuanced than this, but these charts summarize this concept.

XY— BORN MALE	Biological sex	Conscious gender identity	Subconscious gender identity
Heterosexual	Male	Male	Male
Homosexual	Male	Male	Female
Transgender	Male	Female	Female

XX— BORN FEMALE	Biological sex	Conscious gender identity	Subconscious gender identity
Heterosexual	Female	Female	Female
Homosexual	Female	Female	Male
Transgender	Female	Male	Male

Transgender people feel like they are trapped inside a body that is incongruent with their perceived gender. As you can imagine, this leads to a tremendous amount of psychological and emotional distress. Many of them are also stigmatized by society. Sadly, 41 percent of transgender people attempt suicide (compared to 1.6 percent of the general population).[4] They are deeply hurting inside.

That's why many of them attempt to change their body with hormones, drugs, and sex-change surgery. Instead of changing their gender identity to match their biology, they want to change their biology to match their gender identity. An obvious concern with the latter approach is that while it's not possible to mistake your biological sex, it *is* possible to mistake your perceived gender.

The notable exception is someone who is born intersex (formerly called hermaphrodite). They have malformed or sexually ambiguous genitals, and it's not immediately clear whether they are male or female. Doctors encourage the parents to decide on a gender, with their counsel, but it's possible the choice they make leads to gender confusion in later life.

For example, a genetically male child can be born with a severe phallic defect. The doctors surgically resect what's left of the male sex organs and attempt to make his genitals look more female. The doctors and parents hope that by raising the child as a girl, the child will become one.

This approach assumes that gender is wholly a social construction. You can't make a girl, though, by altering a boy's body, infusing him with female hormones, and treating him like a girl. Genetically male children who are born intersex still have a Y chromosome that drives their development into a male child. They also lack ovaries and the accompanying female hormones.

One study followed boys who were reassigned as girls shortly after birth. Years later, they all engaged in male-typical behaviors including aggressiveness, rough-and-tumble play, and sexual arousal by females. Despite being surgically, socially, and legally reassigned as females, they were still boys. Most of them who learned later in life that they were genetically male wished to become men again.[5] Why? Because gender is not merely a social construct, but innately tied to one's biological sex.

Transgender adults who get sex-change operations (transsexuals) fair no better. Although some will say they are content with their new gender, most still have the same emotional and psychological problems they had prior to surgery.[6] Dr. Paul McHugh, former director of the department of psychiatry at Johns Hopkins Hospital, candidly regrets his institution's complicity with sex-change surgeries. He believes, as the field of medicine has known for a century, that being transgender is not a healthy state. "We psychiatrists...would do better to concentrate on trying to fix their minds and not their genitalia," he writes. "We have wasted scientific and technical resources and damaged our professional credibility by collaborating with madness rather than trying to study, cure, and ultimately prevent it."[7]

Though Dr. McHugh and others recognize the problem with transgender people is not with their body but with their mind, many health professionals still don't. According to modern medicine, it's inaccurate (and politically incorrect) to say something is wrong with a transgender person. Therefore, their psychological problems are often left untreated. They think sex reassignment surgery will solve their psychological problems, but they are mystified when their symptoms persist.

That's why many transsexuals regret their surgeries.[8] They have irreversibly changed their bodies without their psychological distress being resolved. This is an indication that the transgender impulse and subsequent surgery is a mistake. That, however, doesn't fit the cultural narrative that you are the gender you believe yourself to be. The LGBT community that once supported their transition no longer accepts them. They vilify and intimidate transsexuals who speak out and warn others.[9] So, whether they change their sex or remain transgender, they remain broken and hurt. They long for hope and healing.

Treat Them with Compassion

The new kind of apologist knows this truth about the brokenness of the transgender person and is transformed by it. That way, before they offer their arguments,[10] they are motivated by compassion for transgender people. Otherwise, what they say won't matter or, worse, will come off as callous and harsh.

The truth and compassion approach is the one Jesus, the perfect apologist, took. He understood people better than anyone else. His knowledge was perfect and, consequently, compassion flowed freely.

The truth we've learned about transgender people is a sober reminder that we live in a fallen world. These people have been hurt. The culture has lied to them and medical professionals have been complicit in their gender-identity confusion. We need to speak truth to them, but it must be motivated by compassion. Here's what we can do.

First, make your relationship with transgender people a top priority. It doesn't have to be *the* top priority, but put it high on the list. Relationships are the bridge we use to communicate with each other, especially things that are difficult to say. Your ability to speak the truth in love will be a function of your relationship with them. By knowing them personally, you'll discover their unique situation. This should evoke the compassion you need to speak with precision and care. Therefore, build your friendship first and make your arguments second.

If you're not close to them, consider that you might not be the right person to speak frankly about their life. This chapter began with a hypothetical conversation with a transgender person, a woman whose gender identity is male. How would you respond if she asks you to call her Michael? The answer depends on your relationship with her. If you're a friend or family member, then speak the truth with compassion. If she is a casual acquaintance or you just met, speaking truth will seem presumptive or out of place.

Second, family rules apply only to those inside the family.[11] It's possible you have a transgender friend who claims to be Christian. Scripture calls them to live according to the commands of Christ. It also authorizes believers to judge each other's behavior to see if it lines up with the biblical standard (1 Corinthians 5:12-13). That means your relationship with them should be similar to relationships with other Christians. You're not making special rules for your transgender friend. You're holding all people who identify as Christian to the same Christlike standard. In this case, their pursuit of a transgender identity rejects a God-given identity. Your prayer and goal is to "restore such a one in a spirit of gentleness" (Galatians 6:1-2 NASB). You would expect them to do the same for you. That's because Christian friends spur one another on toward godly living (Hebrews 10:24).

On the other hand, if your transgender friend doesn't claim to be a Christian, family rules don't apply. We can't expect non-Christians to live like Christians. Of course we want transgender people to recognize their perceived gender is not correct. We also want them to make safe choices. That means we should set proper expectations for ourselves about them. Even though we might ask someone to change how they live, we have to realize they are not motivated to act according to God's commands. If we want them to live like Christ, they need Christ to live in them first.

Third, focus on the gospel. Apologists can craft clever arguments in defense of their views. As a professional apologist, though, I recognize that apologetics is a means to an end and not an end in itself. My initial motivation with a nonbeliever is to present the gospel of Jesus, an offer of pardon for their crimes against God. Only when they reject it or want clarification do I offer an apologetic response.

I take that approach with everyone: a Muslim, atheist, homosexual, or transgender. In most cases where a nonbeliever has changed how he lived, it was because he first committed his life to Christ. Then, the Holy Spirit transformed him from the inside out. The Spirit changed his heart and desires and then changed his life. As the saying goes, God catches his fish first, and then he cleans them. We want our transgender friend or family member to change their relationship with God first. Then, other changes will come more easily.

Transformed

Transgender people are beguiled by a false belief. They don't think their biology determines their gender. Like the emperor's new clothes, the culture is complicit in this deception. Few people are willing to tell them the truth.

The challenge transgender people face is not with their bodies. That's why a physical solution can't resolve the problem. Their only hope for lasting satisfaction and peace is not from a change in their bodies, but a transformation of their souls. Only the Great Physician can do that.

ALAN SHLEMON is an author and public speaker for Stand to Reason and is known for teaching on some of the most controversial issues of our time, such as abortion, evolution, homosexuality, bioethics, and Islam. He has been a guest on both TV and radio, and has spoken to thousands of adults and students across the country at churches, conferences, and college campuses.

— 23 —

An Apologetic for Religious Liberty

JAMES TONKOWICH

Fifty years ago, no one would be writing a chapter in a book on apologetics about how to defend religious freedom in America. Religious freedom was rightly regarded as our birthright—our birthright as human beings and our birthright as American citizens. But in fifty years, the landscape has changed dramatically.

Today politicians, activists, the media, and federal courts denigrate religious conviction as nothing more than "irrational" prejudice springing from "animus" toward those with whom religious people disagree.[1] Why then should people be free to hate? The United States Justice Department in *Hosanna-Tabor Lutheran School v. Equal Employment Opportunity Commission* argued before the Supreme Court that churches and religious organizations should not have the freedom to make hiring decisions based on their internal religious criteria. And a New Mexico Supreme Court justice commented on a ruling against Christian defendants that compromising "the very religious beliefs that inspire their lives" is necessary as "the price of citizenship."[2]

In twenty-first-century America, if we do not defend religious freedom—ours and everyone else's—we are in danger of losing it altogether and along with it every other freedom we hold dear.

Religious Freedom and Human Nature

This is an apologetic to defend religious freedom or, if you wish, religious liberty. That would be obvious except that the soft and slippery phrases "religious toleration" and "freedom of worship" have crept into political, media, and popular speech. The claim is that religious freedom, religious toleration, and freedom of worship all mean the same thing—but nothing could be further from the truth.

Let us look at true religious freedom and then we can consider the counterfeits.

In the face of persecution early in the third century AD, the great Christian apologist Tertullian (AD 160–220) wrote a letter to Scapula, the Roman proconsul at Carthage in North Africa. In his letter, Tertullian presented a new idea in a world of state mandated religious conformity and coercion. He argued for religious freedom based upon intrinsic human rights. Tertullian wrote "[I]t is a fundamental human right, a privilege of nature, that every man should worship according to his own convictions."[3] And therein lies the heart of religious freedom, which separates it from religious toleration or freedom of worship.

Religious freedom is a human birthright. Everyone on the globe is entitled to religious freedom simply by having been born. Governments, if they are just, will recognize that birthright.

From a Christian point of view, we were created in the image of God with freedom. Adam and Eve were faced with a choice to believe God and abstain from eating from the forbidden tree or to believe the serpent and disobey God. In the wake of their bad judgment, we are free to believe or not believe, live in accordance with God's truth or flout it, and we, like Adam and Eve, will be held accountable for the choices we have freely made.

As Christians then, it is our duty to extend to others the freedom God extends to us. God does not coerce us into belief, and we have no right to coerce each other. That is, all people have a right to religious freedom, and since every right has a corresponding obligation, everyone has an obligation to grant religious freedom to everyone else.

Having said that, you don't have to be a Christian to believe in religious freedom. Men and women with no religious convictions, vague religious convictions, and assorted faiths all believe that we have a right to our own minds and our own consciences. People on the political right yell just as loudly as those on the left when they feel someone is unjustly trying to impose their way of thinking or their morality on the rest of us.

The "Don't Tread on Me" flag may be a relic from the American Revolution, but the sentiment is still alive and well today. We hunger for freedom, and freedom begins with freedom over our inner life, that is, with religious freedom.

The American founders, including Thomas Jefferson and James Madison, understood this. They read Tertullian and fully agreed with him. Madison wrote, "The Religion then of every man must be left to the conviction and conscience of every man; and it is the right of every man to exercise it as these may dictate. This right is in its nature an unalienable right."[4]

You and I are the only ones able to decide what we will believe and we are answerable to God. Since the Creator and Ruler of the universe has a claim on us, Madison went on, that claim "is precedent, both in time and in degree of obligation, to the claims of Civil Society." And if religion is beyond the claims of civil society, "still less can it be subject to that of the Legislative Body."

This was the thinking behind the religious freedom provision in the First Amendment to the Constitution: "Congress shall make no law respecting an establishment of religion, or prohibiting the free exercise thereof."

Religious freedom includes the right to believe as you wish, live according to your beliefs, raise your family according to your beliefs, petition the government according to your beliefs, evangelize, and convert from one faith to another, and all without government interference. Is that because of the First Amendment? No. It is because religious freedom is our birthright as human beings. The First Amendment simply forbids the government from robbing us of that inalienable birthright.

Counterfeit Religious Freedom

Religious toleration in marked contrast is not the gift of God given to us by birthright. Religious toleration is the gift of the government extended or taken away based on political expediency and the desire of the state to manage religion and religious believers. As Becket Fund founder Kevin Seamus Hasson put it in his book *The Right to Be Wrong*:

> The authority to choose to tolerate presumes the authority *not* to tolerate. Any government that thinks it is being generous, or shrewd, or pragmatic to put up with dissent faiths necessarily believes it has the power to persecute them if circumstances change. Tolerance, in short, is just a policy choice of the government, not a right of the people. And policy choices can be reversed.[5]

Religious toleration recognizes no inalienable rights and puts everyone's inner life—believers as well as unbelievers—in the hands of the government. In short, it forces us to render unto Caesar the things that are God's (Matthew 22:21).

We can see the difference early in the history of the United States. While the Constitution did not allow Congress to create a "Church of the United States," the individual states could and many did have state churches. Dissenters were tolerated, not free.

In Connecticut the state church was the Congregational Church. Because of that, Connecticut forced Baptists and others to pay taxes to support Congregational churches and clergy. Dissenters were fined for not attending Congregational churches on Sundays. And while their worship was tolerated, they were often denied the use of meetinghouses and their clergy were often denied the ability to perform legally binding weddings.

"[W]hat religious privileges we enjoy," the Baptists in Danbury, Connecticut, wrote to then President Thomas Jefferson in 1800, "we enjoy as favors granted, and not as inalienable rights: and these favors we receive at the expense of such degrading acknowledgements, as are inconsistent with the rights of freemen." Religious toleration is, in short, degrading and most assuredly not the same as religious freedom.

"Freedom of worship" is a restrictive type of religious toleration. Freedom of worship is the government's permission to engage privately in certain god-oriented, free-time activities. You may study the Bible, go to church, pray, say the Rosary, and discuss amongst yourselves all you'd like just as long as you do it in private. Keep it behind the church walls or inside your home, but don't bring your religion out in public.

On a practical level this means no evangelism, no asserting religious-based ideas in the public square, no forming campus organizations based on religious convictions, and no running your business based on your religious faith. Such compromising of our faith is, we're increasingly told, "the price of citizenship."

Religious Freedom and All Freedoms

Yet most of us still believe that freedom rather than servitude marks true citizenship as it marks true humanity. With that in mind, understand that abridging religious freedom by sneaking in language about religious toleration or freedom of worship destroys not just religious freedom but all of our freedoms, since without religious freedom, all the rest are a sham.

The same First Amendment that first and foremost guarantees religious freedom also guarantees freedom of speech, freedom of the press, freedom to assemble, and freedom to petition the government for change. To that list we can add economic freedom, freedom to choose our friends and associates, and the freedom to make a myriad of other legitimate choices.

Consider: What if you are granted "freedom of speech," yet are not permitted to articulate your most deeply held religious beliefs? You could talk about sports, the weather, celebrities, and TV shows, but not about the ideas that inspire and motivate your life. That kind of freedom of speech would be hollow and meaningless.

Freedom of assembly is not free if you cannot assemble over the truths that are most dear to you. Freedom to petition the government does us no good if we can petition the government only for things that have nothing to do with our faith. Traffic laws or banking regulations might be okay topics for petition, but not issues of life or marriage or war or the poor since our advocacy may be the result of our religious convictions.

So it goes with all our freedoms. Take away the right to make up our own minds about matters relating to life, morality, and God and what is left is servitude, not freedom. If the government can control our thoughts, convictions, and consciences, we are in bondage of the worst sort, and living in bondage is contrary to the gift of freedom that goes with our human nature.

Yes, But…

Many have objected that religious freedom is simply an excuse for just about any behavior. Certainly this has been part of the argument against religious freedom in the recent debates about gender, sexuality, marriage, abortion, contraception, and healthcare. Religious freedom, we are told, is simply a pretext for evil forms of discrimination.

First, none of our freedoms are absolute, including religious freedom. Just as freedom of speech does not include yelling "Fire!" in a crowded theater when there is no fire, so freedom of religion has limits. In fact, the history of religious freedom in America is the history of trying to define those limits—a history we continue to write today.

To use an easy example, the government should prevent someone bent on restoring ancient Aztec religion from initiating human sacrifices. Fine, but what about animal sacrifices in suburban neighborhoods? In *Church of Lukumi Babalu Aye v. Hialeah, Florida*, the Supreme Court decided for the animal-sacrificing church. What about the use of drugs in religious rituals? The Supreme Court found against religious worshipers who used peyote in *Employment Division v. Smith*. In response, however, Congress passed the Religious Freedom Restoration Act (RFRA) in 1993.

RFRA affirms the central importance of upholding religious freedom. To do that it stipulates a four-part criterion before the government can infringe on religious freedom. First, the religious belief that inspires the practice in question must be sincerely held. Second, the government, as a rule, may not substantially burden the free exercise of religion. Third, the government may infringe on religious freedom only if there is a compelling government interest in limiting religious practice. And finally, the government is required to use the least restrictive means of realizing its compelling interest—that is, it must tread as lightly as possible.

That is because, as Tertullian wrote to Scapula, "one man's religion neither harms nor helps another man." Or to quote what Jefferson wrote acknowledging Tertullian, "The legitimate powers of government extend to such acts only as are injurious to others. But it does me no injury for my neighbour to say there are twenty gods, or no god. It neither picks my pocket nor breaks my leg."

Thus, even in our law, individual religious freedom comes first, and we insist that the government prove that religious freedom must be restricted before it proceeds.

Another objection to religious freedom is that it causes conflicts. John Shattuck, who served as assistant secretary of state for Democracy, Human Rights, and Labor under President Clinton, made this argument at a 2002 human rights conference at Harvard University. Shattuck said, "Freedom of religion is predicated upon the existence of more than one religion. But a multiplicity of religions has always meant conflict, and religious conflict often led to war and human devastation. This was the state of reality for centuries and millennia, and it is hardly a ringing endorsement of religious freedom."[6]

This idea that religious freedom causes conflict, however, has been completely discredited. Looking at the history of religious freedom and religious oppression, scholars Monica Duffy Toff, Daniel Philpott, and Timothy Shah conclude that governments that do not extend religious freedom to their citizens "encourage pathological forms of religious politics, including religion-based terrorism and religion-related civil wars."[7] That is, religious coercion breeds radicalism, conflict, and violence while religious liberty contributes to civil tranquility.

This would in no way have surprised the American founders who included religious freedom in the Constitution for the sake of "domestic tranquility" in the new republic.

Finally, there are those who object that all this talk about defending religious freedom is simply a way for Christians to impose their way of thinking on everyone else. If that is the reason some Christians defend religious freedom these days, they are dishonest examples of what they advocate.

Religious freedom is about freedom for everyone: religious believers of any and all sorts as well as those who have no religious beliefs. The most important religious freedom to protect is not the freedom of the majority but the freedom of minority religions, unpopular religions, and religions that challenge conventional ideas. To use an example cited earlier, in 1800 the established Congregationalists in Connecticut did not need anyone to protect their religious freedom. It was the despised Baptists who needed protection. Today the law needs to protect Muslim women denied jobs in retail for wearing headscarves,[8] Sihk children wearing ceremonial daggers to school,[9] or Catholic midwives who refuse to participate in abortions.[10] Religious voices that echo the values and priorities of the prevailing culture need no protection; the ones who need it are those who stand against "what everyone thinks" and force everyone to think again.

As for the defense of religious liberty, this has been, through most of history, the role of Christians. And we Christians have no choice but to take up that role once again.

JAMES TONKOWICH is a freelance writer, speaker, and commentator on spirituality, religion, and public life. He is the author of *The Liberty Threat: The Attack on Religious Freedom in America Today* and *Pears, Grapes, and Dates: A Good Life After Mid-Life*. Jim and his wife Dottie have been married for nearly forty years. They have a married son and two fantastic grandchildren. Jim's articles and essays can be found at www.JimTonkowich.com.

Interview with John Njoroge
SEAN MCDOWELL

Would you agree with the claim that we need a new kind of apologetics?

Yes, I would. I actually believe that the vision for a new approach to doing apologetics is long overdue. As paradoxical as this might sound, I believe that we apologists have contributed toward the unfortunate slide of the church toward anti-intellectualism. We have done so by giving an unfortunate impression of what it means to be a Christian intellectual, thus unwittingly encouraging our brothers and sisters to shun the pursuit together with the label.

The weight of this problem was made evident to me recently when I was invited to speak at a major university in an African country in a meeting that was organized by one of the most effective campus ministries in that country. Unfortunately, the ministry has had some bad experiences with apologists, and when they found out that I was an apologist, they canceled the meeting at the last minute.

Thankfully, I was still able to meet with the organizers, and I asked them what happened. Their description of what an apologist does was very sad—it's mostly a person who attacks other Christians and will not hesitate to do so even when the Christians being attacked would welcome an opportunity to align their views better with the Scriptures should the apologist turn out to be right. Essentially, they continued, the priority for an apologist is not reaching the lost or demonstrating God's love to all people; he is mainly concerned with being right and pointing out where others are wrong.

Of course that is a gross mischaracterization of much of apologetics today, but we must ask why we have given the Christian world such a distorted view of what it means to be a disciple of Jesus Christ whose mind and heart have been formed by his person and teaching. We must go further and ask how we can correct this problem while remaining steadfastly committed to the faith once and for all delivered to the saints.

And correct it we must if we intend to be faithful witnesses to the gospel in the coming generations. I come from Africa. The church is growing at a phenomenal rate in that part of the world. For better or for worse, the most popular forms of Christianity in Africa, and in the world as a whole, are the Pentecostal and Charismatic movements. In my experience, these are the very sections of the church in which apologetics is at once visibly absent and most needed.

Why do you think apologetics has a bad name in some circles?

I think there are several reasons for that. First, the church has neglected apologetics for so long that we have, for the most part, perfected a method of doing church that automatically rules it out and may even be antithetical to it. For that reason, many of our church leaders don't even know they need it. Even when they recognize its importance, they think it is for people with a skeptical outlook on life. So the consensus in many of our churches today seems to be that we know what it means to be Christian, and that doesn't have anything to do with apologetics.

Second, I think we apologists bear some of the blame. Apologetics tends to attract people who like to argue and to win. We love a good fight, and we love to prove things. There is nothing wrong with that. But when being right becomes an end in itself—when it is separated from a deep-seated wholeness of the gospel that is grounded in genuine love for God and neighbor—it can easily become a weapon that drives people away from God. It is wonderful to be right, but the obsession to prove that we are right is not always right. The opposite extreme is to cling to a false view of humility. Confidence in what is true is not opposed to humility. The solution is to grow in all areas of our lives and character, not just in knowledge (2 Peter 1:5-9).

Third, I would point to the nature of the education we receive today. Given the staggering amount of information at our disposal, we can't help but specialize in particular fields. Unfortunately, the need to specialize makes it really hard for us to understand each other well enough to lead well-integrated lives. We naturally value what we ourselves do, and that can make it hard for us to have a strong appreciation for what others do. In the context of the church, an expository preacher may think that anyone who does anything different is doing something of lesser value. If I labor to reach the lost, I may be tempted to look down on those who strive to define a role for the gospel in politics, and so on.

Apologists find it hard to play this game within their own field. We are like referees calling out fouls in games in which we are assumed to be nonparticipants. The biblical solution to this problem is simply ingenious—we are called to work together as a body, using our gifts to edify each other. We are incomplete without the gifts and talents of others.

What misperceptions do people often have about apologetics?

Perhaps the most common concern I hear among Christians in Africa is that it is prayer and the power of the Holy Spirit that are needed in evangelism and in the proclamation of the gospel. To focus on acquiring knowledge in spiritual matters is to usurp the power of the Holy Spirit. Knowledge, after all, puffs up, and we all know that you can never argue anyone into the kingdom of God. Sadly, there have been people who were known to have been on fire for God, but the fire all but vanished after they received theological training. This appears to be a confirmation that the search for knowledge is a dangerous thing. I was warned by many sincere believers against going to Bible college and a secular university to prepare for ministry.

What can apologists do to counter these perceptions?

The one practical strategy I have found to be the most effective in teaching apologetics among people who are suspicious of it is to lead with Scripture. This is very helpful in Africa where most people are highly suspicious of any theologizing or intellectualizing of the faith. It is also very helpful among people who have been in the church for a long time and have learned to practice their faith with no reference to apologetics. Such people tend to respect the Word of

God, so if you can show them that what you're trying to do is firmly grounded in Scripture, they are willing to listen. And if anyone wants to argue about this, then he or she has to argue with the Word of God, not with me. Thus it is vitally important that we make a strong biblical case for the indispensability of apologetics in our churches.

Like any other servant of our Lord Jesus Christ, apologists must begin by cultivating Christlikeness so that it becomes abundantly clear that they are motivated by their genuine love for God and neighbor. That's the top priority in our matching orders. As important as we know apologetics to be, it is, in the end, a means to an end, and the end is knowing God. Apologetics may be necessary in our proclamation of the gospel today, but it is not sufficient. We must seek to be formed spiritually by the gospel of the kingdom of God preached by Jesus before we can become bona fide spokespeople for Jesus Christ.

JOHN NJOROGE is a member of the speaking team at Ravi Zacharias International Ministries (RZIM). He speaks frequently on university campuses, churches, and conferences around the world. John is the host of the African versions of RZIM's radio programs *Let My People Think* and *Just Thinking*, which are heard in several countries across the African continent. He is completing a PhD in philosophy at the University of Georgia. He lives in Atlanta with his wife, Leah, and their two boys, Jonathan and Benjamin.

— 24 —

Advocating Intelligent Design with Integrity, Grace, and Effectiveness

CASEY LUSKIN

Each year the scientific case for intelligent design (ID) becomes more compelling as peer-reviewed pro-ID scientific studies and papers by non-ID scientists reveal more evidence of design in nature. Yet simultaneously, prominent cultural and intellectual voices become increasingly louder both in their disdain for ID and their certainty that it is wrong. How can the Christian apologist sort through these starkly contrasting viewpoints and decide whether ID is true, and if true, whether ID is worth expending the effort to defend against seemingly powerful opposition. To put the question another way: *Should ID matter for the apologist?*

This chapter will outline the strong scientific case for ID, and explain why ID is a vital tool for the apologist who wishes to scientifically demonstrate that humanity—and indeed life and the universe—were designed.

Is Intelligent Design True?

Countless students are taught each year by professors with impeccable credentials that there is no evidence for intelligent design, and neo-Darwinian evolution is an unassailable fact. Unless a student proactively researches the topic, she has little chance of disputing her professors' doctrinaire declarations. Is there any hope?

In fact, there is much. With only moderate study, one can articulate the case for ID and answer most common objections. Many excellent books have been written that cover these arguments,[1] but the basics can be sketched here.

The most common objection is that ID is not science but religion. To understand why this objection fails, we must first appreciate how ID theorists argue for design.

Intelligent design is a scientific theory that holds that many features of the universe and living things are best explained by an intelligent cause rather than an undirected process like natural selection. ID aims to discriminate between objects generated by material mechanisms and those caused by intelligence.

ID theorists start by observing how intelligent agents act when they design things. By studying human agents, we learn that intelligent agents generate high levels of information. The type of information that indicates design is generally called specified complexity, or complex and specified information (CSI). Something is complex if it is unlikely. But complexity or unlikelihood alone are not enough to infer design. To detect design, we must also find specification—where an event or object matches a pattern.

To understand these concepts, imagine we're touring famous mountains. First we visit Mount Rainier, a volcano near Seattle. If all the possible combinations of peaks, ridges, and gullies are considered, the exact shape of Mount Rainier is extremely unlikely. But we won't infer design simply because it has a complex shape, which we can easily explain through natural geological processes like uplift and erosion. There's no special pattern to the shape of Mount Rainier, so we don't infer design.

Next, we visit Mount Rushmore. It also has a very unlikely shape, but it matches a recognizable pattern—the faces of four famous presidents. Here we don't just find complexity, but also *specification*. Thus, we infer that Mount Rushmore's shape was designed.

This design argument does not depend on merely refuting evolution or other material causes. Rather, ID makes a positive argument based upon finding in nature the types of information and complexity that, *in our experience*, come from intelligence. As Stephen Meyer explains: "Our experience-based knowledge of information-flow confirms that systems with large amounts of specified complexity (especially codes and languages) invariably originate from an intelligent source—from a mind or personal agent."[2] Yet what do we find at the heart of life? A language-based, information-rich digital code in our DNA.

Another way to show that ID is science is to understand how it uses the scientific method of observation, hypothesis, experiment, and conclusion:

- *Observations:* ID theorists begin by observing that intelligent agents produce high CSI.

- *Hypothesis:* ID theorists hypothesize that if a natural object was designed, it will contain high CSI.

- *Experiment:* Scientists perform experimental tests to determine if natural objects contain high CSI. For example, mutational sensitivity tests show enzymes contain an unlikely ordering of amino acids that matches a precise sequence necessary for function—high CSI. Another empirically testable form of CSI is irreducible complexity, where a system requires a minimum set of multiple interacting parts to function, and cannot evolve in a step-by-step manner. Genetic knockout experiments show some molecular machines are irreducibly complex.

- *Conclusion:* When ID researchers find high CSI in DNA, proteins, and molecular machines, they conclude that such structures were designed.

Contrary to popular conceptions, however, ID is much broader than biology. Physical laws reveal design because they are finely tuned for life's existence.

Universal laws are complex since they exhibit unlikely settings—cosmologists have calculated that our universe is incredibly fine-tuned for life to less than one part in $10^{10^{123}}$ (that's 1 in 10 raised to the exponent of 10^{123}). We don't even have words or analogies to convey numbers this small. Yet these laws are specified because they match an extremely narrow band of values required for advanced life. This high CSI indicates design. As Nobel Laureate Charles Townes observed, "Intelligent design, as one sees it from a scientific point of view, seems to be quite real. This is a very special universe: it's remarkable that it came out just this way. If the laws of physics weren't just the way they are, we couldn't be here at all."[3]

To summarize, scientific discoveries of the past century have shown life is fundamentally based upon:

- A vast amount of CSI digitally encoded in a biochemical language in our DNA.

- A computer-like system of information-processing where cellular machinery reads, interprets, and executes the commands programmed into DNA.

- Irreducibly complex molecular machines composed of finely tuned proteins.

- Exquisite life-friendly fine-tuning of universal laws and constants.

Where, in our experience, do language-based digital code, computer-like programming, machines, and other high CSI structures come from? They have only one known source: intelligence.

The design argument briefly sketched here is entirely empirically based. It offers positive evidence for design by finding in nature the types of information and complexity that we know from experience derive from intelligent causes. One might disagree with the conclusions of ID or disfavor its larger religious implications, but one cannot reasonably claim this argument is based upon religious premises or faith. It's based upon science.

Handling Scientific Objections with Grace and Truth

An apologist could easily convey the aforementioned arguments, but will soon encounter a potentially intimidating swath of second-order objections. Is there any hope to master the issue?

Again, yes. The vast majority of objections to ID fail to address the crux of ID's argument: *Where does new information come from?* Staying focused on that key scientific question will prevent distraction by red-herring objections.

When ID critics do offer evidence-based rebuttals, they typically fall into one of three categories: inadequate, wrong, or they unwittingly confirm ID. Regardless of whether an objection holds merit, any critic offering substantive objections should be treated with graciousness and respect for seeking serious dialogue.

A classic example of an inadequate response is found in how ID critics rejoin arguments for irreducible complexity. They virtually never articulate step-by-step Darwinian accounts of how irreducibly complex molecular machines could evolve. Rather, critics typically cite mere sequence similarity between proteins (called "homology"). Such inadequate explanations ignore that reusage of similar biological parts could reflect common design rather than common descent, and do not demonstrate a Darwinian evolutionary pathway.

Another common rebuttal from critics like Richard Dawkins and Francis Collins is that our genomes contain massive amounts of useless "junk DNA," showing we arose by evolutionary mechanisms rather than design. These claims, however, are wrong. The past decade has witnessed a scientific revolution, with thousands of papers reporting widespread function for so-called junk DNA—a development ID successfully predicted.[4] Even Dawkins has backtracked, now claiming that functionality for genetic junk is "exactly what a Darwinist would hope for—to find usefulness in the living world."

Finally, recent high-profile exchanges between leading ID proponents and critics have affirmed ID arguments. In his 2013 *New York Times* bestselling book *Darwin's Doubt*, Stephen Meyer argues that intelligent design is the best explanation for the origin of the genetic information required to build the many animal body plans that appear abruptly in the Cambrian explosion. This book enjoyed a critical, though serious and respectful, review by UC Berkeley paleontologist Charles Marshall in the top journal *Science*. In a radio debate with Meyer soon thereafter, Marshall conceded that he assumes the existence of the information for the genes necessary to build animals and never explains their origin.[5]

Likewise, leading theistic evolutionist biologist Darrel Falk critiqued Meyer but acknowledged he correctly argues that neo-Darwinism faces strong criticisms from mainstream scientific authorities. Falk also admitted that "the rapid generation of body plans *de novo*" in the Cambrian is a "big mystery," which no evolutionary models can yet explain. Such prominent exchanges confirm that the arguments and evidence are trending in ID's direction.

ID's Research Program

Another common objection is that ID proponents don't do research or publish peer-reviewed scientific papers. These misconceptions are false. The ID research community has published over eighty peer-reviewed scientific publications to date,[6] and has multiple hubs of research.

Biologic Institute, led by protein scientist Douglas Axe, is developing and testing the scientific case for design in biology, conducting experimental research that shows unguided evolutionary mechanisms cannot produce new proteins. The Evolutionary Informatics Lab, founded by William Dembski and Robert Marks, has published multiple peer-reviewed articles testing computer simulations to show that evolution works only when it is actively guided by intelligence. These labs and other researchers have published pro-ID scientific papers in journals such as *Protein Science, Journal of Molecular Biology, Complexity, Journal of Advanced Computational Intelligence and Intelligent Informatics, Cell Biology International, Physics of Life Reviews, Quarterly Review of Biology, Annual Review of Genetics*, and others.

Collectively, this research is converging on a consensus: Natural selection and random mutation can produce minor changes, but many complex biological features—like new protein folds—cannot arise by unguided evolutionary mechanisms. These information-rich structures require an intelligent cause. With researchers both inside and outside the ID camp confirming ID's central arguments, the fundamentals of intelligent design are sound and the future appears bright.

Handling Heated Objections with Grace and Truth

Every ID advocate, from the guru to the newbie, will encounter unfamiliar objections. When this happens, don't worry—there's no shame in honestly admitting when you don't know an answer, and then promising to research the matter. For these situations, apologists have many good resources available. Try scouring credible ID websites like www.evolutionnews.org, www.discovery.org, www.uncommondescent.com, www.arn.org, and www.ideacenter.org to see if the objection has already been tackled.

In addition to evaluating scientific arguments, we can ask: *Does one side make serious arguments and welcome dialogue, while the other persistently resorts to personal attacks that stifle conversation?* This can help reveal which camp is behaving like the evidence is on their side, and which is compensating for a weak position.

When studying the rhetorical dynamics of this debate, I have found that ID critics often fail to address ID arguments, employing labels like "creationist," "anti-science," or "pseudoscientist" and levying ad hominem attacks like "dishonesty" or "liar." Critics use straw-man definitions of ID and focus on irrelevant issues like personal religious beliefs or motives. Such tactics are typically deployed to avoid addressing ID arguments—to shut down discussion and intimidate ID advocates into silence. Conversely, I've found ID proponents generally stay focused on the substantive questions, inviting dialogue and treating critics with respect.

Those who defend ID should emotionally and spiritually prepare to face personal attacks and not be too discouraged when they come. Not only are you in good company, but receiving ad hominem attacks often indicates you made a good argument! After all, people usually resort to emotionally charged rhetoric only because they cannot defend their position.

But how can you reach someone who resists friendly dialogue, lacks arguments, and is lashing out? By following the Bible.

Jesus and the apostles taught us to love our enemies (Matthew 5:44), to repay evil with good and bless those who persecute us (Romans 12:14-21), and to not retaliate when insulted (1 Peter 3:9). Sometimes this can be difficult. But when we respond in a loving, respectful, and informed manner, malicious critics are often surprised and suddenly open to hearing our views. Christ's commands aren't just the right thing to do—they also can be extremely effective in reaching people during heated dialogue.

Additionally, remember that your audience is often much bigger than a few uncivil critics—especially during online debates. Vocal skeptics may stridently oppose your arguments, but objective lurkers in the undecided middle can be positively influenced by a winsome and respectful reply.

The Straw-Man Definition

One common tactic among heated critics is to deploy a straw-man definition of ID, which claims: "ID says life is so complex it couldn't have evolved, therefore was created by a supernatural God." They may cite the 2005 *Kitzmiller v. Dover* case where a federal judge adopted this straw-man definition and ruled that ID is a form of religion—ignoring how pro-ID expert witnesses defined ID in his own courtroom, and ignoring ID's peer-reviewed research.[7] This critics' definition is false for two reasons.

First, it wrongly frames ID as a strictly negative argument against evolution, ignoring the positive case for design discussed previously.

Second, it wrongly claims ID appeals to the supernatural. All ID scientifically detects is the prior action of an intelligent cause. ID respects the limits of scientific inquiry and does not attempt to address religious questions about the identity of the designer.

Some may rejoin ID is hiding its true belief that the designer is God. But ID proponents never hide their personal religious views. I am intentionally open about my Christian faith whether speaking to religious audiences or secular ones. But I make clear that my belief that the designer is the God of the

Bible is not a conclusion of ID; rather, it's a religious belief I hold for separate reasons.

Indeed, the ID movement includes people of many worldviews, including Christians, Jews, Muslims, people of Eastern religious views, and even agnostics. What unites them is not some religious faith but a conviction that there is scientific evidence for design in nature.

Is ID Worth Defending?

The forgoing discussions show that ID is a compelling scientific argument, backed by credible scientists publishing peer-reviewed research, and that it is defensible even against heated objections. But just because something is defensible or true doesn't necessarily mean it's worth spending time and effort defending. Does ID matter enough to defend?

The answer is an unswerving yes. In his book *How We Believe*, atheist psychologist Michael Shermer discusses a study that surveyed "skeptics" for why they do or do not believe in God. *Issues related to scientific evidence for God and design in nature ranked as the number one reason why skeptics doubt God, and also why some believe.*

Apologists who want to demonstrate—especially to scientifically minded skeptics—that life and the universe were designed will find ID is a vital tool. To appreciate the strategic value of ID, however, we must compare ID to other views within the Christian community—creationism and theistic evolution.

ID's Advantage over Creationism

The modern theory of ID was developed in the 1980s and 1990s by scientists seeking a strictly scientific approach to studying origins. Before that time, creationism, which always mixed theology into its arguments, dominated the debate.

Many of ID's founders, such as chemist Charles Thaxton, biochemist Michael Behe, mathematician William Dembski, and philosopher and historian of science Stephen Meyer, realized that the study of information could provide a scientific basis for detecting design in nature—an approach that could appeal to the scientifically minded skeptic. Herein lies ID's advantage over creationism.

While young-earth and old-earth creationists debated the age of the earth, or whether Noah rode a dinosaur or a camel onto the ark, elite materialists were happy to dominate our culture. UC Berkeley law professor Phillip Johnson, another cofounder of the ID movement, helped reframe the origins debate to reach that cultural landscape.

As a legal scholar, Johnson saw that the most important issue was not the age of the earth or differing interpretations of Genesis. Rather, it was a fundamental question asked by everyone: *Are we the result of blind, undirected material causes or purposeful intelligent design?* By using scientific arguments and evidence to show that we are the result of intelligent design, ID directly answers this crucial worldview question.

Of course, various types of creationism can encourage people wanting to reconcile the Bible with science. But for apologists wanting to reach skeptics and scientifically demonstrate design, ID should be of supreme interest.

However, ID doesn't answer every important question. As a science, ID does not attempt to address religious or theological questions about the designer's identity or the proper meaning of Genesis. Of course many good philosophical, theological, and historical arguments address those important issues—but they go beyond ID.

Apologists should thus take ID for what it's worth: It's a compelling scientific argument showing that life and the universe were designed. Yet recently, another camp has arisen within the Christian community that claims science does not support ID, and ID doesn't matter. This camp is called theistic evolution (TE).

ID's Advantage over Theistic Evolution

Theistic evolutionists (who sometimes call themselves "evolutionary creationists") are Christians who believe that God used material evolutionary mechanisms to create life. To understand how ID interfaces with theistic evolution—and why ID is a better approach—we must first define evolution.

Evolution can mean something as benign as (1) "life has changed over time," or it can entail more controversial ideas, like (2) "all living things share common ancestry," or (3) "natural selection acting upon random mutations produced life's diversity." ID does not conflict with the observation that natural selection causes small-scale changes over time (meaning 1), or the view that all organisms are related by common ancestry (meaning 2).

However, the dominant evolutionary viewpoint today is neo-Darwinism (meaning 3), which contends that life's entire history was driven by unguided natural selection acting on random mutations—a blind, purposeless process with no direction or goals. It is this specific neo-Darwinian claim that ID directly challenges.

To the extent that theistic evolutionists accept neo-Darwinian evolution (and many do), ID conflicts with that view. (Conversely, a theistic evolutionist who thinks life's history *does* appear guided is *not* a neo-Darwinian and is an ID proponent—perhaps even unwittingly.) An important distinction between TE and ID is therefore:

- TE adopts entirely materialistic evolutionary models where life's history appears unguided (e.g., neo-Darwinism), and denies that we scientifically detect design.

- ID claims we scientifically detect design in biology and that unguided models like neo-Darwinism are inadequate.

TE advocates often think these differences are inconsequential, but ID proponents think they are crucial.

Neo-Darwinism, as defined by scientists, is a blind process of natural selection acting upon random mutations without any guidance by an external agent. When theistic evolutionists say "God guided evolution," they mean that somehow God guided an evolutionary process such that (as Francis Collins writes) it "would *appear* a random and undirected process."[8]

Whether it is theologically or philosophically coherent to claim that "God guided an apparently unguided process," I will leave to the theologians and the philosophers. ID avoids these problems by maintaining that life's history *doesn't appear unguided* and that we can scientifically detect that intelligent design was involved.

Theistic evolutionists sometimes try to obscure these differences, as when the leading TE group BioLogos asserts, "It is all intelligently designed."[9] For BioLogos, however, this is a strictly theological view for which they can provide no supporting scientific evidence. ID proponents wonder how one can speak of "intelligent design" if it's entirely hidden and undetectable. "We're promoting a scientific theory, not a theological doctrine," replies ID, "and our theory detects design through scientific observations."

Some theistic evolutionists may further reply, "Since we all believe in some form of design, our differences are small." ID proponents retort: "The differences are critical."

According to standard Darwinism, unguided material mechanisms created not just our bodies but also our brains, behaviors, and deepest desires—including our moral and religious impulses. TE surrenders to such dubious materialistic claims, claiming, as two TE advocates argued, that God's work in creation "is signed using invisible ink." This view directly clashes with Paul's declaration in Romans 1:20 that God is "clearly perceived" in nature.

And there's the rub. ID claims the scientific evidence shows life was designed. This validates Romans 1:20 and directly confronts atheism. But theistic evolutionists deny that we clearly perceive scientific evidence for design in nature, ceding to materialists some of the most important apologetic territory in the debate over religion—territory the Bible says properly belongs to theism. Even one BioLogos article admits, "Evolutionary creationism does not necessarily add apologetic value to the Christian faith."[10]

To be clear, I'm *not* saying that if one accepts Darwinian evolution then one cannot be a Christian. The grand Darwinian story is a disputable or secondary matter, and Christians may hold different views. But just because something is disputable doesn't mean it's unimportant.

TE may not be absolutely incompatible with Christianity, but it offers no scientific support for faith. Perhaps this is why William Provine writes: "One can have a religious view that is compatible with evolution only if the religious view is indistinguishable from atheism."[11]

Christian apologists should avoid TE because it is scientifically wrong, theologically unsound, and apologetically weak. ID, on the other hand, shows evidence of design in nature and offers other important advantages.

The ID Advantage

People hunger for compelling scientific arguments that can bolster their faith and persuade skeptical friends. In meeting this demand, ID offers apologists the best of both worlds:

- Unlike creationism, ID accepts the best evidence offered by mainstream science and makes a strictly scientific argument.
- Unlike theistic evolution, ID doesn't challenge orthodox Christian theology and embraces the use of science to argue for design.

True, ID has apologetic limits: it's a scientific theory that holds that some aspects of nature are best explained by an intelligent cause. If one desires to take a person to Christ on the cross, ID is not enough. But if one seeks convincing scientific arguments to show the universe and life require a designer, then, as ID's motto says, we must simply "follow the evidence wherever it leads."

The skeptical public is eager to hear about this evidence, and with some study, patience, and grace, the apologist's task of informing them shouldn't be too difficult.

CASEY LUSKIN is an attorney with graduate degrees in science and law. He works as research coordinator at Discovery Institute, and is cofounder of the Intelligent Design and Evolution Awareness (IDEA) Center. He has coauthored or contributed to multiple books, including *Traipsing Into Evolution, Intelligent Design 101, God and Evolution, Science and Human Origins, More than Myth, The Unofficial Guide to Cosmos,* and the curriculum *Discovering Intelligent Design.*

— 25 —

The Scientific Naturalist Juggernaut and What to Do About It

SCOTT SMITH

A s Western evangelicals, we live in the midst of largely secular cultures that have been deeply influenced by evolutionary science and its related worldview, naturalism. That is the view that the natural or physical/material is all that exists. There is no supernatural realm nor are there any immaterial beings[1] or any nonphysical "essential natures," like a human soul that all humans universally have in common. There are only particular bits of matter in particular combinations, and it's the view of what's real behind naturalistic evolution (NE).[2]

The Implications of Naturalism

Naturalism has practical implications for our lives. Here are just a few.

First, if there aren't any nonphysical things, then we don't think with the mind; instead, the brain thinks and believes. So people might say that computers think (maybe better than we do) or that robots can achieve consciousness (and maybe they should be protected as persons).[3]

Second, we live in cultures that separate facts, which is what science tells us, from mere values, opinions, or beliefs, which are all that ethics and religion can give us. That suggests that morality and religion are private and *up to us*, which leads us straight to relativism in both areas, but science (based on naturalism) gives us knowledge and therefore is public. How then are we to come together politically and legally as societies? We tend to discount religious appeals for public policy proposals as something that should be kept private. While we may tolerate differences in opinions and preferences, our public policy basis must be something public.

Third, any laws that discriminate on the basis of there being a nature to something cannot be tolerated. Take marriage, for example. Evangelicals and Catholics have argued that marriage has an essential nature to it, designed by God for the union of a man and a woman. But if there are no essential natures, and since this is a religious appeal, marriage can be redefined as an evolutionary development or a cultural artifact.

Naturalism is deeply embedded in Western cultures, especially in academia, the media, and government. This does not mean that everyone in such positions is an atheist. But these pressures will tend to shape believers to bifurcate their lives as Christians from their everyday lives. So naturalism undermines Christians' discipleship and loyalty to Jesus.

Strategies for Undermining Naturalism

What then can we do about naturalism? For one, we have to be aware of it and its effects.[4] In this essay, I will highlight three basic strategies for undermining naturalism, which I think can be extremely useful for pre-evangelism.[5] Then, I will look at what we need to do to help defeat naturalism's influences in our churches.

First,

1. If naturalism is true, then all that exists can be known by the five senses.

2. But there's more to what's real than what can be known by the five senses.

3. Therefore, naturalism is not true.

Scientists (and others) use their senses to make observations, to know what's real, which is good and invaluable. But isn't there more to what's real than what is physical? Consider numbers. We can represent the number five in many ways: *five, 5, v, V, cinco*, which we can detect with our sense of sight. But suppose we deleted those representations and all others. Would that destroy the number five itself? It doesn't seem so.

Or how about moral truths? What if there were no examples of murder at present? Or what if we destroyed all sentences that contain the words "murder is wrong"? Would murder still be wrong? It surely seems so. These are but two examples of things that seem to be nonphysical, yet do not fit with what naturalism says is real. And I think there are many more such things (like souls, thoughts).[6] If so, naturalism is false.

Second, we can think about choices we can make, and we can decide which one to do. We can choose to study hard or go be with friends, for example. We could have chosen the other option if we wanted. Or if we're on a jury, we weigh the evidence and render our verdict. These actions involve our ability to make decisions freely.

But with naturalism, everything is physical and subject to the laws of physics and chemistry. There's room for only one kind of cause—*state-state causation*, in which a given physical/chemical state causes another. These laws and states *dictate* all that happens *without room for real choices (free will)*. So,

1. If naturalism is true, then people do not have real free choices.

2. But we know that we do have free choices.

3. Therefore, naturalism is not true.

Many even forthrightly proclaim that naturalistic evolution is proven fact. But if NE were true, there's no way we could be rational in *deciding* it is true. So NE undermines itself.

Third, even if NE were true, we'd still be irrational to believe it.[7] Our brains would produce our thoughts and beliefs, which would be physical things, the result of just physical/chemical processes. If we survive, then our genetic traits can be passed on.

But this suggests that natural selection is not concerned with truth, for all that matters is that we survive and reproduce. *However* that happens is not important; *that* we survive is. Suppose a hominid named Paul sees a large tiger nearby. Does it matter that he believes what is true in order to survive? Not really. He could believe all sorts of implausible things, but as long as he isn't eaten, he survives. So, why think that the results of physical/chemical processes have anything to do with truth?[8]

Later in life, even Darwin realized this problem. He expressed his "horrid doubt" that "always arises whether the convictions of man's mind, which has been developed from the mind of lower animals, are of any value or at all trustworthy. Would anyone trust in the convictions of a monkey's mind, if there are any convictions in such a mind?"[9] If our beliefs don't aim at truth, *why should we trust what our brains tell us, including the theory of NE itself?*

So naturalism has deep problems. It is not true that science has disproven Christianity. Yet many young people leave the church when confronted by atheists in schools. They need good training in apologetics to help them think through naturalism and to know reasons why they should believe Christianity is true.

I sense a further problem at work among many Western evangelicals. Often we think we are being biblically faithful, but if so, why are so many people leaving our churches? Why does there seem to be such a lack of God's supernatural presence and power? I think a key reason is that *we have been deeply affected by naturalism but don't realize it.*

Naturalism is broader than its philosophical description. It is an attempt to steal our focus from God's authority, love, and power. It's a denial of his personal investment in each heart and mind.

The early Christians knew intellectually and experientially the reality of Jesus's presence and resurrection power. They abided in him and let his words abide in them (John 15:7). They also knew the reality of the unseen world, including angels, demons, and spiritual battle.

Unlike them, often we don't expect God to show up miraculously or in power. Nor do we expect to encounter or be influenced by demons. We usually don't expect God to speak to us and be *intimate* with us.

Defeating Naturalism's Influences in Our Churches

These traits are not strange developments. They are the natural outgrowth of what we have received as truly biblical. Our evangelical forefathers in the faith made several key moves, and we have been shaped by what they embraced.[10]

First, we inherited a long history in which science garnered great prestige. To be respectable, all scholars, including theologians, should do their work as a science. Evangelicals readily embraced this mindset, seeking to show that Christianity is scientific. Yet, that outlook put an empirical focus on theology, which, over time, tended to discount souls, angels, or demons as real.

Second, the modern scientific outlook tended to see creation as a grand mechanism that operates by natural laws. From the 1700s and following, people saw the universe as a closed system of matter in motion. Three tendencies resulted: (1) Over time, it became harder to conceive how God could act in a "closed" universe without also introducing new, additional energy into it. So miracles became suspect. (2) Creation is fundamentally made of matter; while some still would hold to humans being a unity of a body and an immaterial soul, that distinction has become harder to sustain over time. (3) While American evangelicals generally remained orthodox theologically, this move suggested a God who was distant or functionally deistic. Over time, the results have been to conceive of God as not being intimate, acting miraculously, or speaking with us, and to think of humans as basically physical beings.

Third, science was wed to Francis Bacon's inductive methodology, which was revered by evangelicals and others. In his view, science focuses just on empirically observable, physical causes, not any (supposed) nonphysical ones. So his methodology pushed us toward a more thoroughgoing view of creation as just physical stuff.

Fourth, modernity also bequeathed an attitude of (overly) high confidence in human reason's powers to know universal truths, even with certainty. In

America, "commonsense realism" was the expression of that mindset, and it was deeply embraced by evangelicals and the broader culture. That Christianity is true was a matter of common sense, so those evangelicals thought science's discoveries simply would support Christianity. It then became easy to think they could read God's truths right off the pages of Scripture and nature, since their reason was so capable of knowing truth. If this view is pushed, and if God is distant, then there would not be a great felt need to rely on the Holy Spirit to lead us into all truth or give us insight into things that God has not revealed in Scripture.[11]

But when Darwin's theory of evolution by natural selection became accepted by the "new" science, these naturalized kinds of moves were readily adapted into a thoroughgoing naturalistic worldview.[12] It became easier for people to drop God from their worldview, making for an easy reception of Darwinian thought.

Often we evangelicals seem ignorant of those influences and how we've been shaped by them. Instead, we simply accept our *inherited* understanding of the faith to be the same as that which was once for all delivered to the saints. But it is not. While the faith we inherited was basically doctrinally faithful, nonetheless the supporting scientific and philosophical views of God, creation, and humanity have been altered significantly. These mindsets stand in sharp contrast to those of the early church, which knew God intimately and experienced his presence and power as a lived reality. They knew the reality of the unseen realm.

But we do not. By and large, Western evangelicals have been deeply *naturalized*, or *de-supernaturalized*, so that even we, along with the culture, often accept the supposed split between facts and values. Overall, we've been left with a shell of the faith, one we still proclaim as the gospel truth, but one that has been gutted in many practical ways of its supernatural substance. No wonder then that many evangelicals tend to not experience the Lord's presence or resurrection power. No wonder that many people are turned off by what they see in our churches, for if we don't live in fullness of Spirit and truth, we'll live in our flesh. And the way we live becomes hypocritical and turns people off.[13]

In addition, our American evangelical forefathers bequeathed to us a strong distrust of religious experience. Their mindset arose from addressing several factors, such as (1) liberal theology's claim that Scripture is a record of people's experiences of God; (2) new religious movements in the nineteenth century, such as Mormonism and spiritualism; and (3) the rise of Pentecostalism, which they saw as anti-intellectual and against reason.

They also had a strong preference for the written, objective Word.[14] Scripture could be studied by reason and science since it is empirically accessible and unchanging, unlike experiences. Their values for scientific knowledge and what could be known by reason shaped their attitudes toward religious experience as something rather inferior to Scripture. Their ideal was to eliminate *anything* subjective and rely on what is objective (the Bible).

But relationships inherently involve subjectivities, whether with humans or God. Throughout Scripture, God deeply desires to be our God, for us to be his people, and for him to dwell in our midst. He has adopted us into his family, poured out his love within our hearts, and invited us into the intimacy shared by the members of the Trinity.

The effects of these cultural, historical, and philosophical moves our forefathers made in response to modernity's influences were naturalistic in that they distance God from us. We would not tend to expect miracles in a closed, mechanistic view of creation or deism. Plus, there would not be a felt need to do so if the Bible is obviously true to everyone. Moreover, we probably would not expect God to speak to us personally or show up supernaturally.[15]

These moves work together to keep Western evangelicals shackled to a form of Christianity that is orthodox doctrinally but deeply de-supernaturalized practically. But the early church was convinced of the reality of God's power and presence, and they turned the world upside down. Can we Western evangelicals hope to do that? Not without a deep repentance from our unwitting captivity to naturalism.

SCOTT SMITH, PhD in religion and social ethics, University of Southern California, is professor of ethics and Christian apologetics in the MA in Christian apologetics program at Biola University. He is the author of *In Search of Moral Knowledge: Overcoming the Fact-Value Dichotomy* and other books and essays.

— 26 —

Water that Satisfies the Muslim's Thirst

ABDU MURRAY

Night at the Islamic Center

I took my thousandth sip of water trying to quench my dry throat. Nervous energy filled Canada's second largest Islamic center that Saturday night in Toronto. I had been invited there to speak at a symposium on the topic, "The Word of God." The experience was far different from when I had walked into mosques as a youth. Until 2000, I was a serious Muslim who wanted non-Muslims, especially Christians, to see the beauty of Islam. But that night I found myself hoping to present the gospel to the dear Muslims who had invited me there. All of the more than one thousand people in attendance knew I was a former Muslim, which added to everyone's anxiety and the dryness of my mouth. And recent events and often-shaky interactions between Christians and Muslims in the West didn't help much.

Yet, I was strangely optimistic. In fact, all the Christians from Maple Community Church—the organization that sponsored my appearance there—were filled with optimism. The church had cultivated relationships with the Muslim community and the Muslims I met greeted me warmly. But our optimism's source wasn't merely social. It sprang up from the biblical attitudes we had prayed for. Yes, we knew there would be disagreements between my Muslim counterpart and me that evening. But we saw those Muslims not as enemies to be vanquished but as fellow beings made in God's image for whom Christ offers living water.

It's very difficult to maintain that perspective these days as we're baited with fear and anger toward the "other." Christian apologists certainly aren't immune to such baiting. Recently a well-known apologist contritely confessed to me that in light of ISIS's atrocities, he's having difficulty not hating Muslims. Sobering words, aren't they? We may not express hostility through slurs or epithets, but it can seep through our apologetics if we destroy not only the argument a Muslim may offer but also the emotions of the Muslim who offers it. Such enmity, whether open or subtle, drowns out the good news our Muslim neighbors need to hear.

That night, we prayed to emulate the apostle Paul's attitude toward non-Christians: "Walk in wisdom toward outsiders, making the best use of the time. Let your speech always be gracious, seasoned with salt, so that you may know how you ought to answer each *person*" (Colossians 4:5-6, emphasis added).

So much could be said about this passage, but there's something particularly important for apologists to note. Paul doesn't say that we ought to know how to answer each question. He specifically teaches us to answer each *person*. In the many open forums I've been in, the questions are often similar in content. But the intent behind each question is always different because the questioner is always different. Paul tells us that we aren't in the question-answering business. We're in the people-answering business. Today's apologist must understand that questions don't need answers; *people* need answers.

The hundreds of Muslims I spoke to that cold Toronto evening needed answers about who has the true "Word of God." From my own journey from Islam to Christ, I knew this is an extremely touchy subject because Muslims hold the Qur'an so dear.[1] But I also knew that the key to providing the answers they needed was to address their deepest spiritual thirst. I'm convinced that the key to apologetics today is to identify what non-Christians thirst for most and show how the Christian faith alone can slake that thirst.[2]

Drawing from a Common Well

And so that night, I drew from a deeply held belief—shared by Christians and Muslims—to make my case that the Bible, the Word of God, was the uncorrupted and reliable revelation to us about God the Word made flesh. Muslims and Christians share a deep belief in God's greatness, and it was a powerful place to start our evening.

Allahu Akbar! we hear Muslims all over the world say with religious fervor. It literally means "God is Greater." In the West, we associate this phrase with terrorism because radicals shout it when committing their atrocities. But peace-loving Muslims (the vast majority of Muslims worldwide) also use this phrase routinely. Muslims say it during their five daily prayers and whenever else a situation—good or bad—may warrant it. When they get good news, Muslims will praise God as great. When they receive bad news, Muslims proclaim *"Allahu Akbar,"* putting their hope in a deity greater than their circumstances. For the Muslim, I pointed out, God's greatness is the cornerstone of belief.

Of course, God's greatness also is a cornerstone of Christianity. The eleventh-century theologian, St. Anselm of Canterbury, argued for God's existence based on the idea that God is the "Greatest Possible Being." Indeed, long before St. Anselm, God's greatness formed the basis for Christian faith. As Psalm 145:3 says, "Great is the LORD, and greatly to be praised, and his greatness is unsearchable."

I argued that two divine attributes flow from God's greatness: omnipotence and trustworthiness. If God lacked either of these qualities, he would no longer be the Greatest Possible Being. The audience's collective facial expressions signaled their agreement so far. That common belief opened the Muslims' ears so that I could discuss some of our deepest differences with gentleness and respect.

Will the Real Word of God Please Stand Up?

A key difference that comes up in nearly every conversation with a Muslim is the Bible's authenticity. Muslims claim that the Bible—specifically the Torah, Psalms of David, and the Gospel of Jesus—were God's revelations, but were corrupted over time with blasphemous ideas like the Trinity, Incarnation, and atonement. And, so Muslims believe, God revealed the Qur'an in seventh-century Arabia to correct those corruptions and bring humanity back to true monotheism.

I argued that, ironically, the Qur'an itself doesn't leave such a claim open to Muslims. I recalled how during my own journey to Christ I discovered Qur'anic verses that actually extol the Bible's reliability:

> And We caused Jesus, son of Mary to follow in their footsteps, confirming that which was (revealed) before him in the Torah, and We bestowed on him the Gospel wherein is guidance and light, confirming that which was (revealed) before it in the Torah—a guidance and an admonition unto those who ward off (evil). *Let the People of the Gospel judge by what Allah hath revealed therein.* Whoso judgeth not by that which Allah hath revealed: such are the evil-livers (Sura 5:46-47, emphasis mine). [3]

These verses expressly command Christians to judge by "the Gospel" and that failure to do so is nothing short of evil. If Muslims take those words seriously, then how could it be that the Gospel was corrupted before the Qur'an was revealed? Does it make any sense for God—the Greatest Possible Being—to command Christians to judge by a hopelessly corrupt book?

Several verses later, the Qur'an identifies the Gospel and the Torah as the foundations of true worship:

> People of the Book [a euphemism for Christians and Jews]! Ye have no ground to stand upon unless ye stand fast by the Law, [Torah], the Gospel, and the revelation that has come to you from your Lord. (Sura 5:68).

I asked those gathered that evening: How could these books be the foundation upon which Christians and Jews are to stand if they contain damnable blasphemies? In verse after verse, the Qur'an itself undermines the Islamic claim that the Bible had been changed. In fact, at least one Muslim scholar agrees:

Contrary to the general Islamic view, the Qur'an does not accuse Jews and Christians of altering the text of their scriptures, but rather of altering the truth which those scriptures contain. The people do this by concealing some of the sacred texts, by misapplying their precepts, or by "altering words from their right position." However, this refers more to interpretation than to actual addition or deletion of words from the sacred books.[4]

Lest there be any ambiguity, the Qur'an makes plain in at least two places that "None can change God's words" (Sura 6:115 and Sura 18:27). This comports with the Qur'an's declarations that Jesus's disciples, not those who opposed Jesus, were victorious in the struggle for the hearts and minds of the faithful:

Behold! Allah said: "O Jesus! I will take thee and raise thee to Myself and clear thee (of the falsehoods) of those who blaspheme; *I will make those who follow thee superior to those who reject faith, to the Day of Resurrection*: Then shall ye all return unto Me, and I will judge between you of the matters wherein ye dispute" (Sura 3:55, emphasis mine).

O ye who believe! Be ye helpers of Allah: as said Jesus the son of Mary to the Disciples, "Who will be my helpers to (the work of) Allah?" Said the Disciples, "We are Allah's helpers!" then a portion of the Children of Israel believed, and a portion disbelieved: *But We gave power to those who believed against their enemies, and they became the ones that prevailed* (Sura 61:14, emphasis mine).[5]

I continued my case by summarizing the manuscript evidence supporting the Christian claim that the Bible we have today contains the same message as the original revelation. As has been comprehensively shown by others, finds like the Dead Sea Scrolls have supported the Old Testament's authenticity, while nearly six thousand Greek manuscripts and over twenty-four thousand manuscripts in Greek and other languages (some dating to possibly the first and second centuries) support the New Testament. Based on the strength of this evidence, New Testament scholars Dan Wallace, Ed Komoszewski, and James Sawyer conclude:

> The gospels are historically credible witnesses to the person, words, and deeds of Jesus Christ. What the evangelists wrote was based on a strong oral tradition that had continuity with the earliest eyewitness testimony. In essence, the gospel did not change from its first oral proclamation to its last written production.[6]

Easing the Tension

At this point, the spiritual tension rose a bit because the implications were clear. If the Qur'an calls the Bible a reliable revelation of God, and the Qur'an and the Bible conflict over important points like the Trinity, deity of Christ, and the crucifixion, how can both books be trusted on these matters?

I stood on that platform hoping to cool the rising heat by offering the Muslims a drink of something that would satisfy their hearts' and souls' desire to worship a God who is great. I repeated that if God is truly great, he would be all-powerful and trustworthy. From there, I asked them to consider a profound dilemma I struggled with for years when I was a Muslim considering the gospel, yet wanting to affirm that *Allahu Akbar*.

If the Bible was once God's revealed Word, but became corrupted, only two possibilities emerge: either God *couldn't* protect the Bible or he wouldn't protect it. If God couldn't preserve the Bible, then he's not all-powerful. But no Muslim in that auditorium would even entertain such a blasphemy. Indeed, if God is unable to preserve his self-revelation in the Bible, why think that he's able to preserve the Qur'an? If God does not have the power to protect his self-revelation, then we cannot claim that he is truly great.

But the second option isn't any better. If God was just unwilling to prevent the Bible's corruption, he'd be untrustworthy. He would have allowed horrible blasphemies to lead millions to hell. And if he's willing to allow the Bible's corruption, what gives a Muslim any confidence that God wouldn't allow the Qur'an to become corrupted as well? No Muslim can believe that God was too impotent to preserve the Bible nor that was he so callous and untrustworthy that he chose not to.

And so I presented for my Muslim friends the one remaining option if they wanted to maintain that God is great—the Bible could not have been corrupted. If God is great—and both the Muslim and the Christian believe he is—then he can protect the Bible, he would protect the Bible, and history tells us that he did protect the Bible. While this may seem to leave the Muslim in a desert of doubt, it really doesn't. The Bible's preservation as the Word of God fulfills the Muslim's thirst to worship a God who is all-powerful and trustworthy. And it is that very Word of God that gives all of us—Muslim and Christian alike—a true picture of the Greatest Possible Being.

Listening with Our Eyes

We simply must understand what Muslims care about and hear the heartbeat of their concerns. It's a crucial step toward getting them beyond their stereotypes of Christianity so that they can see Jesus for who he really is. The night of that symposium, as I walked through the Islamic center, I saw writ large on their walls in numerous places the phrase, "Love for all, hatred for none." What a beautiful sentiment to aspire to. Having listened with my eyes to the Muslims' aspirations, I found something with which I could turn their ears into eyes so that they could see the fountain Jesus offers in his Incarnation of the Greatest Possible Being.

The God who is great enough to preserve his word is also a God who expresses the greatest attributes we all aspire to, but in the greatest possible ways. The greatest attribute is love, isn't it? Doesn't every other great attribute flow from love? Justice without love drowns out mercy. Mercy without love washes over justice. Love is indeed the greatest possible attribute or ethic. The Muslims I spoke to that evening aspired to that universal ethic: "Love for all, hatred for none." Wouldn't God himself—who is infinitely greater than us—express "love for all, hatred for none" far better than we ever could?

As I closed my remarks, I pointed out that if God is the Greatest Possible Being, then he must express the greatest possible ethic in the greatest possible way. And there is no greater expression of love than self-sacrifice. We mere humans do it all the time. It's how we know our spouses, our brothers, our sisters, or our parents truly love us. Mustn't the God—the Greatest Possible Being—also express love in such a great way?

But when we express love through sacrifice for others, our natural inclination is to do it only for those who love us or for strangers at best. It goes against everything within us to sacrifice ourselves for those who hate us. But if "love for all, hatred for none" is the greatest ethic, then God—whose love flows from an infinite fountain—would sacrifice not just for those who love him, but for those who hate him. And such a great God is nowhere to be found but at the cross of Christ.

In the Christian faith, God the Word became flesh. And as the Word that God has preserved tells us, "God shows his love for us in that while we were still sinners, Christ died for us" (Romans 5:8). And those words tell us that the Greatest Possible Being expressed the greatest possible ethic—love—in the greatest possible way—self-sacrifice.

That reality is what soothes parched lips that have uttered *Allahu Akbar* without the foundation of the gospel. Blaise Pascal, the seventeenth-century Christian thinker whose words are as relevant as ever for today's apologist, reminds us:

> Men despise religion. They hate it and are afraid it may be true. The cure for this is first to show that religion is not contrary to reason, but worthy of reverence and respect. Next make it attractive, *make good men wish it were true, and then show that it is.*[7]

We can easily apply this to our engagement with Muslims. They thirst to worship a God who is the Greatest Possible Being. The gospel offers them such a God. Apologetics offered as a cool cup of spiritual water can make our Muslim friends wish the gospel were true even as we show them that it is.

ABDU MURRAY, JD, a former Muslim, is a Senior Itinerant speaker with Ravi Zacharias International Ministries, and the president of Embrace the Truth International, an apologetics-evangelism ministry dedicated to engaging non-Christians with the credibility of the gospel in ways that touch the mind and the heart. Abdu is the author of *Grand Central Question: Answering the Critical Concerns of the Major Worldviews*. He lives in Michigan with his wife and three children.

— 27 —

But…What About Other Religions?

TANYA WALKER

Imagine for a moment that you are having a great conversation with a friend who isn't a Christian. You are sharing why you believe in God and what a difference Jesus has made in your life. As the conversation goes on there is a moment of silence. Your friend stops, apparently deep in thought, and your heart is beating as you think, *Wow! We're really getting somewhere here.* And then they say, "But…what about other religions?"

If your heart sinks at this point, thinking that the conversation is veering off course, this chapter is for you. Far from a detour, questions about different worldviews can be an amazing opportunity to consider what is so unique and so profound about the claims of the person of Christ.

The question of other religions is, in part, born out of a growing awareness of diversity. Of course, religious pluralism is not a new phenomenon, but the rise of new technologies and the reality of the migration patterns of past decades have brought about an unprecedented juxtapositioning of strongly held and diverse beliefs from people of every background.

The challenges of the resulting culture are multifaceted and impact individuals in different ways. Like any question of apologetic relevance, we need to be aware that hidden within a seemingly straightforward question might be not one but multiple strands of thought. The following lines expand on three of these: errors of logic, concerns about character, and the question of destination.

An Error of Logic

One response to the dizzying plurality of claims has been to deny the truth-value of any claim at all. "There is no such thing as truth." That is, "There is no such thing as an overarching, 'true for everyone' type truth," is what some insist. "Truth is subjective or relative to each person."

There is much that is interesting about postmodern philosophy, but the complete denial of truth faces insurmountable difficulties. It is impossible to deny truth without at once affirming it. Those who say "There is no such thing as truth" are in fact affirming that "*The truth is*, there is no such thing as truth." Similarly, the claim that truth is subjective or relative to each person, written in full, often reads, "It is *objectively*, *absolutely* the case that truth is subjective and relative to each person's point of view." These are contradictory statements.

For those who seek to make the claim that it is relatively true, for them, that truth is relative, it is unclear what their objective would be in seeking to share that relative perspective. They are sharing nothing more than a personal preference, not an idea to be examined. More importantly, they do not bypass the challenge of contradictory claims being made by others.

Whilst some respond to pluralism with attempts to deny truth, others look to counter the relational and epistemological challenges of diversity with an opposite endeavour: the desire to draw all beliefs together under the banner of truth. "All roads lead to God." Or, in other words, "There is no need to distinguish between competing truth claims. Every viewpoint is actually just a different way to the same ultimate reality."

For some who make this claim, the issue may simply be a lack of knowledge about the major religions and philosophies of this world. Many are under the impression that the differences between religions are only superficial, masking a fundamental similarity at heart. The reality is that the major religions of this world are fundamentally different and only superficially similar, raising the need to examine their competing claims.

For others, the issue is not one of knowledge but of logic. They are aware of the contradictory claims of various worldviews, but they do not consider this a hindrance to them all being true. Of course there is an understandable desire for anyone living in our fragmented world to search for an all-inclusive philosophy of truth. But the basic foundations of logic refuse us this longing.

It may appear, for example, that saying "all roads lead to God" is all-inclusive. But that statement actually excludes all those who say that "some" or "only one" road leads to God. If we argue that "some roads lead to God" (we're not sure, for example, about Hitler, Genghis Khan, and a few others), we exclude all who say that "all" or "only one" road leads to God. And if we say that "only one road leads to God," we exclude all who say that "all" or "only some" roads lead to God.[1] There is no way around this.

The law of noncontradiction dictates that when two things are contradictory, they cannot both be true. If we insist that contradictory beliefs are true, we obliterate the distinction between *truth* and *belief*. We may believe all sorts of things that are false, but truth by its nature is exclusive in that it draws boundaries between what accurately corresponds to reality and what does not.

There is perhaps for some a fear of having to grapple with differing claims and to come to specific conclusions. We are a generation that has seen much discord in diversity. Nevertheless, rather than attempting the logically impossible in redefining the nature of truth, our energies are better spent in cultivating gracious and gentle manners of engaging with those who hold differing views. A more respectful, open, and thorough engagement with diverse philosophies may mean that we are better able as individuals and as society to access relative claims, to examine them against the various tests for truth, and to come to evidence-based conclusions, without entailing discord.

It is of course the case that thinking through these points of logic with others is not the same thing as preaching the gospel. Gently and respectfully exposing these ingrained errors, however, may form an important part of the process of clearing ground for the gospel to be heard. It may not always be a necessary step along the way, but for some it may be the beginning of the light dawning.

Concerns of Character

A second concern related to preaching the exclusivity of Christ in a plural age is the fear that such a message is arrogant (or, indeed, the outright accusation of others that it is in fact so). You may have encountered the angry charge: "It's so arrogant of you to say that *you* have the truth and that everyone else is wrong." How do we counter this charge? I have found it helpful to think of three headings: *truth, content,* and *manner*.

If it is simply the very belief in an exclusive truth that has drawn the charge, a discussion on the nature of truth might be relevant. The fact is that each of us makes exclusive truth claims. As I discussed earlier, even those attempting to denounce truth entirely end up affirming truth in the process, and attempts to include everyone fail. It is, in short, impossible to keep from making truth claims and impossible to make those claims all-inclusive. As a result, if the charge to arrogance exists purely on the basis of an exclusive truth claim being made, the accusation would have to double as a confession.

But we need to look a little deeper here. Whilst a charge to arrogance is not appropriate if it's simply for making a truth claim, *content* and *manner* may make it very relevant indeed.

It could be that the charge of arrogance has come because our message has been misunderstood. The *content* of what people understand us to be sharing is vitally important. Too many people think that the Christian message is a self-righteous message of judgment that says that God saved Christian people because they are morally superior to everybody else. Unsurprisingly, Christians are then viewed as smug and arrogant. We need to ask ourselves: have we actually communicated the gospel truth that Christians are not morally superior people who deserve salvation but rather sinners who realized they need saving?

Or it could be that the *manner* in which we are communicating is actually arrogant and condescending. If you are someone who gets this charge a lot, it might suggest that something is amiss. It might be helpful to ask the next person who tells you that you are arrogant whether they would mind talking to you a little more about that. Is the issue, for example, the fact that you make a claim that is exclusive in nature? Or something of the content of what you have shared? (This would be a helpful way of seeing whether what they have heard you share is an accurate reflection of the gospel.) If it turns out that your manner and your communication has caused the charge, it would be a good time to apologize.

Peter writes so clearly in 1 Peter 3:15-16 that we are to be prepared to give an answer but to do this with gentleness and respect. If this is not our natural mode, we need to repent and to ask the Holy Spirit to change us and help us. Maybe we need a fresh revelation of what the gospel is, and a greater, genuine love for the lost (as opposed to a desire to win the argument). The manner in which we communicate the gospel is not a minor add-on to the gospel itself. Very often it is the nature of the communication that determines whether the gospel gets a hearing at all.

Despite these nuances, it remains true that it is not arrogant to make truth claims, it is not arrogant to pursue a knowledge of that truth, and to argue that we've found it. It is important that the *content* of our message is a genuine reflection of the gospel, and that the manner in which we communicate it doesn't become a stumbling block.

A Question of Destination and the Uniqueness of Jesus Christ

Sometimes people ask me "Is Jesus the only way?" and of course the question alludes to a journey. It occurs to me that when attempting to be helpful in giving directions, some facts are more relevant than others. In this case, perhaps none more so than one: the question of destination. When asking "Is Jesus the only way?" it begs at least one further question, which is "To what?" or "To where?"

In our society, it is not uncommon to hear the statement "All religions lead to God." Although it's not a logical statement, I find the second part of it—the "lead to God" bit—very interesting. There seems to be an awareness, however subconscious, however little thought through, that only God himself is the appropriate destination. Where does this thought come from?

I am struck by the lack of consideration given to the fact that the major religions and philosophies of this world, in their own words and on their own terms, claim to lead us to very different destinations. Atheism tells us that God does not exist and that life is a product of blind matter, time, and chance. Not only is there no "lead to God" bit, there is no destination point. The endgame is that we pass away into nothingness. Buddhism and Eastern spiritualties in their various forms end their journey in the release into cosmic singularity—the recognition and awareness that there are no distinctions in reality. Islam invites us into a different destination again, and a different means of getting there. It tells us that if we are good enough, we will be allowed into paradise, but the paradise it offers is a very specific one. The focus is on emotional, physical, and sexual wellbeing. Islamic scriptures, in their descriptions of that place, very rarely mention Allah.[2]

Don't all religions lead to God? No, they don't even claim to.

I have found it helpful at times to ask, "What is the destination you are aiming for? What is the destination you *hope* would be true?" It seems to me that in the search for truth and meaning, many of us are not primarily or only looking for logical answers, but for a response to the existential longing for *true life*.

Jesus says that he has come so that we might have life and life in all its fullness—life abundantly. The Message translation puts it as "real and eternal life, more and better life than [you] ever dreamed of" (John 10:10). But what I find so intriguing about this is that Jesus tells us not just that he will give us life, not just that he will change and transform our lives, not just that he will show us the way to life, but that he himself *is* the life (John 14:6). In other words, *he is the destination*. There *is* one faith that does claim to lead to God: Jesus stands unique across the ages. He is not simply the means through which we might get to some other destination. He is not a means to an end. Relationship with Jesus *is* the end.

Conclusion

We are living in an age where pluralism is not just a fact of a globally diverse population. The clamour of multiple voices and ideas, all seeking to be heard at one and the same time, is a reality of our immediate contexts. This chapter has drawn out some (by no means all) of the relevant strands of a conversation that might arise when someone asks a question about other religions. But although thinking through these strands might be helpful, one of the challenges to communicating well above the noise is the challenge of resisting neat boxes and stereotypes. There is no substitute for really listening to the question and to the questioner. If we fail to give the individual person in front of us the respect of our attention, we fail to do the one thing that can cut straight through the noise and to the heart.

I hope that as you read this book you will find yourself not only better equipped at the level of ideas to share your faith with non-Christian friends, but that we would all be reminded again of the preciousness and uniqueness of each individual seeker and their journey toward Christ. As has been said, there is only one way to God, but "there are as many ways to Jesus as there are people that come."[3]

TANYA WALKER, PhD, is an apologist for Ravi Zacharias International Ministries (RZIM) and a guest lecturer at the Oxford Centre for Christian Apologetics. She speaks internationally on issues of faith, primarily as an evangelist, but also to equip the church.

Notes

Introduction: A New Kind of Apologist—McDowell

1. www.reformationproject.org/.

Introduction to Part 1: A New Approach to Apologetics—McDowell

1. For a great article that discusses how Jesus was both an apologist and philosopher, see Douglas Groothuis, "Jesus: Philosopher and Apologist," *Christian Research Journal* 25, no. 2 (2002): www.equip.org/article/jesus-philosopher-and-apologist/.

2. Dallas Willard, "Jesus, the Logician," *Christian Scholars Review* 28, 4 (1999): 607.

Chapter 1: Christians in the Argument Culture—Muehlhoff

1. Deborah Tannen, *The Argument Culture: Moving from Debate to Dialogue* (New York: Random House, 1998), 3.

2. The late Christopher Hitchens expresses this hostility when he writes, "As I write these words, and as you read them, people of faith are in different ways planning your and my destruction...Religion poisons everything." *God Is Not Great: How Religion Poisons Everything* (New York: Hachette Book Group, 2007), 13.

3. Dave Barry, *Dave Barry Turns 50* (New York: Ballantine Books, 1999), 30.

4. Reuel Howe, *The Miracle of Dialogue* (New York: The Seabury Press, 1963), 30.

5. Ibid, 110.

6. Carol Gilligan, *In a Different Voice: Psychological Theory and Women's Development* (Cambridge, MA: Harvard University Press, 1982), xi.

7. Jeff Goodall, "The Steve Jobs Nobody Knew," *Rolling Stone*, issue 1142, October 27, 2011, 41.

8. David Hubbard, *Proverbs* (Dallas, TX: Word Publishers, 1989), 29.

9. C.S. Lewis, *The Four Loves* (New York: Harcourt Brace Jovanovich, 1960), 96.

10. While Muslims and Christians often disagree on how to answer these questions, there are times when the answers are similar. Christians and Muslims believe God is one (monotheistic) not a thousand like the Hindu gods or no god found in Buddhist teachings. There is also agreement that when a person dies, she or he is not caught in a cycle of rebirth (samsara) governed by the principle of karma commonly held by Buddhists and Hindus. While differing on the standards of judgment, both Muslims and Christians believe each of us after death face our Creator.

11. Cornelius Plantinga Jr., *Not the Way It's Supposed to Be: A Breviary of Sin* (Grand Rapids, MI: Eerdmans, 1995), 69.

Chapter 2: Apologetics and New Technologies—Auten

1. Lori Greene, "Enough About Disruption: We're in the Golden Age of Communications," *Huff Post Business*, December 21, 2014, www.huffingtonpost.com/communications-week/enough-about-disruption-w_b_6024734.html.

2. Gregory Koukl's *Tactics: A Game Plan for Discussing Your Christian Convictions* is an excellent primer on principles of gracious and tactful apologetic interaction.

Chapter 4: Motivating Others to "Give an Answer"— Mittelberg

1. "Six Reasons Young Christians Leave Church," September 28, 2011, *Barna Group*, www.barna.org/teens-next-gen-articles/528-six-reasons-young-christians-leave-church.

2. Mark Mittelberg, Lee Strobel, and Bill Hybels, *Becoming a Contagious Christian* training course (Grand Rapids, MI: Zondervan, 1995).

3. Sean McDowell, *GodQuest* (Vista, CA: Outreach, 2011). See www.godquestoutreach.com.

4. For more on how to motivate and organize a church for evangelism and apologetics, see my book *Becoming a Contagious Church* (Grand Rapids, MI: Zondervan, 2007).

Chapter 5: Social Justice and a New Kind of Apologist—Wytsma and Gerhardt

1. Matthew 5:14,17.

2. Dibin Samuel, "Mahatma Gandhi and Christianity," *Christianity Today*, August 14, 2008, www.christiantoday.co.in/article/mahatma.gandhi.and.christianity/2837 .htm.

3. Kilns College (School of Theology and Mission) offers MAs in social justice, in leadership and innovation, and (beginning fall 2016) in theology and culture through both residential (in Bend, OR) and distance learning. For information, please visit www.kilnscollege.org.

4. Videos of these questions and answers by not only Antioch pastors and leaders but by a wide range of guest speakers and friends of Antioch are videotaped and can be viewed and heard at http://askquestions.tv.

5. For a fuller treatment of this topic, see Ken's book *Pursuing Justice* (Nashville: Thomas Nelson, 2013).

6. Psalm 9:16 NIV.

7. Psalm 45:6 NIV.

8. Psalm 146:6-9.

9. Deuteronomy 16:20 NASB.

10. Jeremiah 22:3 (among others).

11. Micah 6:8.

12. E.g., Isaiah 58.

13. Jeremiah 22:16.

14. Found in Luke 4:18-19, as prophesied of him in Isaiah 61:1-2.

15. Matthew 25:31-46, part of Jesus's last recorded discourse prior to his crucifixion.

16. According to Paul Copan, "The Christian faith has this-worldly implications. If it doesn't, it's not Christian." Paul Copan, *Is God a Moral Monster?* (Grand Rapids, MI: Baker Books, 2011), 12.

17. Matthew 6:10.

18. Colossians 1:15-20.

19. 2 Corinthians 5:18-21.

20. Ephesians 2:10.

21. David Kinnaman, *Unchristian: What a New Generation Really Thinks About Christianity…and Why It Matters* (Grand Rapids, MI: Baker Books, 2007), 27.

22. Dr. John Perkins, personal conversation with Ken Wytsma, August 13, 2012.

23. Colossians 1:15-20.

24. 2 Corinthians 5:18-21.

25. For more information about AJS, please visit www.ajs-us.org.

Chapter 6: "Don't Blame Us, It's in the Bible"—Kimball

1. www.awkwardmomentsbible.com/order/. Accessed May 6, 2015.

Chapter 7: Shepherd Is a Verb—Myers

1. Linda A. Hill, "Where Will We Find Tomorrow's Leaders?" *Harvard Business Review*, January 2008, 126.

2. Researchers have found that of twenty-five available strategies teachers can use to build affinity with their students, one strategy—making learning fun—accounts for more than 50 percent of their affinity-building activity. In other words, while teachers trained in educational methodology may *know* of lots of ways to build relational bridges with students, they tend to restrict themselves to a very narrow range of strategies. See Joan Gorham, Derek H. Kelley, and James C. McCroskey, "The Affinity-Seeking of Classroom Teachers: A Second Perspective," *Communication Quarterly* 37, no. 1 (Winter 1989): 16-26.

3. "'Nones' on the Rise," *PewResearchCenter*, October 9, 2012, www.pewforum.org/Unaffiliated/nones-on-the-rise.aspx.

4. Ravi Zacharias, statement from *Grow Together: A Conversation-Starter Film*, Summit Ministries, 2015.

5. "5 Reasons Millennials Stay Connected to Church," *Barna Group*, September 17, 2013, www.barna.org/barna-update/millennials/635-5-reasons-millennials-stay-connected-to-church#.VMFh4EeoqSp.

6. Karen Weller and David Weller, "Coaching and Performance: Substantiating the Link," *Leadership in Action* 24, no. 2 (May/June 2004): 20.

7. David Clutterbuck and David Megginson, *Making Coaching Work: Creating a Coaching Culture* (London: CIPD, 2005), quoted in Peter Hawkins and Nick Smith, *Coaching, Mentoring and Organizational Consultancy: Supervision and Development* (Berkshire, England: Open University Press, 2006), 106.

8. Josh McDowell, statement from *Grow Together: A Conversation-Starter Film*, Summit Ministries, 2015.

9. Stratford Sherman, "How Tomorrow's Leaders Are Learning Their Stuff," *Fortune*, November 27, 1995.

10. Raymond D. Aumack, "The Story of St. Patrick," www.iaci-usa.org/pdf/3-11%20enews%20stpatrick.pdf.

11. "Solomon Stoddard," *Wikipedia*, http://en.wikipedia.org/wiki/Solomon_Stoddard.

12. Arnold Dallimore, *Spurgeon: A New Biography* (Carlisle, PA: Banner of Truth Trust, 2000).

Chapter 8: A Practical Plan to Raise Up the Next Generation—Kunkle

1. C.S. Lewis, *Surprised by Joy* (New York: Harcourt Brace & Company, 1955), 207.

2. Susan Wise Bauer, "What is Classical Education?" Available online at www.welltrainedmind.com/classical-education/.

3. It's certainly not the only, or even primary, indicator of academic success, but standardized test scores from the Association of Classical and Christian Schools indicate classically trained students clearly outperform their publicly educated counterparts: www.accsedu.org/what-is-cce/statistics_at_a_glance.

4. It is a short 38-page booklet of theological Q&A for kids, published by Great Commission Publications. You can order it online at www.gcp.org/ProductDetail.aspx?Item=020030.

5. Of course, this doesn't mean they won't begin asking why questions earlier or that you cannot begin teaching apologetics at younger ages. But generally, they are most definitely ready to begin apologetic training in fourth or fifth grade.

6. The research was conducted by Kara Powell and Brad Griffin. Read more online at http://stickyfaith.org/articles/i-doubt-it.

7. Norm Geisler and Frank Turek wrote an excellent book answering these four questions titled *I Don't Have Enough Faith to Be an Atheist* (Crossway, 2004). I suggest every high schooler read this book before they graduate. There is also an excellent starter apologetics book for middle-school students titled *Living Loud: Defending Your Faith* (B&H Publishers, 2002), that Geisler coauthored with Joseph Holden.

8. Daniel Dennett, *Breaking the Spell: Religion as a Natural Phenomenon* (New York: Penguin Group, 2006), 53.

Chapter 9: The Multiethnic Church—Gray

1. Timothy Keller, "The Gospel and Our Prejudice," *Redeemer.com*, accessed March 31, 2015, http://download.redeemer.com/grace_and_race/The_Gospel_and_Our _Prejudice.pdf.

2. Scot McKnight, *A Fellowship of Differents* (Grand Rapids, MI: Zondervan, 2015), 20.

3. Quoted in Mark DeYmaz, "Building the Church: In Multi-Ethnic Expressions," *NAE Insight*, Spring 2013, www.nae.net/nae-newsletter-archive/spring-2013/97 4-building-the-church.

4. Christopher J.H. Wright. *The Mission of God* (Downers Grove, IL: InterVarsity, 2006), 191.

5. William Barclay, *The Letters to the Galatians and Ephesians,* Daily Study Bible (Philadelphia, PA: Westminster John Knox Press, 1976), 107.

6. Ibid.

7. Ibid.

8. Ibid., 113.

9. N.T. Wright, *Paul and the Faithfulness of God* (Minneapolis: Fortress Press, 2013), 1494.

10. See my book, *The High-Definition Leader: Building Multiethnic Churches in a Multiethnic World* (Nashville: Thomas Nelson, 2015).

Chapter 11: Using Hollywood Blockbusters to Share Your Faith—Esposito

1. Steven S. Cuellar, "The 'Sideways' Effect: A Test for Changes in the Demand for Merlot and Pinot Noir Wines," *Wines and Vines,* January 2009, www

.winesandvines.com/sections/printout_article.cfm?article=feature&content =61265.

2. Earl Doherty, *Jesus, Neither God nor Man: The Case for a Mythical Jesus* (Ottawa, Canada: Age of Reason Publications, 2009), Kindle edition.

3. Acts 10:9-16.

4. Philippians 3:5-6; 1 Corinthians 15:9.

5. Paul wrote 1 Corinthians somewhere between AD 53 and AD 57, according to most scholars. In chapter 15, Paul gives us an oath and proclaims Jesus's death and resurrection, and he then appeals to the fact that many of the eyewitnesses who saw the risen Jesus were still alive and could be questioned about the events. If Jesus was crucified in AD 30 or AD 33, that means that it had been only twenty years or so between the resurrection and Paul's letter to the Corinthian church—and it's the same amount of time between the sixties and the making of *Forrest Gump*.

Chapter 12: The Urban Apologist—Brooks

1. Jen Manuel Krogstad, "A View of the Future through Kindergarten Education," Pew Research Center, July 2014.

2. Blacklivesmatter.com/about/.

3. Avery Dulles, "John Paul and the Mystery of the Human Person," *National Catholic Review*, February 4, 2004.

Chapter 15: Why More Women Should Study Apologetics—Sharp

1. Essentially, revitalized, since Peter commanded the defense of the faith in 1 Peter 3:15 and Paul consistently gave defenses, as recorded by Luke in the book of Acts.

2. Gary R. Habermas, *Dealing with Doubt*, chapter 1, e-book available from: www .garyhabermas.com/books/dealing_with_doubt/dealing_with_doubt.htm. Accessed April 26, 2015.

3. C.S. Lewis, "On Learning in Wartime," *The Weight of Glory* (New York: Macmillan, 1980), 28.

4. C.S. Lewis, *Mere Christianity* (New York: Macmillan, 1980), 125.

5. From the story of Mary and Martha, Luke 10:38-42.

6. Mark Twain quote as utilized by the Freedom from Religion Foundation's billboard campaigns. Available from: http://ffrf.org/news/news-releases/item/2817-ffrf-bill boards-revere-hartfords-famed-irreverents-twain-and-hepburn. Accessed May 7, 2015.

7. Stated by Bill Maher on a September 2008 episode of *The View* television talk show.

8. Richard Dawkins from *The Root of All Evil* television program on Channel 4 UK, 2006.

9. Sam Harris, *The End of Faith* (New York: W.W. Norton, 2005), 173.

10. Quoted and adapted from J.P. Moreland and Klaus Issler, *In Search of a Confident Faith* (Downers Grove, IL: InterVarsity Press, 2008), 54.

11. J. Gresham Machen. *What is Faith?* (Carlisle, PA: The Banner of Truth Trust, 1991), 47-48.

12. Moreland and Issler, *In Search of a Confident Faith,* 18.

13. Jennifer Aaker and Andy Smith, *The Dragonfly Effect* (San Francisco, CA: Jossey-Bass, 2010), xx.

Chapter 16: A Christian Political Apologetic—Marshall

1. Steve Corbett and Brian Fikkert, *When Helping Hurts: How to Alleviate Poverty Without Hurting the Poor...and Yourself* (Chicago: Moody, 2012).

Chapter 17: An Assessment of the Present State of Historical Jesus Studies—Licona

1. See my review of Murdock's book *The Christ Conspiracy: The Greatest Story Ever Sold* at www.risenjesus.com/a-refutation-of-acharya-ss-book-the-christ-conspiracy. Murdock replied and I replied in turn at http://risenjesus.com/licona-replies-to -acharya-part-2. See also my review of the video *The God Who Wasn't There* by Brian Flemming, which is based largely on Doherty's arguments: www.risenjesus.com /answering-brian-flemmings-the-god-who-wasnt-there. These three were accessed December 18, 2014.

2. See Bart D. Ehrman, *Did Jesus Exist? The Historical Argument for Jesus of Naz-areth* (New York: Harper Collins, 2013). Also see R. Joseph Hoffmann's criti-cal response to Richard Carrier's reply to Ehrman at http://rjosephhoffmann

.wordpress.com/2012/04/23/mythtic-pizza-and-cold-cocked-scholars/. Accessed December 18, 2014.

3. 1 Corinthians 9:19-22. Also compare how Paul relates to the Jews in Acts 17:1-3 compared to the Greeks in 17:16-33. In the former he used the Scriptures whereas in the latter he relates his message to one of their idols and quotes from one of their poets.

Chapter 18: How to Question the Bible in a Post-Christian Culture—Morrow

1. I am indebted to New Testament professor Darrell Bock for first introducing me to this phrase in a lecture I once heard him give.

2. Bart D. Ehrman, *Jesus, Interrupted: Revealing the Hidden Contradictions in the Bible* (New York: HarperOne, 2010), 268.

3. For a more in-depth treatment of these issues and many other popular challenges to the Bible, see my book *Questioning the Bible: 11 Major Challenges to the Bible's Authority* (Chicago: Moody Publishers, 2014).

4. Gary Habermas, "The Resurrection of Jesus Time Line: The Convergence of Eyewitnesses and Early Proclamation," in *Contending with Christianity's Critics: Answering New Atheists and Other Objectors*, ed. Paul Copan and William Lane Craig (Nashville: B&H Publishing, 2009), 124.

5. Richard Dawkins, *The God Delusion* (Boston: Houghton Mifflin, 2008), 31.

6. Christopher J.H. Wright, *The God I Don't Understand: Reflections on Tough Questions of Faith* (Grand Rapids: Zondervan, 2008), 92.

7. Ibid.

8. I go into more detail in chapter 9 of my book *Questioning the Bible*.

Chapter 19: Entrepreneurs—Richards

1. In a 1944 lecture called "Is Theology Poetry?" It is reprinted in the C.S. Lewis collection, *The Weight of Glory* (San Francisco: HarperOne, 2001).

2. *Where Good Ideas Come From: The Natural History of Innovation* (New York: Riverhead Books, 2010).

3. Malcom Gladwell, *Outliers: The Story of Success* (New York: Little, Brown and Company, 2008).

4. For examples, see Jay W. Richards *Money, Greed, and God: Why Capitalism Is the Solution and Not the Problem* (San Francisco: HarperOne, 2009).

5. Quoted in Robin Klay and John Lunn, "The Relationship of God's Providence to Market Economies and Economic Theory," *Journal of Markets and Morality* 6, no. 2 (2003): 541-64.

6. For a detailed discussion, see Richards, *Money, Greed, and God*, chapter 8.

7. Julian Simon, *The Ultimate Resource 2* (Princeton: Princeton University Press, 1996).

Chapter 20: Telling the Truth About Sex in a Broken Culture—Stonestreet

1. Some studies suggest that purity pledges are successful in delaying but not preventing premarital sex. Other studies found similar rates of STDs between teenagers who had taken pledges and those who hadn't. See, for example, David Knox and Caroline Schacht, *Choices in Relationships: An Introduction to Marriage and Family* (Belmont, CA: Wadsworth, 2015), 244. The greatest success of purity pledges were with those students who were already "highly religious." See Jenny Kutner, "Virginity Pledges Don't Work—Unless You're Super Religious," *Salon*, July 16, 2014, www.salon.com/2014/07/16/study_virginity _pledges_dont_work_unless_youre_super_religious/.

2. Jared C. Wilson, "They Will Know You Are Conference Christians by Your Porn?" *The Gospel Coalition* (blog), April 10, 2015, www.thegospelcoalition.org/blogs/ gospeldrivenchurch/2015/04/10/they-will-know-you-are-conference-christians -by-your-porn/.

3. See Ezra Klein, "Nine Facts about Marriage and Childbirth in the United States," *Washington Post*, March 25, 2013, www.washingtonpost.com/blogs/wonkblog/ wp/2013/03/25/nine-facts-about-marriage-and-childbirth-in-the-united-states/.

4. "Sexual Assault Statistics," *National Center on Domestic and Sexual Violence*, www .ncdsv.org/images/sexualassaultstatistics.pdf.

5. Rob Jackson, "When Children View Pornography," *Focus on the Family*, www .focusonthefamily.com/parenting/sexuality/when-children-use-pornography/when -children-view-pornography.

6. Rod Dreher, "Sex After Christianity," *American Conservative*, April 11, 2013, www .theamericanconservative.com/articles/sex-after-christianity.

7. I've borrowed this phrase from Owen Strachan. See "Back to Your Posts: A Response to Dalrymple on Marriage," *Patheos* (blog), November 27, 2012, www .patheos.com/blogs/thoughtlife/2012/11/back-to-your-posts-a-response-to-dalry mple-on-marriage/.

8. Dreher, "Sex After Christianity." Dreher is relying on the work of Sarah Ruden, *Paul Among the People: The Apostle Reinterpreted and Reimagined in His Own Time* (Colorado Springs: Image, 2010).

Chapter 21: Being Authentically Christian on the LGBT Issue—Stanton

1. American Psychological Association, "Sexual Orientation and Homosexuality: Answers to Your Questions for a Better Understanding," (Washington, DC: APA, 2008).

2. Camille Paglia, *Vamps and Tramps: New Essays* (New York: Vintage Books, 1994), 72.

Chapter 22: Transgender—Shlemon

1. Simone de Beauvoir, *The Second Sex* (New York: Vintage Books, 2011), 283.

2. William Bigelow, "Planet Fitness Bans Woman for Protesting Man in Locker Room," *Breitbart*, March 8, 2015, www.breitbart.com/big-government/2015/03/08/planet -fitness-bans-woman-for-protesting-man-in-locker-room/. Accessed April 1, 2015.

3. Katy Steinmetz, "The Transgender Tipping Point: America's Next Civil Rights Frontier," *Time*, June 9, 2014.

4. Jaime Grant et al., *Injustice at Every Turn: A Report of the National Transgender Discrimination Survey*, Washington: National Center for Transgender Equality and National Gay and Lesbian Task Force, 2011.

5. William G. Reiner and John P. Gearhart, "Discordant Sexual Identity in Some Genetic Males with Cloacal Exstrophy Assigned to Female Sex at Birth," *New England Journal of Medicine* 350 (2004): 333-41.

6. John Meyer and Donna Reter, "Sex Reassignment. Follow-up," *Archives of General Psychiatry* 36 (1979): 1010-1015.

7. Paul McHugh, "Surgical Sex," *First Things* 147 (2004): 34-38.

8. Stella Morabito, "Trouble in Transtopia: Murmurs of Sex Change Regret," *The Federalist*, November 11, 2014, http://thefederalist.com/2014/11/11/trouble-in -transtopia-murmurs-of-sex-change-regret/. Accessed April 1, 2015.

9. Ibid.

10. I'm referring to the classical sense of an *argument*, a point of view with reasons to back it up. I don't mean being argumentative.

11. I owe this way of putting this principle to my pastor, Larry Osborne.

Chapter 23: An Apologetic for Religious Liberty—Tonkowich

1. See *United States v. Windsor* in which the Supreme Court struck down the fed-eral definition of marriage as one man and one woman in the 1993 Defense of Marriage Act because they felt that the Congress that passed it (85-14 in the Sen-ate, 342-67 in the House) and then-President Bill Clinton were motivated "by an improper animus or purpose" in order "to disparage and to injure," to "demean," to "impose inequity," and to "humiliat[e]" the children of same-sex couples.

2. See Albert Mohler, "'It Is the Price of Citizenship'? An Elegy for Religious Lib-erty in America," *Christianity.com*, www.christianity.com/christian-life/political -and-social-issues/it-is-the-price-of-citizenship-an-elegy-for-religious-liberty-am erica.html?p=0.

3. Tertullian, "To Scapula," chapter 2.

4. James Madison, *Memorial and Remonstrance Against Religious Assessment* (1785).

5. Kevin Seamus Hasson, *The Right to Be Wrong: Ending the Culture War Over Reli-gion in America* (San Francisco: Encounter Books, 2005), 57.

6. Quoted in William L. Sauders, "The First Freedom, *Touchstone*, April 2008.

7. Monica Duffy Toft, Daniel Philpott, and Timothy Samuel Shah, *God's Century: Resurgent Religion and Global Politics* (New York: W.W. Norton, 2011), 220.

8. Richard Wolf, "Muslim's Case Takes 'Look' at Abercrombie & Fitch Policy," *USA Today*, February 24, 2015, www.usatoday.com/story/news/nation/2015/02/24/ supreme-court-abercrombie-muslim/23882405/.

9. Eric Wilkinson, "Student Allowed to Bring Religious Knife to Class," *King5*, October

23, 2014, www.king5.com/story/news/local/2014/10/22/sikh-kirpan-auburn-schools-knives/17746565/.

10. Russ Jones, "Court to Decide if Catholic Midwives Can Refuse to Perform Abortions," *ChristianHeadlines.com*, November 12, 2014, www.christianheadlines.com/blog/court-to-decide-if-catholic-midwives-can-refuse-to-perform-abortions.html. (This case is in the United Kingdom.)

Chapter 24: Advocating Intelligent Design with Integrity, Grace, and Effectiveness—Luskin

1. See http://www.discovery.org/csc/books/.

2. Stephen C. Meyer, "The Origin of Biological Information and the Higher Taxonomic Categories," *Proceedings of the Biological Society of Washington*, 117(2): 213-39 (2004).

3. Cited in Bonnie Azab Powell, "'Explore as Much as We Can': Nobel Prize Winner Charles Townes on Evolution, Intelligent Design, and the Meaning of Life," UC Berkeley NewsCenter, June 17, 2005.

4. See Jonathan Wells, *The Myth of Junk DNA* (Seattle, WA: Discovery Institute Press, 2011).

5. See Casey Luskin, "A Listener's Guide to the Meyer-Marshall Radio Debate: Focus on the Origin of Information Question," *Evolution News and Views,* December 4, 2013, www.evolutionnews.org/2013/12/a_listeners_gui079811.html.

6. See "Bibliographic and Annotated List of Peer-Reviewed Publications Supporting Intelligent Design," Center for Science and Culture, April 2015, www.discovery.org/f/10141.

7. For further rebuttals see "The Truth About the Dover Intelligent Design Trial," www.traipsingintoevolution.com.

8. Francis Collins, *The Language of God* (New York, NY: Free Press, 2006), 205 (emphasis added).

9. "How is BioLogos Different from Evolutionism, Intelligent Design, and Creationism?," http://biologos.org/questions/biologos-id-creationism.

10. Rachel Held Evans, "13 Things I Learned at the BioLogos Conference,"

BioLogos Forum, June 16, 2010, http://biologos.org/blog/13-things-i-learned-at-the-biologos-conference/P80.

11. William Provine, "No Free Will," in *Catching up with the Vision,* ed. Margaret W. Rossiter (Chicago, IL: University of Chicago Press, 1999), S123.

Chapter 25: The Scientific Naturalist Juggernaut and What to Do About It—Smith

1. Still, someone *might* allow for mental states to emerge from physical ones. But this is not the main view. Plus, they are free riders; they don't cause anything and depend entirely upon the physical.

2. There's no room for *theistic* evolution.

3. Consider the movie *Chappie* or, from *Star Trek: The Next Generation,* Captain Pickard's defense of the android, Data, who was to be taken apart and studied, www.youtube.com/watch?v=vjuQRCG_sUw, accessed March 18, 2015.

4. See also J.P. Moreland, *Kingdom Triangle* (Grand Rapids, MI: Zondervan, 2007).

5. In addition, there are many good resources for addressing naturalism in science and philosophy: Nancy Pearcey, *Finding Truth: 5 Principles for Unmasking Atheism, Secularism, and Other God Substitutes* (Colorado Springs, CO: David C. Cook, 2015); William Lane Craig, *On Guard* (Colorado Springs, CO: David C. Cook, 2010); and perhaps my *In Search of Moral Knowledge* (Downers Grove, IL: InterVarsity Press, 2014).

6. See also J.P. Moreland, *The Soul* (Chicago, IL: Moody, 2014).

7. See Alvin Plantinga, *Where the Conflict Really Lies: Science, Religion, and Naturalism (New York:* Oxford University Press, 2011).

8. Our belief about what a chemical reaction will produce can be true, but the chemical reaction itself seems unrelated to truth.

9. Charles Darwin, Letter to W. Graham, Down, July 3, 1881, http://darwin-online.org.uk/content/frameset?pageseq=334&itemID=F1452.1&viewtype=side, accessed March 18, 2015.

10. See especially George Marsden, *Fundamentalism and American Culture,* 2nd ed. (New York: Oxford University Press, 2000).

11. Though not through "commonsense realism," Europeans still embraced the

Enlightenment's high confidence in human reason (apart from special revelation) to know truth.

12. Marsden, *Fundamentalism and American Culture*, 226, helps show how the definition of science had changed from the study of fixed laws to the developing systems.

13. Especially younger people, who are very sensitive to hypocrisy.

14. Marsden, *Fundamentalism and American Culture*, 113. This ties closely with their emphasis upon objective, scientific knowledge by empirical means and their high confidence in reason.

15. I wonder if cessationism might have much the same kinds of practical effects. I cannot pursue this here, but if it does, then that suggests that cessationism also might be naturalistic. How so? Jesus taught us that we will know false from true prophets (and teachings) by their fruits or effects (Matthew 7:15-23).

Chapter 26: Water that Satisfies the Muslim's Thirst—Murray

1. Unless otherwise noted, all Qur'an quotations are from Abdullah Yusuf Ali, *The Holy Qur'an: Translation and Commentary* (Damascus: Ouloom AlQuran, 1934).

2. I extensively discuss how to offer the credibility of the gospel to Muslims (as well as atheists and pantheists) based on our shared questions in my book, *Grand Central Question: Answering the Critical Concerns of the Major Worldviews* (Downers Grove, IL: InterVarsity Press, 2014).

3. Muhammad M. Pickthall, *The Glorious Qur'an: Arabic Text and English Rendering* (Des Plaines, IL: Library of Islam, 1994).

4. Mahmoud Ayoub, "Uzayr in the Qur'an and Muslim Tradition," in *Studies in Islamic and Judaic Traditions*, ed. W.M. Brinner and S.D. Ricks (Atlanta, GA.: Scholars Press, 1986), 5.

5. For more Islamic sources that support the authenticity of the Bible, see Section III of Murray, *Grand Central Question*.

6. J. Ed Komoszewski, M. James Sawyer, and Daniel B. Wallace, *Reinventing Jesus: How Contemporary Skeptics Miss the Real Jesus and Mislead Popular Culture* (Grand Rapids, MI: Kregel, 2006), 259.

7. Blaise Pascal, *Pensées* (London: Penguin, 1995 [1966]), 4 (emphasis added).

Chapter 27: But...What About Other Religions?—Walker

1. Michael Ramsden, "One God, Many Paths?," The Veritas Forum at Pepperdine University, February 9, 2015 (paraphrased).

2. Surah 56:10-14 describes a level of physical proximity to Allah for some in paradise, but does not signify relational closeness.

3. Os Guinness, "Why Does Truth Matter?," *Pulse*, no. 11, Summer 2012, 14.

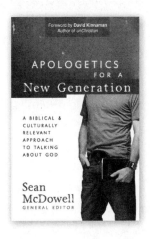

Apologetics for a New Generation
A Biblical and Culturally Relevant Approach to Talking About God

Many teenagers leave home for college but don't take their faith with them. Popular writer and speaker Sean McDowell offers a solution for this problem: a new way of approaching faith that addresses the questions the emerging generation is asking and that incorporates a radically humble and relational approach.

An impressive list of contributors including Dan Kimball (*They Like Jesus but Not the Church*), Brian Godawa (*Hollywood Worldviews*), and Josh McDowell show that today's apologetics must employ...

- a clear connection with everyday life
- an invitation for people to express their doubts and wrestle with tough questions
- a culturally savvy understanding of the way secular people view Christians
- an engaging methodology that captures the imagination before engaging the mind
- a strong emphasis on the resurrection and how it changes everything

This resource is imperative for leaders who are ready to engage a new generation with the claims of Christ.

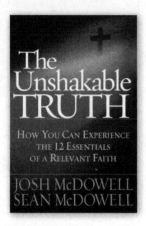

The Unshakable Truth®

How You Can Experience the 12 Essentials of a Relevant Faith

Josh McDowell joins his son Sean to comprehensively address a vital issue: *why an entire generation of young Christians—and millions of older believers—is confused about what they believe, why they believe it, and how it's relevant.*

The Unshakable Truth is uniquely positioned for younger Christians because it presents apologetics *relationally,* focusing on how Christianity's doctrines affect relationships. The authors...

- ground every assertion in the overarching story of creation, incarnation, and re-creation.

- distill 12 crucial "faith statements"—for example, "A personal Creator God exists."

- explain *why* each statement is trustworthy, *how* it applies to real life, and—using examples, stories, and experiences—*what* its relevance is.

A spiritual gold mine for parents, youth workers, pastors—anyone wanting to reveal Christianity's relevance to today's life and culture.

Understanding Intelligent Design
Everything You Need to Know in Plain Language

This compact guide lays out the basics of Intelligent Design, popularly known as ID. William Dembski, the dean of the intelligent–design movement, and Sean McDowell especially target readers whose understanding may have been confused by educational bias and one-sided arguments and attacks.

Commonsense and no-nonsense, with pointed examples, the authors explain

- the central theories of ID, showing why the presence of *information* and meaningful *complexity* require the involvement of intelligence

- why ID adheres to the scientific method and is a valid field of scientific inquiry

- why scientific evidence increasingly conflicts with evolutionary theories

- how *both* evolutionary theory and ID have religious/philosophical underpinnings, and why this causes so much controversy

- how *both* systems of thought have radical implications for our culture—and what readers can do about it

Clarifying crucial issues, this key resource gives nonspecialists a solid grasp of one of today's foundational religious–scientific–cultural concepts.

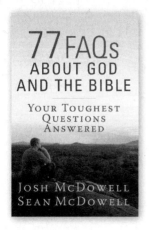

77 FAQs About God and the Bible
Your Toughest Questions Answered

Real-life, on-the-street Christian apologetics is what readers expect from Josh McDowell. Here, he and his son, Sean, reflect their ongoing research and close engagement with our culture in answers to classic questions such as…

- Is there scientific proof God exists?
- How can a loving God send people to hell?
- Why does God allow suffering?
- Is the New Testament historically reliable?
- Aren't there errors and contradictions in the Bible?

…and questions that arise from today's culture:

- If God is so loving, why can't he be more tolerant of sin?
- Is God sexist?
- Is religion the real cause of violence in the world?
- How can teachings from the ancient cultures of the Bible be relevant to our culture?
- What's the difference between the Bible and the Koran?

77 FAQs offers the concise, accessible presentations that readers want and need in an apologetic resource—answers they'll turn to for help in everyday life.

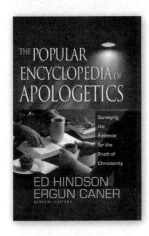

The Popular Encyclopedia of Apologetics

Surveying the Evidence for the Truth of Christianity

Ed Hindson and Ergun Caner have brought together a who's who of apologetic experts—including Lee Strobel, Norm Geisler, Josh McDowell, and John Ankerberg—to produce a resource that's both easy to understand and comprehensive in scope.

Every entry provides a biblical perspective and mentions the key essentials that believers need to know about a wide variety of apologetic concerns, including...

- issues concerning God, Christ, and the Bible
- scientific and historical controversies
- ethical matters (genetic engineering, homosexuality, ecology, feminism)
- a Christian response to world religions and cults
- a Christian response to the major worldviews and philosophies of our day

Included with each entry are practical applications for approaching or defending the issue at hand, along with recommendations for additional reading on the subject.

To learn more about Harvest House books and
to read sample chapters, visit our website:

www.harvesthousepublishers.com

HARVEST HOUSE PUBLISHERS
EUGENE, OREGON